CRIME, HISTORY, AND HOLLYWOOD

CRIME, HISTORY, AND HOLLYWOOD

Learning Criminal Justice History through Major Motion Pictures

Willard M. Oliver

Nancy E. Marion

CAROLINA ACADEMIC PRESS

Durham, North Carolina

Library of Congress Cataloging-in-Publication Data

Oliver, Willard M.
Crime, history, and Hollywood : learning criminal justice history through major motion pictures / Willard M. Oliver and Nancy E. Marion.
p. cm.
Includes bibliographical references and index.
ISBN 978-1-59460-975-6 (alk. paper)
1. Motion pictures and history. 2. Crime in popular culture. 3. Crime--United States--History--20th century. 4. Criminal justice, Administration of--United States--History--20th century. I. Marion, Nancy E. II. Title.

PN1995.2.O45 2012
791.43'658--dc23

2012016546

Carolina Academic Press
700 Kent Street
Durham, North Carolina 27701
Telephone (919) 489-7486
Fax (919) 493-5668
www.cap-press.com

Printed in the United States of America

To
James F. Hilgenberg, Jr.,
who shares my love of history and has been a good mentor,
colleague, and friend.
and
Joyce Hilgenberg,
a beautiful lady and friend to the family,
Requiescat in Pace.
W.M.O.

CONTENTS

Acknowledgments

In 2003, one of the authors (Oliver) began teaching in the College of Criminal Justice at Sam Houston State University, in Huntsville, Texas. One of the classes, which was part of the core curriculum, was the History of Criminal Justice. As I had previously authored a book on the subject (*A History of Crime and Criminal Justice in America*, 2nd Edition, with James Hilgenberg, Jr., Carolina Academic Press), I regularly taught the class for our criminal justice majors. With each passing semester, more and more students would challenge me on my presentation of history. They would tell me in some major motion picture they had watched, they saw something different than what I was conveying in my lectures. I told them the film was historically inaccurate and, expecting to move on, continued to lecture. Yet the students would usually stop me and ask me to explain in more detail why it was wrong. Thus, I found myself taking more and more time to teach the historical inaccuracies of Hollywood films than actually teaching criminal justice history.

I toyed with the idea of teaching one of my criminal justice history courses through the use of film, but decided that students would come away with a very sparse knowledge of criminal justice history overall. Still, students continued to challenge my read of history with their read of Hollywood films. Finally, in the summer of 2006, I was asked to teach a special topics course on whatever I liked. I decided to try teaching the concepts that are now found in this book, *Crime, History, & Hollywood*. By teaching students the real history, as well as the techniques that Hollywood uses to subvert real history which make films more simple and enjoyable to watch, I could teach them how to analyze a film for its accuracy. What happened next amazed me.

Students came to class fully prepared to discuss and criticize the historical accuracy of the films we watched in class. Either they had dog-eared a page in the book and drew upon that to point out a historical discrepancy in the film or they surfed the web for critical reviews of the films to see what others had to say. Many found historical websites or those maintained by historians that also reviewed our films in question, and from these, the students brought to class many observations, small and large, that I had overlooked in my own analysis. Then, when these mistakes were brought up in class, the students often became engaged in debates as to whether the historical inaccuracies were mistakes or intentional on the part of the director. And sometimes at issue were debates over whether something was historically inaccurate or not. Further, students with specific interests brought into class observations based on their particular knowledge of such things as baseball, guns, and automobiles; observations that further led to the recognition of historical inaccuracies.

Thus, in the end, after having taught this same class multiple times, and with each film shown, learning new mistakes from my students, I would be remiss in not thanking them for making this book possible. Still further, I should acknowledge Sam Houston State University and the College of Criminal Justice for allowing me the opportunity to teach such a class in the first place.

The authors would also like to thank Beth Hall from Carolina Academic Press for her support of seeing this idea into a book and to Kelly Miller, also at Carolina Academic Press, for putting up with all my questions about photographs. And, as always, our thanks extend to our families.

CRIME, HISTORY, AND HOLLYWOOD

Introduction

Motion picture producers ... are in the business of entertaining people and not of educating them.

— August Vollmer, First Professor of Police Science

It has become rather commonplace today to find major motion pictures used in the classroom at all levels of education, including higher education. Films have served as a useful pedagogical tool because they are familiar to students, entertaining and can serve as a common experience for classroom discussion (Cheatwood & Petersen, 2007; Mattheisen, 1989). Films also have the capability of not only entertaining, but often inspiring, and they have the ability, like other fiction, to teach important truths about the strength and frailties of the human condition (Carnes, 1995).

Historians have been at the forefront of using film in the classroom due to their capability of presenting enhanced visualizations of historical events. Hollywood history, according to Carnes (1995), "fills irritating gaps in the historical record and polishes dulling ambiguities and complexities" (p. 9). Carnes (1995), however, laments that "for many, Hollywood history is their only history" (p. 9). Another historian, O'Connor (1988), has also noted that "however unfortunate, it appears likely that even well-educated Americans are learning most of their history from film or television" (p. 1201). After viewing a historical film, viewers often come away with the belief that the history presented on screen was accurate and because the viewing of films is a passive experience, they often do not consider engaging in an active challenge to this truth. This can be further exacerbated by the fact that many filmmakers, "wholly smitten by their creations, proclaim them to be historically 'accurate' or 'truthful' and many viewers presume them to be so" (Carnes, 1995, p. 10). This appears to be true for Hollywood's presentation of criminal justice history as well.

The reality, however, is that Hollywood has one overriding goal in the production of their films and that is to make a profit. And, in order to make a profit, they have to make films that people want to go see. Hence, presenting accurate history is not the overriding goal for making major motion pictures. In the early 1930s, August Vollmer, the first professor of police science, was asked to conduct a study to determine if films caused crime, especially among juveniles. Writing in 1949, Vollmer summed this up nicely when he said, "Motion picture producers ... are in the business of entertaining people and not of educating them. In order to serve the public as entertainers they give the people what they want, and the best evidence to them of what people actually want is box office receipts" (p. 33). That was true in the early 1930s, it was true in 1949, and that is still true today.

In light of this truth, that means the use of film in teaching criminal justice history is suspect at best. Yet, there appears to be value in teaching students, who often take what they see in a motion picture as historical fact, and educating them on how to separate fact from fiction, true history from Hollywood entertainment. Thus, learning how to dispel myths can lead to something far more useful from an educating perspective, and that is an automatic response to actively question Hollywood's representation of criminal justice history through an analysis of its historical representation. Stoddard and Marcus (2006), perhaps explain it best when they state "through pedagogy that promotes teaching students how to assess how well a film meets the burden of historical representation through analysis and democratic deliberation, students can form a more complex and diverse understanding of ... U.S. history" (p. 34).

Film Studies

The use of film as a pedagogical tool in the classroom has been widely used in academia, including such disciplines as English (Costonzo, 1992), communications (Bochner, 1995), science (Borgwald & Schreiner, 1994), and both sociology and political science (Powers, Rothman, & Rothman, 1996; Stoddard & Marcus, 2006). The academic discipline of history, as previously mentioned, has widely used film to teach history in its journals and publications, both broadly (Carnes, 1995; Jackson, 1990; Marcus, 2005; O'Connor, 1988; Rebhorn, 1987; Toplin, 1996a, 1996b) and in more specific time periods such as twentieth century history (Briley, 1990) or the middle ages (Attreed & Powers, 1997). In fact, in the area of history, the use of film has become so pervasive, there is even a journal dedicated to this subject matter: *Film & History* (2009).

The academic disciplines of criminal justice and criminology have also developed a healthy body of literature dealing with the pedagogical use of film in the classroom. A number of these publications have addressed the topic of crime films rather broadly (Clarens, 1997; Rafter, 2000; Reiner, Livingstone, & Allen, 2000; Rockell, 2009), or a specific genre of films, such as silent movies (Brownlow, 1990). Much of the research, however, has been dedicated to the coverage of specific types of crimes in film such as serial killers (Jarvis, 2007), psychopaths (Rafter, 2005), gangsters (McCarty, 1993; Munby, 1999; Yaquinto,

1998), prostitutes (Campbell, 2005), and sex crimes (Rafter, 2007). Many of the articles have also focused on a specific component of the criminal justice system, including law enforcement (Crawford, 1999; King, 1999; Leishman & Mason, 2003; Mawby, 2003), lawyers (Denvir, 1996; Greenfield & Osborn, 2003), courts (Bergman & Asimow, 2006; Chase, 2002; Kuzina, 2001), and prisons (Bennett, 2006; Bordt & Lawler, 2005; Crowther, 1989; Hesse, & Przemieniecki, 2009; Parish, 1991; Wilson & O'Sullivan, 2005). Moreover, some articles have focused on either a specific agency in film, such as the Federal Bureau of Investigation (Herzberg, 2007), or a specific area of justice research in film, such as peacemaking (Braswell, 2003).

Many recent articles regarding film and criminal justice have focused their attention on specific films and the elements of crime and criminal justice conveyed in those motion pictures, including *Bowling for Columbine* (Robbers, 2005), *Gangs of New York* (O'Brien, Tzanelli, & Yar, 2005b), *Chicago* (O'Brien, Tzanelli, & Yar, 2005a), *Catch Me If You Can* (Tzanelli, Yar, & O'Brien, 2005), *Criminal Justice* (Cheatwood & Petersen, 2007), *The Shawshank Redemption* (Fiddler, 2007), and the English film *The Blue Lamp* (McLaughlin, 2005). Many articles have also dealt more directly with the teaching of specific criminal justice classes, describing how films can be incorporated into those courses (Nickoli, Hendricks, Hendricks, & Osgood, 2003; Rockell, 2009), such as crime scene investigations (Lacks, 2007), the death penalty (Patenaude, 2001), criminal justice ethics (Pino, Brunson, & Stewart, 2009), and even criminal justice literature (Engel, 2003). Finally, Cook and Babcot (1993) mention that films can also be incorporated into the classroom in order to display historical and current attitudes toward crime, criminals, victims, and the criminal justice system (police, courts, and corrections).

Despite what appears to be a healthy body of literature in the area of film and criminal justice, little has been written on the teaching of criminal justice history through major motion pictures. Therefore, it is the intent of this book to fill in this gap in the literature. In order to do so, it first turns to an overview of the common techniques Hollywood employs in creating (criminal justice) history films.

Hollywood's History

Hollywood's presentation of historical films related to criminal justice is quite extensive. Criminal justice history often provides Hollywood motion picture directors and producers with a subject that is often amenable to the film industry's common usage of crimes, courtroom scenes, and mysteries that can resolve themselves in less than two hours. As the public apparently enjoys these types of films, there have been many events in criminal justice history portrayed on the silver screen. Hollywood, however, faces a number of dilemmas when trying to convey criminal justice history (or any history) in a two hour film that often lead to a misrepresentation of history. It is important that students of criminal justice film history understand these limitations and techniques before viewing and assessing the historical representation of the film.

It should, perhaps, be first noted that very often Hollywood simply makes mistakes. In many cases these types of mistakes are not intended or taken as *artistic license,* but are simply mistakes that viewers often catch or historians dispute. The Internet Movie Database (IMDB) typically recognizes anachronisms, revealing mistakes, continuity, and factual errors. Most of those cited have to do with filming issues or minor historical issues that do not add to the historical record, nor do they necessarily take away from the history presented, but it is important to make note of these mistakes. For instance, in the film *Amistad,* when a small row boat is rowed to shore the side of it reads "La Amistad." On the way back to the main ship it reads "LA AMISTAD." A simple filming mistake (although one wonders how?) that does not impact historical accuracy in any way, it is simply a filming mistake. Another example of historical mistakes in the same film, Baldwin's glasses have a purple tint to them—a sign of modern anti-glare coating. An anachronism, assuredly, but one that does not necessarily detract from the film's historical accuracy.

One of the most common techniques employed by Hollywood is oversimplification of historical events. Life is often very complex and it is the many complexities and ambiguities that make history intriguing and exciting. Yet, Hollywood often avoids these complexities due to the time constraints and the difficulties in presenting these complexities and ambiguities in a cogent manner. Therefore, they will often oversimplify reasons for motives, multiple events, and myriads of outcomes for the easier one motive, one event, and one outcome. A good example of this is the movie *Tombstone,* which portrays the events of the gunfight at the O.K. Corral, but presents a very limited explanation for why the gunfight occurred.

Associated with this oversimplification is the use of combining multiple historical characters into one, creating a composite character intended to represent a group of individuals all voicing similar viewpoints or who took similar actions. In addition, and still related, is the elimination of historical characters. This is often done through the composite or by simply removing individuals from the historical record to simplify the story and to retain few primary subjects on screen. Hollywood is most effective in conveying a story when there is approximately two to five main characters. Although real history often has more players, Hollywood will eliminate many of them for simplicities sake. One example is in the 1919 fix of the World Series, in which Hugh S. Fullerton and Christy Mathewson were the first to suspect the scandal. Yet in the movie *Eight Men Out*, writer and director John Sayles chose to minimize Hugh S. Fullerton's role, eliminate the historic Mathewson altogether, and inflate the role of Ring Lardner, even making him appear as the "side kick" to Hugh Fullerton—something entirely fictitious.

Another technique employed by Hollywood is the use of fictional characters. Directors simply make up people and place them in the story often to either emphasize an aspect of history that was actually absent in the historical record or to create a bridge to the story, creating continuity in and amongst other disparate characters that did exist in the historical record. This is often taken even further with historical situations, creating romances between historical figures that did not exist in order to make the film a love story or creating a false confrontation between two historical figures to represent an adversarial element to the movie. Further, Hollywood will often fictionalize certain aspects of a true historical figure for many of the same reasons detailed above. Examples of these include the movies *Mississippi Burning* and *September Dawn*. In the former, FBI agent "Anderson" (played by Gene Hackman) has an affair with the wife of Deputy "Pell," and when discovered, she is severely beaten by several members of the Ku Klux Klan. The characters in this movie were all loosely based on real individuals, Anderson based on FBI Agent John Proctor and Deputy Pell on Deputy Price. Fictitious names aside, the real FBI Agent never had an affair with the Deputy's wife, nor was she ever beaten. The fictitious characters were played for simplification and the affair to have a love-arc in the storyline. In the case of *September Dawn*, the lead male is a Mormon and the lead female is part of the wagon-train and the two fall in love only to meet tragedy at the end of the movie. This is no record of any love interest between these two individuals in real life, nor could there have been—Emily Hudson and her father had left the wagon train before it even reached Utah, where the Mountain Meadows Massacre occurred.

Two other common techniques are the use of time compression and false sequencing. In the case of the former, Hollywood will often take events that historically occurred over weeks, months, or years, and present them as occurring within a day or two. The latter, false sequencing, is where Hollywood will present the historical record out of true time sequencing in order to have a greater effect and impact on the viewer. Examples of both of these are found in the movie

Tombstone. For instance, after the gunfight at the O.K. Corral, Earp brothers Virgil and Morgan were quickly attacked. In real life, the shootout occurred October 26, 1881; Virgil was not attacked until December 28, and Morgan was not killed until March 18, 1882. In addition, at the end, when Wyatt Earp goes on his vendetta, it appears to occur just shortly after the shootout and over a few days or a week. The true vendetta began several months after the shootout and lasted for several months (not to mention only four were killed — the movie makes it appear that dozens were gunned down).

Finally, one of the most serious allegations against Hollywood is the fact that it conforms it's films to the widest audience available or, simply put, those most likely to go to the movies. In America that means catering films to the white middle class, thus Hollywood has been accused of making films to appeal to whites by ensuring that lead characters are mostly white and that race issues are presented from the white perspective (even if the lead characters are another race), previously referred to as "whitewashed" by two researchers (Shohatt & Stam, 1994). The two movies they draw heavily upon as examples for this are *Glory* (the story of the all black 54th Massachusetts Infantry, shown through the eyes of its white leaders) and the movie *Amistad* (See Chapter 1).

Despite these criticisms, there are some positive aspects in the way Hollywood presents criminal justice history. For many this is often their only exposure to a historical subject; if it was not for Hollywood they would have no knowledge of the subject matter. Motion pictures tend to attract many to the topic, it makes history exciting, and it can make the past relevant to the present and future. Hollywood also celebrates great persons in its films, conveying the persona of key figures in American history. Finally, it should be noted that the mere fact Hollywood is willing to put forth big budget films on criminal justice history, whether done well or not, is a positive thing.

There are negative aspects to Hollywood's presentation of criminal justice history as well. Hollywood will often claim in its advertising or in interviews that what is depicted in their historical movies are accurate and truthful, which they are often not (as suggested above and evidenced below). Unfortunately, many viewers will believe these historical depictions are accurate for without the knowledge of history, they will know no difference. Whenever challenged on the historical representation of their criminal justice history, Hollywood often hides behind the veil of *artistic license.* Directors will claim they are not making historical films so much as art, and that any historical inaccuracies are not fair criticisms since that was never their aim in the first place. Thus, in the end, the greatest criticism of these portrayals is that they fail to live up to the true historical representation of criminal justice history.

Format of the Book

In order to gain a better understanding of how criminal justice history is presented in major motion pictures, ten films were selected for this book. The films were selected as good representations of criminal justice subject matter, mostly centered on specific crimes, their investigation, and courtroom outcomes. Films made across a wide range of times were also selected, and ones that represented American history from the mid-1800s (*Amistad*) and into the 1970s (*All the President's Men*). The most important aspect of the film selection was that they were based on actual historical events. While films such as the *Shawshank Redemption* and *Twelve Angry Men* are excellent criminal justice films, they are not based on true historical crimes or events.

Each film (chapter) will open with an introduction to the historical event and film. It will then present the true historical events that the film was based on. Next, it will present a review of the film's narrative and how Hollywood portrayed the historical event. It should be noted here that the viewing of the film would best complement this section of each chapter. Then a review of the historical accuracy of each film will be detailed, mentioning the various types of historical inaccuracies employed in each film. Finally, each chapter will present a conclusion to the accuracy of the film, a list of books for further reading on the topic, and the endnotes.

References

Amistad (Dreamworks, 1997) (Steven Spielberg, Director.)

Attreed, L. & Powers, J.F. (1997). Lessons in the Dark: Teaching the Middle Ages with Film. *Perspectives, 35,* 11–16.

Bennett, J. (2006). The Good, the Bad, and the Ugly: The Media in Prison Films. *Journal of Criminal Justice, 45,* 97–115.

Bergman, P. & Asimow, M. (2006). *Reel Justice: The Courtroom Goes to the Movies.* New York: Andrews McMeel Publishing.

Bordt, R.L. & Lawler, M.J. (2005). Teaching a Course on Prisons: A Design, Some Resources, and a Little Advice. *Journal of Criminal Justice Education, 16,* 180–192.

Borgwald, J.M. & Schreiner, S. (1994). Science and the Movies: The Good, the Bad, and the Ugly. *Journal of College Science Teaching, 23,* 367–371.

Braswell, M. (2003). A Picture is Worth a Thousand Words: Teaching Peacemaking and Justice Themes in a Film Course. *Contemporary Justice Review, 6,* 293–299.

Briley, R. (1990). Reel History: U.S. History, 1932–1972, as Viewed Through the Lens of Hollywood. *History Teacher, 23*, 215–236.

Brownlow, Kevin. (1990). *Behind the Mask of Innocence: Sex, Violence, Prejudice, Crime: Films of Social Conscience in the Silent Era*. Berkeley, CA: University of California Press.

Campbell, R. (2005). *Marked Women: Prostitutes and Prostitution in the Cinema*. Madison, WI: University of Wisconsin Press.

Carnes, M.C. (1995). *Past Imperfect: History According to the Movies*. New York: Henry Holt & Co.

Chase, A. (2002). *Movies on Trial: The Legal System on the Silver Screen*. New York: The New Press.

Cheatwood, D. & Petersen, R.D. (2007). The Film *Criminal Justice*: Race, Gender, and University Experience in Students' Perceptions of Racism and Guilt. *Criminal Justice Review, 32*, 26–46.

Clarens, Carlos. (1997). *Crime Movies*. New York: Da Capo Press.

Cook, K.L. & Bacot, H. (1993). Movies in the Classroom: Popular Images of Criminal Justice, Criminology, and the Law. *Journal of Criminal Justice Education, 4*, 199–209.

Crawford, C. (1999). Law Enforcement and Popular movies: Hollywood as a Teaching Tool in the Classroom. *Journal of Criminal Justice and Popular Culture, 6*, 46–57.

Crowther, Bruce. (1989). *Captured on Film: The Prison Movie*. London, England: B.T. Batsford Ltd.

Denvir, J. (1996*). Legal Reelsim: Movies as Legal Texts*. Champaign, Illinois: University of Illinois Press.

Engel, S. (2003). Teaching Literature in the Criminal Justice Curriculum. *Journal of Criminal Justice Education, 14*, 345–356.

Fiddler, M. (2007). Projecting the Prison: The Depiction of the Uncanny in *The Shawshank Redemption*. *Crime, Media, Culture, 3*, 192–206.

Film & History. (2009). Available at http://www.uwosh.edu/filmandhistory/index. php

Greenfield, S. & Osborn, G. (2003). Film Lawyers: Above and Beyond the Law. In *Criminal Visions: Media Representations of Crime and Justice*. P. Mason (Ed.), Cullompton, England: Willan.

Herzberg, B. (2007). *The FBI and the Movies: A History of the Bureau on Screen and Behind the Scenes in Hollywood*. Jefferson, NC: McFarland.

Hesse, M.L. & Przemieniecki, C.J. (2009). Prison Sci-films, Technocorrections, and Educational methods. *ACJS Today, 34*, 1–11.

Jarvis, B. (2007). Monsters Inc.: Serial Killers and Consumer Culture. *Crime, Media, Culture, 3*, 326–344.

Jones, H. (1997). *Mutiny on the Amistad.* New York: Oxford University Press.

King, N. (1999). *Heroes in Hard Times: Cop Action Movies in the U.S.* Philadelphia, PA: Temple University Press.

Kuzina, M. (2001). The Social Issue Courtroom Drama as an Expression of American Popular Culture. *Journal of Law and Society, 28,* 79–96.

Lacks, R.D. (2007). The 'Real' CSI: Designing and Teaching a Violent Crime Scene Class in an Undergraduate Setting. *Journal of Criminal Justice Education, 18,* 311–321.

Leishman, F. & Mason, P. (2003). *Policing and the Media: Facts, Fictions, and Factions.* Cullompton, England: Willan.

Lemisch, J. (1999). Black Agency in the *Amistad* Uprising: Or, You've Taken our Cinque and Gone." *Souls: A Critical Journal of Black Politics, Culture, and Society, 1,* 57–70.

Linder, D. (2000). "The Amistad Case." Available at http://www.law.umkc.edu/faculty/projects/ftrials/amistad/AMISTD.HTM.

Marcus, A.S. (2005). 'It is as it Was': Feature Film in the History Classroom. *The Social Studies, 96,* 61–67.

Mattheisen, D. (1989). Finding the Right Film for the History Class. *Perspectives, 2,* 13–14.

Mawby, R. (2003). The Screen Machine: Cinematic Representations of Prison. In *Criminal Visions: Media Representations of Crime and Justice.* P. Mason (Ed.), Cullompton, England: Willan.

McCarty, John. (1993). *Hollywood Gangland: The Movies' Love Affair with the Mob.* New York: St. Martin's Press.

McLaughlin, E. (2005). From Reel to Ideal: The Blue Lampand the Popular Cultural Construction of the English 'Bobby.' *Crime, Media, Culture, 1,* 11–30.

Munby, J. (1999). *Public Enemies, Public Heroes: Screening the Gangster from Little Caesar to Touch of Evil.* Chicago, IL: University of Chicago Press.

Nickoli, A., Hendricks, C., Hendricks, J., & Osgood, E. (2003). Pop Culture, Crime, and Pedagogy. *Journal of Criminal Justice Education, 14,* 149–162.

O'Brien, M., Tzanelli, R., & Yar, M. (2005a). Kill-n-Tell (& All That Jazz): The Seductions of Crime in Chicago. *Crime, Media, Culture, 1,* 243–261.

O'Brien, M, Tzanelli, R., & Yar M. (2005b). 'The Spectacle of Fearsome Acts': Crime in the Melting p(l)ot in *Gangs of New York. Critical Criminology, 13,* 17–35.

O'Connor, J.E. (1988). History in Images/Images in History: Reflections on the Importance of Film and Television Study for an Understanding of the Past. *American Historical Review, 93,* 1200–1209.

O'Connor, J.E. (1990). *Images as Artifact: The Historical Analysis of Film and Television.* Malabar, FL: Krieger Publishing Co.

Osagie, I. F. (2003). *The Amistad Revolt.* Athens, GA: University of Georgia Press.

Parish, James R. (1991). *Prison Pictures from Hollywood.* Jefferson, NC: McFarland & Company, Inc.

Patenaude, A.L. (2001). 'May God have Mercy on your Soul!' Exploring and Teaching a Course on the Death Penalty. *Journal of Criminal Justice Education, 12,* 405–425.

Pino, N.W., Brunson, R.K., & Stewart, E.A. (2009). Using Movies to Illustrate Ethical Dilemmas in Undergraduate Criminal Justice Classes. *Journal of Criminal Justice Education, 20,* 194–202.

Powers, S., Rothman, D., & Rothman, S. (1996). *Hollywood's America: Social and Political Themes in Motion Pictures.* Boulder, CO: Westview Press.

Rafter, N. (2005). Badfellas. In *Law and Popular Culture.* M. Freeman (Ed.), Oxford: Oxford University Press.

Rafter, N. (2007). Crime, Film and Criminology: Recent Sex-Crime Movies. *Theoretical Criminology, 11,* 403–420.

Rafter, N. (2001). *Shots in the Mirror: Crime, Films and Society.* Oxford: Oxford University Press.

Reiner, R., Livingstone, S., & Allen, J. (2000). No More Happy Endings? The Media and Popular Concerns about Crime Since the Second World War. In *Crime, Risk, and Insecurity.* T. Hope and R. Sparks (Eds.), London, England: Routledge.

Robbers, M.L. (2005). The Media and Public Perception of Criminal Policy Issues: An Analysis of *Bowling for Columbine* and Gun Control. *Journal of Criminal Justice and Popular Culture, 12,* 77–95.

Rockell, B.A. (2009). Challenging What They all Know: Integrating the Real/Reel World into Criminal Justice Pedagogy. *Journal of Criminal Justice Education, 20,* 75–92.

Schneider, A. (1998). Advising Spielberg: A Career Studying the *Amistad* Rebellion. *The Chronicle of Higher Education,* A12.

Shohat, E. & Stam, R. (1994). *Unthinking Eurocentrism: Multiculturalism and the Media.* London: Routledge.

Sprau, R. (2001). I Saw it in the Movies: Suggestions for Incorporating Film and Experiential Learning in the College History Survey Course. *College Student Journal, 1,* 35–44.

Stoddard, J.D. & Marcus, A.S. (2006). The Burden of Historical Representation: Race, Freedom, and 'Educational' Hollywood Film. *Film & History, 36,* 26–35.

Toplin, R.B. (1996a). The Historian and Film: Challenges Ahead. *Perspectives, 34,* 7–10.

Toplin, R.B. (1996b). *History by Hollywood: The Use and Abuse of the American Past.* Champaign, IL: University of Illinois Press.

Tzanelli, R., Yar, M., & O'Brien, M. (2005). 'Con Me if you Can': Exploring Crime in the American Cinematic Imagination. *Theoretical Criminology,* *9,* 97–117.

Vollmer, August. (1949). *The Criminal.* New York: The Foundation Press, Inc.

Wilson, D. & O'Sullivan, S. (2005). Re-Theorizing the Penal Reform Functions of the Prison Film. *Theoretical Criminology, 9,* 471–491.

Yaquinto, Marilyn. (1998). *Pump 'em Full of Lead: A Look at Gangsters on Film.* New York: Twayne Publishers.

CHAPTER 1

AMISTAD AND THE TRIAL OF THE AMISTADS (1839)

Portrait of Sengbe Pieh, the leader of the Amistad Captives, who was renamed Joseph Cinque by his Portuguese captives. The painting is by Nathaniel Jocelyn in 1840, and the original painting is held by the New Haven Colony Historical Society, New Haven, CT.

Mendi people have got souls ... All we want is make us free.
— Kali, a Mende child, in a letter
to former President John Q. Adams

Introduction

On June 27, 1839, the Spanish schooner *La Amistad* ("The Friendship") left the port of Havana, Cuba for the port of Puerto Principe, located on the other side of Cuba. The captain of the *Amistad* was Ramon Ferrer, and his passengers included two slave traders, Jose Ruiz and Don Pedro Montez. They had just purchased 49 newly imported Africans from the slave auction in Havana. The slaves had been captured months earlier along the coastal countries of Africa and transported across the Atlantic Ocean to Havana. One of the slaves was Sengbe Pieh of Dombokoro (modern day Sierra Leone), a man destined to be the leader of his tribe. After being captured by other Africans working for the slave traders, he was locked into chains, purchased by Jose Ruiz and Pedro Montez. He then found himself in the slave hold of the *Amistad* with 48 other prisoners.

As the *Amistad* sailed east toward Puerto Principe, Sengbe managed to obtain a metal file and free himself from his chains. He quickly freed the others and they armed themselves with cane knives they had found in the ship's hold. Rebelling against the slavers, they killed Captain Ramon Ferrer and the ship's cook. They then forced Ruiz and Montez to return the ship to their homeland by steering toward the rising sun.

During the day, the *Amistad* sailed east, heading toward Africa, but at night, Montez slowly turned the ship west. Before the sun arose, he slowly steered the ship back east so the Africans would not know of his scheme. Thus, the ship began to make a zigzag pattern north, catching the attention of many other ships. Eventually running out of supplies, the *Amistad* was forced to go ashore for supplies. Little did they know, they had sailed as far north as Long Island Sound. A United States Revenue Cutter, the *Washington*, having heard of the wayward *Amistad*, stopped to investigate and took possession of the ship, towing it to New London, Connecticut. Thus arose the case of the *Amistad*, and its 49 slaves, which centered on whether the individuals captured were African or Spanish, as well as slave or free. Eventually it was two court cases and a hearing before the United States Supreme Court that ultimately decided their fate.

The *Amistad* was a minor event in American history and despite numerous books on the events,[1] the story received little attention until motion picture director Steven Spielberg decided to make a film titled *Amistad*, which was released in 1997.[2] The film, although ultimately not very successful at the box office, brought the name of the *Amistad* and the plight of the African slave trade to the attention of the American public and their story became more widely shared. Additional publications have since been released chronicling the *Amistad* revolt.[3] Funds were also generated to create a replicated schooner named *La Amistad*, that would sail from port to port in America, sharing the story of the 49 slaves that garnered the attention of many renown abolitionists at the time as well as two presidents, the then current serving President Martin Van Buren and former President John Quincy Adams.[4]

While the motion picture served to bring the story of the *Amistad* to many Americans, the film was also rife with historical errors and mistakes. Spielberg employed every technique for conveying a criminal justice historic event and trial as detailed in the introduction in the film. Thus, this chapter will explore the true story of the *Amistad*, review the motion picture's portrayal of that history, and discuss the historical mistakes and errors of that film.

Amistad: The History

In January of 1839, Spanish slave traders operating off the coast of Dombokoro (modern day Sierra Leone), paid Africans to capture other Africans for entry into the illegal slave trade. The capture of these Africans for purposes of slavery was in direct violation of the 1817 treaty between Spain and Britain, which prohibited the importation of slaves into any of the Spanish colonies, including Cuba. A small raiding party of four Africans lurked on the outskirts of the small village of Mani in Upper Mende country, watching for potential victims. They spotted a young man, Sengbe, a farmer, who was working in the fields late that day. They descended upon him, wrestled him to the ground, and bound him tightly. Sengbe Pieh was the son of the local chief who was married with three children, one son and two daughters. He was destined to become the chief himself one day.[5]

Sengbe was first taken to a nearby village where he was kept tied up with the leader of the raiding party. He was sold off to another tribesman and he remained in captivity for a month before being marched to the coast, a ten day's journey. There he was sold to the notorious Spanish slaver Pedro Blanco and taken to the slave stronghold known as Lomboko, an island located near Sulima on the Gallinas coast.[6] He remained on the slave-trading island for two months, waiting for other slaves to join him before there were enough to transport across the Atlantic.

By late April, with enough Africans collected, Sengbe, along with 600 other African men, women, and children, were then transferred to the slave ship *Tecora*. The ship set sail, crossing the infamous Middle Passage of the Atlantic Ocean, bound for the Spanish Colony, Cuba. The slaves were kept naked and chained in a prone position in the slave hold area of the cargo ship. The conditions were horrendous and many of the captured died on the passage across the Atlantic Ocean; their bodies being thrown overboard without ceremony.

The *Tecora* arrived in early June of 1839 at the port of Havana, Cuba. The Africans were transferred to the *Barracoon* (slave market), where they were kept in chains for another week as they were prepared to go on the auction block, which consisted of a brutal washing and forced feeding. It was there that Don Pedro Montes and Jose Ruiz purchased 53 slaves, including four children, along with the Mende leader, Sengbe, They were again transferred to the slave hold, this time on aboard *La Amistad*, and the schooner set sail on June 28, bound for Puerto Principe, Cuba.

Don Pedro and Jose Ruiz had chartered the ship from Ramon Ferrer, the captain of *La Amistad*. The schooner had originally been an American transport ship called the *Friendship*, but when it changed hands to the Spaniards, the name was changed to Spanish. In addition to the captain and two slavers, the crew consisted of two black slaves, a cabin boy by the name of Antonio, a mulatto cook by the name of Celestino, and two Spanish seamen. The ship carried not only the slaves as goods, but it also carried a number of valuable items ranging from gold and jewelry to fine dishes and elegant cloth.

The trip should have only lasted three days, but strong gale winds blew in and the *Amistad* found itself still at sea on the fourth day, July 2, 1839. That night, Sengbe led a slave revolt based on rumors circulating among those in the hold that the Spaniards were cannibals and they were to be eaten.[7] The story, later told by the Africans, was that the mulatto cook "told the slaves that they would be chopped to pieces and salted as meat for the Spaniards when the ship arrived at its destination."[8] Fearing they would be eaten, Sengbe had decided that "we may as well die trying to be free, as to be killed and eaten."[9]

Sengbe managed to obtain some type of metal object, often described as a metal nail, spike, or file, and began working on his chains.[10] Sengbe managed to free himself, then quickly freed the others in the slave hold. They armed themselves with cane knives (machetes), and during the overthrow of the ship, they killed the Captain, Ramon Ferrer, and the mulatto cook, Celestino. They also wounded the Spaniard Montez, but he surrendered and was not further harmed. The two Spaniard seamen, during the struggle on deck, managed to escape overboard by climbing into the stern boat and rowing away.

Now in charge of the ship, Sengbe demanded that Montes and Ruiz sail the ship east toward the rising sun, what the Africans knew to be the direction home. By day, Montes steered the ship east, but by night he gradually changed course west until just before sunrise, when he would again turn east. Six weeks of this zigzag pattern caused many ships to notice the *Amistad's* erratic behavior, which brought them to New York, just off Long Island Sound, fast running out of supplies and fresh water.[11]

Sengbe ordered a boat to row to shore to gather fresh food and water. Upon reaching shore and heading inland, four of the Africans, naked save for the blankets they had around them, startled two sea captains, Peletiah Fordham and Henry Green, who were shooting birds along the Long Island coast. The Amistads tried to communicate with the two men through hand gestures. They motioned them to the top of a sand dune where they pointed to *La Amistad,* which shocked the two sea captains for the conditions the ship was in—the sails were tattered and there was no flag flying off the stern. The leader of the small foraging party showed Fordham and Green the gold necklace he was wearing and gestured that the valuables would be theirs if they provided food and provisions for the ship.

At this point, the negotiations were interrupted by the appearance of the U.S. Revenue Cutter Service (predecessor to the U.S. Coast Guard) ship, the *Washington.* Having heard the stories of an errant ship from a number of seamen who had sighted the *Amistad,* as well as two pilot boats that had actually encountered the Amistads themselves, they searched for and finally discovered the *Amistad* anchored off the New York coast.[12] Upon boarding the ship, the officers found Mendes and Ruiz locked in the hold, pleading for help. The four Africans on shore saw the new ship and abandoned Fordham and Green, trying to row back to the *Amistad*. Sengbe, realizing the situation was lost, leaped over the side of the ship and began swimming away. The sailors gave chase, firing warning shots over the head of Sengbe, but he continued to swim away. The seamen continued to follow until Sengbe had exhausted himself and they pulled him aboard the stern boat. Sengbe remained so defiant in the face of captivity that he was placed in chains and separated from the rest of the Amistads.

After firing shots across the bow of the stern boat that was trying to return to the *Amistad,* the seamen took the other four Africans into custody. The Amistad captives, except for Sengbe, were all placed back in the slave hold with Montes and Ruiz, with several of the U.S. Revenue Cutter service seaman to assist, the *Amistad* was towed by the *Washington* to New London, Connecticut.[13] Lieutenant Gedney sent word of the salvaging of the *Amistad* to the U.S. Marshal in New Haven, who notified United States District Court Judge Andrew Judson of the situation.

It was now August 27, 1839. For nearly two months the *Amistad* had been sailing east by day and west by night, zigzagging north off the North American coastline. Their fate was largely undetermined for there was no proof they were free and only the word of Montes and Ruiz that they were property. The estimated value of the ship, the cargo (which included gold and silk) and the slaves was considered to be worth approximately $70,000, so ownership became the crucial question, and the courts became the forum in which ownership would be decided.[14]

On August 29, 1839, Judge Judson opened a criminal trial on board the *Washington* based on the complaints by Montes and Ruiz accusing the Amistads of murder and piracy.[15] Montes and Ruiz demanded the return of the Spanish property, namely the Amistad captives. They presented evidence that the Amistad captives were Spanish slaves for they had a manifest listing their names, all in Spanish. Sengbe was now Cinque.

Lieutenant Gedney, captain of the *Washington,* demanded of the court salvaging rights and compensation for the return of *La Amistad*. Judson decided to refer the case to circuit court as a federal case and he placed the Amistads in the county jail in New Haven. There the Amistads became somewhat of a sideshow as thousands of people visited the jail every day to look at the people from Africa. The four children immediately became a hit with the crowds and the public became more sympathetic to their plight.

Others had also become sympathetic to the plight of all the Amistads and many abolitionists worked behind the scenes to assist the Amistad captives.

Businessman and abolitionist leader Lewis Tappan became heavily involved by helping to form the "Amistad Committee," which secured the assistance of lawyer and abolitionist Roger Baldwin (who one day would become the governor of Connecticut). In addition, two other noted lawyers and abolitionists were part of the team, and these included Seth Staple and Theodore Sedgwick. Staple left the case early on and Sedgwick remained helpful, but was not at the forefront of the case. Baldwin became the lawyer for the Amistads.

The circuit court case opened September 14, 1839, with Judge Judson now serving alongside Judge Smith Thompson, as the circuit court judge.[16] The focus of the case centered on the Amistads status as property and their citizenship. After three days of legal wrangling from both sides, the circuit court issued its decision. The judges determined that they had no jurisdiction in the case regarding the charges of murder and piracy. The crimes were committed in Spanish waters, on board a Spanish ship, by and amongst alleged Spaniards. As for the property rights, it was the wrong court as well, and thus it was remanded to the district court. As soon as the circuit court case was concluded, Judge Judson convened the district court case, releasing the captives on bail and stating that the property claim needed to be explored further. Baldwin protested the bail decision, which suggested the prisoners were in fact slaves, thus the Amistads were returned to jail. The case was then moved for hearing to November.

The biggest deficiency for the defense was the fact the lawyers could not communicate with their clients. Dr. Josiah Gibbs, a Yale professor and noted scholar who also happened to be an abolitionist, worked with the Amistads and determined that their language was Mende. He then learned how to count to ten in Mende and, armed with that knowledge, went down to the docks, walking daily amongst the throngs of people hoping to find someone who recognized the language. In October, Dr. Gibbs finally came across a British sailor who recognized his native language and began speaking to the professor. James Covey was the seaman and he had been born and raised in Africa. He was captured by slavers as a teenager, but rescued by a British ship targeting the slave trade. He learned English and decided to sign on with the British Navy, which is why he found himself in New Haven, Connecticut. Hearing his native language he responded. His assistance secured, he became the translator for the Mende.

The trial began on November 19, 1839, in Hartford, Connecticut, presided over, again, by Judge Judson.[17] The case had to be postponed until January 7, 1840, as some of the key witnesses could not be present. Once the court case resumed, testimony from both sides was again entered into the court record. This time, however, Sengbe was given the opportunity to speak through the translator. He eloquently relayed his and the other Amistad's stories about being kidnapped, beaten, and treated with indignity, and how they simply had defended their rights as free men. Emotion would overcome him during his testimony and he would rise and shout in English, "Give us free! Give us free!" This emotional outburst and the story of the Amistad were not only revealed to the court, but it was revealed to the entire United States, as newspapers widely reported the story and testimony.

After several more days of testimony, Judge Judson issued his decision on January 13, 1840, declaring the Amistads had been born free and kidnapped in violation of international law. Any crimes they had committed, murder and piracy, had been committed in Spanish held waters and were therefore not under the purview of U.S. law. The Amistads were ordered released and "delivered to President Van Buren for transport back to Africa."[18] District Attorney William S. Holabird, on advice from the Van Buren Administration, immediately appealed the decision.

While the Amistads were technically free, they had no means to return home. They were taken into the care of the abolitionists and moved to better living conditions in a home in Farmington, Connecticut. There were now only 36 Amistads remaining.

Once the decision was appealed, the Amistads could not leave until the outcome of appellate decision, which went before the United States Supreme Court. Baldwin appealed to former President John Quincy Adams to assist the defense.

John Quincy Adams had been the sixth president of the United States, serving from 1825 to 1829, losing reelection to Andrew Jackson. Continuing his life of politics, he was elected to the House of Representatives and was serving in that capacity as the Representative of the 12th District, Massachusetts. The appeals from Baldwin, Tappen, and others were not initially acted upon, but after receiving two letters from the Mende children, one passage denoted in the epigraph at the beginning of the chapter, Adams decided to sign on in defense of the Amistads.

Baldwin represented the Amistads before the United States Supreme Court hearing where seven justices presided. None of the Amistads were present at the hearing and, while John Quincy Adams sat at the defense's table, he did not address the court until the last day, February 24, 1841. This was indeed a historic moment, for in many ways his presence pitted the former president against the current president, Martin Van Buren.

Adams delivered his testimony, speaking for four and one-half hours, leaving the court enraptured and glued to their seat by his testimony. After recessing to deliberate, Chief Justice Story announced, on March 9, 1841, that the Africans were free.[19] He noted the Court's decision was based upon the more narrow arguments of lawyer Roger Baldwin, rather than the more "interesting" comments of John Quincy Adams. To be sure, the decision was pointedly not a repudiation of slavery, but rather an acknowledgement that these Africans had been illegally kidnapped and were entitled to freedom, even by the laws of Spain. The Amistads were free, but there was no one waiting to return them to Africa.

The abolitionists' efforts then turned to raising adequate funds to return the kidnapped Mende back to their homeland. As they struggled to raise the necessary funds, many of the Amistads became depressed, and found themselves involved in brawls, assaults, and one committed suicide, drowning himself in a pond. Eventually, in November of 1841, the ship *Gentleman* was chartered at the cost of $1,840, and the remaining Amistads, along with several missionaries, made the 50 day voyage across the Atlantic Ocean. A mission was established, although not without difficulties. Some of the Amistads, finding nothing left for them in their native country, remained with the mission; others were never heard from again. The last of the Mende to return to the mission was Sengbe. After leaving the mission to return to his village, he found it mostly destroyed and the people scattered. His wife and children were gone and for years he searched for them. He never found them. In 1879, Sengbe, now a sick old man, returned to the mission and died the following day. He was buried in the mission's cemetery, among the many abolitionists who had died supporting the mission.

Amistad: The Film

In 1997, film director Steven Spielberg, in conjunction with DreamWorks, released the film *Amistad*.[20] The film was rated "R" for scenes of brutal violence and had a December release. It featured an all-star cast, with Morgan Freeman headlining the production, playing a free-black abolitionist character known as "Joadson." Matthew McConaughey played the part of lawyer Roger Baldwin, Anthony Hopkins as John Quincy Adams, and Djimon Hounsou as Sengbe (Cinque). The film had a production budget of $40 million, but only managed to gross $44 million; it was not a major hit with the American audience.

The film opens with the *Amistad* on a dark and stormy night, and an African (later identified as Sengbe) who is in chains, obtains a spike and manages to free himself from his manacles. He then frees others and they began to grab swords from a crate. The freed slaves climb the stairs, gain the deck of the ship, and one slave kills a sailor with a knife while another slits the throat of a sailor. A third seaman is killed and finally the captain is run through with a sword by Sengbe. Intermixed in the violence, the crew manages to shoot one slave and stabs and kills a second. The scene shifts to the name of the boat, *La Amistad,* before shifting scenes and showing the boat on still water with the caption "1839."

The film next shows Sengbe and another freed African arguing about how to proceed. Sengbe prevails and orders the two Spaniards to sail the ship toward the sun. Montes sails toward the sun during the day, but at night turns the ship back in a westward direction. Sengbe is shown watching the stars one night, realizing what is happening, and orders Montes to turn the ship back east, as shown by the depiction of the compass. Montes shows Sengbe in the morning that the ship is still sailing toward the sun.

The scene shifts to nighttime and the four children are singing and playing, when Sengbe orders them to be quiet. They hear music and soon another ship, replete with an elegant dining spread, guests in evening wear, and a musical quartet, passes by, giving the Africans hardly a glance.

A caption states "six weeks" in the next scene and the *Amistad* is shown running out of supplies with tattered sails when land is sighted. Eight of the Africans row ashore on a small stern boat named *La Amistad.* They then break the ice with their buckets as they gather water, when suddenly a bicyclist goes by and keeps on going when he sees the Amistads. At that point, a U.S. flagged ship comes upon the *Amistad,* and those on shore return to the stern boat and begin rowing back to the ship. Realizing the stern boat with U.S. seamen were going to block their way, Sengbe jumps in the water and tries to swim away, nearly drowning, before being pulled onto the boat.

The *Amistad* and captives all arrive at a port in chains. The town lies in a blanket of snow and it is obviously cold by the condensed breath. The Amistads are escorted to the jail at night while two white men inside the jail, dressed in suits, look on, concerned.

The scene then shifts to Isabella II, Queen of Spain, a young child who is advised about the situation. It then shifts to Martin Van Buren, campaigning for reelection on a whistle stop tour by train. He says he is unconcerned with the plight of "44 Negroes." Another scene shows Morgan Freeman, who plays a free black abolitionist character named "Joadson," talking with a newspaper publisher about the Amistads. Finally, another scene shows the jailers taking the Amistads to court.

The courtroom is packed and Judge Judson enters and takes his seat. District Attorney Holabird charges the Amistads with murder and piracy; Tappan shows up with a writ for the Amistad's release; Secretary of State Forsyth shows up announcing he represents the diplomatic interests of Spain; Lieutenant Gedney, of the *U.S.S. Washington*, shows up claiming savaging rights; and finally the two Spaniards, Pedro Montes and Juan Ruiz, show up with a lawyer representing their property rights. The court then quickly convenes and Roger Baldwin is shown approaching Tappan, begging for the case, although he appears to know little of Tappan, and Tappan doesn't know Baldwin. When asked, Baldwin states he is a real estate lawyer.

The film shifts to John Quincy Adams "sleeping" in some legislative room and as he leaves, he is told that Tappan wants to visit with him. They talk about the Amistads outside of a large white state building, but Joadson does most of the talking, telling John Quincy Adams about Adam's own life. Adams excuses himself and says he won't help.

Roger Baldwin is next shown as a starving lawyer, being fed by Tappan, who has no resort but to use this lawyer. They argue about how to present the case and Baldwin sees it as a case of property, Tappan as a cause of righteousness. Tappan brings up the case of Christ, and Baldwin explains that Christ lost his case.

The scene again shifts to the jail, where a group of Christians arrive and sing "Amazing Grace" to the Amistads, who think they are entertainers. Baldwin and Joadson then arrive at the jail with Dr. Gibbs in tow. They try to talk to the Amistads, who are arguing over tribal areas of the jail. Baldwin then shows the Amistads some evidence, such as a sword, and asks them if it belongs to them. Gibbs is supposed to translate, but he is played for humor as his translation is entirely different than what the Amistads are saying.

The film returns to the courtroom and Baldwin begins by saying the case is about geography. He tries speaking with the Amistads in English and then Spanish, it being clear they speak neither. Suddenly the lawyer for the Spaniards arrives with a manifest showing the "Spanish" names of the Amistads. Judge Judson enters it into evidence and the Africans are returned to jail.

After a brief jail scene, Baldwin and Joadson are seen exploring the *Amistad* looking for evidence. Baldwin finds several maps of Cuba, as well as the African coast. Joadson, while looking in the ship's hold, suffers an anxiety attack. Because of this, Baldwin discovers the true ship's manifest, showing the names of the Africans being crossed off and the new names, all Spanish, being handwritten into the ledger. The scene then cuts to the courtroom, where Baldwin introduces this evidence, causing consternation on the part of Holabird and elation on the part of Tappan. While celebrating outside of the courthouse, Baldwin is briefly assaulted.

Several scenes then shift to show the political diplomacy between Queen Isabella II of Spain and Martin Van Buren. Van Buren, shown campaigning via train and kissing babies, is then placed in the White House with Forsyth, who explains that the Amistad dilemma could spark a civil war. The answer to the dilemma is to remove the current judge and replace him with a young, insecure Catholic, who is trying to hide his religion—Judge Coglin. The idea being he could be manipulated by the administration. Baldwin is then shown going into a rage when he learns about the replacement.

The film next shows Joadson speaking with John Quincy Adams, who advises that the key to the case is who can tell the best story. In order to learn the Amistad's story, Dr. Gibbs is shown educating Baldwin how to count to ten in Mende, so they can roam the docks counting in the hopes that someone will understand the language and could serve as an interpreter. That person is found by Joadson in the British sailor James Covey. Baldwin and Joadson then take Covey to the jail to translate and they find one of the Africans has died and others are in a chanting rage, while the guards are inside the jail with rifles and bayonets along with the Christians, who are singing.

The translation begins with Baldwin explaining the judge had been replaced and asking Sengbe about his story of slaying the lion. Baldwin then asks how Sengbe arrived in America and Sengbe, through a flashback, tells his story of being captured, taken to Lomboko, carried across the Atlantic in the *Tecora*, and sold into slavery. They show scenes of the slavers throwing some of the Africans overboard and flogging the captives, while the scene pans out to show the *Tecora* flying the American flag. Eventually Sengbe ends where the film begins, escaping his chains and taking the ship, while the film reverts to the courtroom, where it suggests that Sengbe gave the same testimony before the new judge. Sengbe's testimony is followed by a British captain, who details his experience with the slave trade, while Sengbe is shown having an anxiety attack before standing and shouting in English, "Give us free!"

The film shifts to the jail, juxtaposed against scenes of a Catholic Church. One of the captives in the jail shows Sengbe a Bible and tells the story of Jesus, while the new judge enters the church, kneels, makes the sign of the cross, and begins to pray. This is quickly followed by the Amistads being marched to the courtroom in chains, where the Judge states the Amistads are free, orders the arrest of Ruiz and Montes, and Baldwin et al. celebrate.

After a White House dinner featuring Senator John Calhoun talking about the plight of the South and the coming Civil War, the scene returns to the jail, where the Amistads are celebrating with drums, dancing, and a bonfire. Baldwin tells Sengbe the case must be retried in the Supreme Court and Sengbe strips naked in protest. Baldwin, distraught, writes to John Quincy Adams for help. He decides to work with Baldwin and Sengbe on the case. There is a back and forth between Sengbe and Adams before Sengbe is invited to Adam's house for a visit, where he sees an African violet.

The film then moves to Adams speech before the Supreme Court and their decision that the Amistads are to be freed. A quick wrap-up of the slave fortress being blown up by the British is shown, followed by the Amistads sailing home. A note says that Sengbe found his village destroyed and his family missing, never to be seen again. The film then fades to credits.

Amistad: Hollywood's Rendering

Amistad presents a good example of the various types of techniques and mistakes Hollywood makes when presenting criminal justice history. From the opening scenes on board *La Amistad* to the film's credits, Spielberg's portrayal of factual events is rife with historical inaccuracies. To begin with, the film opens with Sengbe and the other slaves' revolt. The night is dark and stormy, rain pelts the ship, and winds blow. Recorded history only suggests that there were heavy winds that had delayed the ship in making its port fall on the third day, but there is no report of a major storm. Sengbe then frees himself with what appears to be a nail or spike, unchains the others, and opens a crate of fancy swords. In reality they were cane knives (machetes), not Spanish swords. As they move on deck, the film depicts four of the seaman, including the captain, being killed in the revolt, while two of the slaves are killed. In actuality, only two of the slavers, Captain Ferrer and the cook, Celestino, were killed, along with the two slaves involved in the revolt.

In regard to the technique of simplifying reality, in these very same scenes, Spielberg immediately focuses on the revolt without any explanation or background as to why the slaves were revolting. While the film later alludes to the fact they are attempting to "be free," the reality is more complex: rumors, circulated by Celestino, had spread among the captured Africans that the Spanish captors were cannibals and the true reason for their captivity was to be served. Fear of being eaten motivated their overthrow of the ship. In addition, among the captives on board the *Amistad* were four small children, who in the early scenes are shown on the boat. Once the slaves are removed from the ship the film no longer presents the children's story, yet in reality, it was they who elicited the most sympathy for the Amistad captives, not Sengbe.[21]

The film continues to show a number of entirely fictitious scenes that are apparently inserted into the film because they play well on screen, creating somewhat oddly humorous encounters. One example is when the *Amistad* is zigzagging across the Atlantic Ocean; one night, the boat comes across another boat with a formal dinner party and quartet playing music. The dinner party appears to hardly notice the *Amistad* and when they do, are wholly unconcerned as three dozen Africans stare at them as their ships pass. In truth, the *Amistad* did come across other ships, but never one with such an elaborate dining party.

In another scene, the Amistads go on shore at Long Island Sound with eight men (historically it was only four) to gather water when they spy a gentleman on a bicycle who rides by them. When they try to flag him down, he rides even faster to get away, creating a somewhat comic scene. History records the four men met two sea captains out hunting, not a man bicycling through the woods on Long Island. Still further, when this scene is shown, the eight men in the film are all cold, wearing blankets, and they have to break through a layer of ice to get to the water. Later, when they arrive in New London, Connecticut there is snow on the ground. In reality, these events transpired in August when there was no chance for either ice or snow to be present.

Once the Amistads are brought into the jail in New London, a number of the characters begin to be introduced and various techniques are used to deal with the main characters to be portrayed. In terms of both combining multiple characters into one and the creation of fictional characters, *Amistad* manages to achieve both through one of the first characters introduced—Joadson. Morgan Freeman, a wonderful actor, plays the part of Joadson in the film, a character who is a freed black who has become an abolitionist. Although of all the historical characters, Lewis Tappan was perhaps the most reknown of the abolitionists, the film uses Joadson (poorly) to represent all abolitionists.[22] The biggest issue with the Joadson character is that he is entirely fictitious for there was no one named Joadson in the actual historical events, nor was there a black abolitionist assisting the Amistads. He simply never existed. This fact is then made worse at several points in the film because of the ineptitude of Freeman's character. At one point he tells Baldwin that taking the case was just about money. In another scene he has the former President, John Quincy Adams, tell him his story of becoming free; keeping in mind that Joadson is supposed to be the freed slave. In short, despite all efforts to represent the freed slaves in the film, the character serves no narrative purpose.

One other element of the Joadson character was the application of Professor Josiah Gibbs counting to ten in Mende on the docks to him. In the film, Professor Gibbs is painted as a bumbling and idiotic professor who was unable to translate Mende. In reality, Professor Gibbs never attempted to translate for the lawyer Baldwin, but rather learned how to count to ten in Mende, then suggested to Baldwin that he could secure a translator by counting to ten in Mende down by the docks in and amongst the sailors. It was Professor Gibbs who located the translator on the docks, not the fictitious Joadson.[23]

Beyond the fictitious Joadson character, the film *Amistad* also fictionalizes some aspects of real characters. One such example is found in the lead lawyer for the Amistads, Roger Baldwin. Early in the film he appears to be a hungry real estate lawyer, looking to make money on the Amistad case, and having to be instructed on the abolitionist movement.[24] In real life, Baldwin was a well-to-do lawyer who did not need the money, was well-respected in the community, and was already a key player in the abolitionist movement—he needed no instruction. Still further, Baldwin appears not to know who Tappan is and vice versa, yet in reality both of these men were prominent in the community because of their involvement in the abolitionist movement, making them well aware of one another. Baldwin also had experience in representing the abolitionist cause in court, for in one case he defended a client who was a runaway slave and he won the case.[25] In fact, Baldwin was not a real estate lawyer, but a very successful business lawyer. Finally, it should be noted that in real life there were three prominent lawyers for the Amistads, not just Roger Baldwin. The other two lawyers were Seth Staples and Theodore Sedgwick. All three of the lawyers were Yale graduates. Staples did remove himself from the case as he was placed in charge of developing a new school—what would become the Yale Law School. Yet, the film does not depict either of these lawyers assisting in the case.

Another example of partially fictionalizing a historical person is found in another prominent character in the film, former President John Quincy Adams, played so well by Anthony Hopkins. The film portrays John Quincy Adams as reluctant to become involved, but in reality he assisted Baldwin throughout the trial via letters, answering questions and offering suggestions to the defense.[26] Therefore, when Baldwin wrote the last ditch letter soliciting John Quincy Adams's help, it was not really necessary. Further, John Quincy Adams did meet Sengbe once, but not as depicted in the film—not in jail, not at the Supreme Court hearing, and not in his own home. Thus, when Sengbe has to teach John Quincy Adams about his forefathers, it is entirely a Hollywood fabrication (why would John Quincy Adams need to know about his "forefathers" for his own father was one of them!).

As the court proceedings begin, a number of characters barge into the courtroom to represent some interest before the court. That first court hearing was actually held on the *U.S.S. Washington,* and not in a New London courtroom, as was suggested. The various interested parties also did not barge into the court proceedings as they do in the movie. The judge would not have tolerated such behavior. One of these individuals also happens to be John

Forsyth, the Secretary of State to President Martin Van Buren. He arrives to represent the diplomatic interests and remains present at the opposition table throughout the trial, and is present at the Supreme Court hearing. In reality, Forsyth never visited any of the court proceedings, including those before the Supreme Court.

The presentation of the court proceedings is also a good example of time compression. In reality there were two court proceedings, the first in the district court, which is shown in the film, and the second in the Federal Circuit Court, which we do not see. Judge Judson would preside over both of these cases, which made it more interesting for the fact he was pro-slavery, did not like the abolitionists, but yet he would still find in favor of the Amistads. In the film, however, the original judge, Judson, is replaced by Judge Coglin, who was supposed to be a political pawn for the Van Buren administration and a devout Catholic. This character did not exist, yet the director dedicates some time to developing the story of the replacement judge.[27]

One scene that was played for high effect in regard to the replacement judge comes when Sengbe and another African are looking through a Bible while in jail. Even the Bible they are looking through is historically inaccurate for it was the Gustave Dore illustrated Bible, first published in 1866, thus not available to them in 1839. That error aside, as Sengbe is shown the story of Jesus, Judge Coglin enters a Catholic Church, with all of its imagery of the crucifix, and kneels to pray. The scene then cuts back and forth between Sengbe learning the story of Jesus and the Judge praying for divine guidance. Since the character did not exist and so much time is spent on the replacement judge's Catholicism (or rather his attempt at hiding the fact he is Catholic), one can only speculate as to what was intended by Spielberg in this unnecessary addition to the film. Hadden speculates that the reason for the fictitious Catholic judge is "that it allowed gratuitous shots of a Catholic Church and a further inquiry into the religious hypocrisy of any human professing Christianity while forcing men to remain in bondage, which was a pure plot device in the middle of the movie."[28]

Another scene in the film that generates a number of historical errors, although it plays well to show the abuses of slaves across the Middle Passage, is depicted by the slave ship *Tecora*. The *Tecora* brought Sengbe to Cuba from Africa, along with approximately 600 other Africans. Some of the minor mistakes in the film are when the Portuguese sailors on board the *Tecora* are heard speaking early in the film, they speak with Mexican accents. In another scene, the ship's compass shows the signs of direction in English, when they would have most likely been in Spanish (e.g., NO (*nor-este*) for NW). These are most likely unintentional mistakes, but there is one that was most likely well intended. The film graphically shows slavers throwing many Africans overboard due to low food supplies, while at the same time viciously flogging others. The film then pans out to show the *Tecora* flying the American flag. This was no doubt juxtaposed for the effect of viewers to feel a sense of collective guilt, American guilt, for such abuse against the African slaves. In reality, however, the *Tecora* would not have flown the American flag, but rather the flag of Spain, for it was a Portuguese vessel sailing into Spanish territory.

The presentation of the Van Buren Administration raised a number of interesting mistakes, some also minor, some major. The minor ones included the depiction of the U.S. Capitol with what looks to be the current dome, but in 1839 it was actually still the very small copper dome. Also, when they show the U.S. House of Representatives hard at work, they depicted the U.S. flag on the wrong side of the speaker. The film also shows President Van Buren running for reelection, but it was actually the following year, 1840, that he would have run; they showed him doing whistle-stops and kissing babies, two things that were late 19th Century conventions.[29] In one scene, when Van Buren enters the room, the band plays "Hail to the Chief," yet the idea for this first came from First Lady Jane Tyler in 1841, two years after the events transpire in the film. Perhaps the most egregious mistake regarding President Martin Van Buren is the fact he is played as a bumbling, inept fool, one who has to be educated about why the Amistads pose a threat to his administration, about international relations with Spain, and about the supposedly impending Civil War. Yet it is historically recorded that Van Buren was very knowledgeable and politically astute and would not have needed such artificially employed education sessions.

Toward the end of the film, when it depicts the Supreme Court hearing, the camera pans to show all nine justices, but on that particular day, two of the justices were absent. Also in the courtroom scene, it shows Sengbe in handcuffs next to Baldwin. Sengbe, nor any of the Amistads, were present at the Supreme Court hearing. Other mistakes during this scene occurred when Adams gives his final speech in the movie: he mentions the "Executive Review," of which no publication existed. In addition, he talks about having Cinque over to his house, a scene shown earlier in the film, which is entirely false, and while he does mention the words "Civil War" in his closing arguments, it was not about any impeding American Civil War, but rather, it was spoken in the context of Spain's Civil War.

The film also employs the false sequencing of time on a number of occasions. One example comes at the end of the court hearing when "Judge Coglin" orders Ruiz and Montes arrested and charged with slave trading. This is an example of time sequencing for effect, for historically Judge Judson had already charged them with assaulting the captives, tried them, and had sentenced them for the crime, while the main case was still proceeding. Waiting to show them ordered into custody at the end of the trial was simply for effect. Another example comes at the end of the film; after hearing that the Supreme Court decision favored the Amistads, there is a scene showing that the slave trade fortress was finally found and ordered to be blown apart. The film shows with great effect the walls of the fortress crumbling from cannon fire. The abrupt shift to the slave fortress being destroyed seems to suggest it occurred shortly after the release of the Amistads and before they sailed for home. In reality, it was not found and destroyed by the British until 1849, seven years after the Amistads returned to Africa.

As demonstrated above, the issues of oversimplification, fictitious characters and scenes, time compression and sequencing, have all been evidently used in the film *Amistad*. In regard to the "whitewashed" technique, this is highly evident in the simple fact that the main characters in the film are primarily white, not black.[30] There are, however, numerous examples that are more subtle, but highly evident of whitewashing. A minor example is when John Quincy Adams shows Sengbe his African violet. An obvious reference to something familiar to Africans, but in reality, African violets were not from the area of Africa the Amistads came from and John Quincy Adams could never have owned one for they were first discussed in America in 1891 and brought over several years later. A simple example, but somewhat telling, for the director tried to introduce all things African into the film, even if highly fictitious.

The more striking examples, however, are the number of jail scenes that are highly fictitious in the film. The first full depiction of the jail shows the Africans fighting over territory in the jail, equating it to tribal territory. This is unlikely, for at that time tribes did not have as much contact or disputes over territory; that would be created later by European colonization. Even more ludicrous, however, was when Baldwin brings in items from the *Amistad* to see if they belonged to the Amistads, including a sword. It is truly doubtful that Baldwin would have been allowed to bring a sword into a jail. Later, the celebration of the court's decision in the Amistad's favor when the Africans are shown with fires raging, drums and other instruments being played, and the captives dancing. It is highly unlikely that they would have had access to the musical instruments, and most assuredly they would not have allowed dancing in the jail, much less fires. Then, when the court does not free them due to the court challenge, Sengbe rips off his clothes in protest and dances naked. There is no evidence in the historical record of this action. One other scene takes place after one of the slaves dies in custody and they pass the body around and refuse to let the jailors take the body. The reality is the captives simply wanted to bury the body themselves, hence the protest, but there was no funeral ceremony, as depicted in the film. The purpose of most of these fictitious scenes is to present the Amistads as savages, not as they truly were, but as white Americans would perceive them.[31]

Further evidence for this comes from the fact that Sengbe does not speak until the last third of the film and then only to say "Give us free." It is indeed a powerful scene, but one that makes Sengbe look unintelligent. According to Foner, the primary reason for the lack of speaking on the part of the Mende is because the film was originally going to have the Amistads speak in Mende with English subtitles.[32] However, screenings of the film found this to be unacceptable on the part of viewers, so rather than have the Mende speak in English, the majority of their speaking parts were cut from the final film.

Regardless of the film director's decision, the reality is Yale professors and students were hired to teach the Amistads English and Sengbe could read and write far more than "Give us free." In fact, "the historical records paint Sengbe Pieh as an excellent rhetorician" and "his comportment and his rousing speeches made New Englanders line up for hours in the cold just to secure seats in the courtroom."[33] Once again, it would appear that presenting the Amistads as less intelligent than the historical record suggests was simply because that is how whites would most likely perceive the captured Africans of that time period.

Perhaps the strongest evidence of the film *Amistad*, a film about African slaves fighting for their freedom, being "whitewashed" comes from the fact that the blacks throughout the film are at times savage, others submissive, but regardless, they have to rely entirely on the help of the white characters in the film to gain their freedom.[34] Only once, when Sengbe has many questions for Baldwin and John Quincy Adams, does he appear to be thoughtful and intelligent, but then it is used for comic effect and the white characters still know better in the end. One author, Dalzell, suggests that perhaps the reason for this form of portrayal is based on our collective guilt over slavery, and that "with its story of revolt, it fulfills our need, still deeply felt, to witness and vicariously participate in the overthrow of slavery."[35] Whether or not that is the case or the intent, it is clear that a film principally about Africans is primarily told through the eyes of whites—America's largest film audience.

Conclusion

In the end, it must be said that the film *Amistad* is a prime example of the quandary of Hollywood presenting history. On the one hand, if it were not for the film, the majority of Americans would have no knowledge of this important piece of criminal justice history. On the other hand, the history as presented is so rife with errors it is a poor historical representation. The average American watching this film would come away with a general idea about the *Amistad* affair, but if this was, in fact, their only frame of reference for this historical event, their history would be so burdened with historical inaccuracies as to render it almost invaluable.

Clifton Johnson, the founder of the Amistad Research Center at Tulane University, perhaps summed it up best when he spoke of the historical inaccuracies found in the film: "What [filmmakers] call dramatic license, I call historical error."[36] He then clearly spelled out the problem with the film when he explained that after having labored for 40 years to share the Amistad's story, he would now "spend the rest of my life correcting the errors" made in Spielberg's film.[37]

Further Reading

Abraham, A. (1998). *The Amistad Revolt: An Historical Legacy of Sierra Leone and* the United States. Washington, D.C.: U.S. Information Agency.

Adams, J.Q. (1969). *Argument of John Quincy Adams Before the Supreme Court of the United States, in the Case of the United States v. Cinque & Others: Africans Captured in the Schooner Amistad.* Westport, CT: Greenwood Press.

Barber, John W. (1840). *A History of the Amistad Captives.* New Haven, Connecticut: E.L. & J.W. Barber.

Cable, Mary. (1971). *Black Odyssey: The Case of the Slave Ship Amistad.* New York: Viking Press.

Jackson, D.D. (1997). "Mutiny on the Amistad." *Smithsonian,* December: 114–124.

Johnson, C.H. (1990). "The Amistad Case and Its Consequences in U.S. History." *Journal of the New Haven Colony Historical Society,* 36, 3–22.

Jones, H. (1998). "All We Want is Make Us Free." *American History,* January–February, 22–28.

Jones, H. (1997). *Mutiny on the Amistad: The Saga of the Slave Revolt and Its Impact on American Abolition, Law, and Diplomacy.* New York: Oxford University Press.

Kohn, Bernice. (1971). *The Amistad Mutiny.* New York: McCall.

Kromer, Helen. (1973). *The Amistad Revolt, 1839: The Slave Uprising Aboard the* Spanish Schooner. New York: Franklin Watts.

Linder, D. (2000). "The Amistad Case." Available at http://www.law.umkc.edu/faculty/projects/ftrials/amistad/AMISTD.HTM.

Martin, Christopher. (1970). *The Amistad Affair.* New York: Abelard-Schuman.
Niles, Blair. (1941). *East by Day.* New York: Farrar & Rinehart.
Osagie, I. F. (2003). *The Amistad Revolt.* Athens, GA: University of Georgia Press.
Owens, William A. (1953). *Black Mutiny: The Revolt on the Schooner Amistad.*
    Philadelphia: Pilgrim Press.

Endnotes

1. Barber, John W. (1840). *A History of the Amistad Captives.* New Haven, Connecticut: E.L. & J.W. Barber; Kohn, Bernice. (1971). *The Amistad Mutiny.* New York: McCall; Kromer, Helen. (1973). *The Amistad Revolt, 1839: The Slave Uprising Aboard the Spanish Schooner.* New York: Franklin Watts; Martin, Christopher. (1970). *The Amistad Affair.* New York: Abelard-Schuman; Niles, Blair. (1941). *East by Day.* New York: Farrar & Rinehart; Owens, William A. (1953). *Black Mutiny: The Revolt on the Schooner Amistad.* Philadelphia: Pilgrim Press.

2. Osagie, I. F. (2003). *The Amistad Revolt.* Athens, GA: University of Georgia Press.

3. Osagie, I. F. (2003). *The Amistad Revolt.* Athens, GA: University of Georgia Press; Zeinert, Karen. (1997). *The Amistad Revolt and American Abolition.* North Haven, Connecticut: Shoe String Press.

4. The Amistad Freedom Schooner. (2010). Available online at https://amistadamerica.net/Home_Page.php. Downloaded January 2011.

5. Jones, H. (1997). *Mutiny on the Amistad.* New York: Oxford University Press; Linder, D. (2000). "The Amistad Case." Available at http://www.law.umkc.edu/faculty/projects/ftrials/amistad/AMISTD.HTM; Osagie, I. F. (2003). *The Amistad Revolt.* Athens, GA: University of Georgia Press.

6. Abraham, A. (1998). *The Amistad Revolt: An Historical Legacy of Sierra Leone and the United States.* Washington, D.C.: U.S. Information Agency.

7. Jones, H. (1997). *Mutiny on the Amistad.* New York: Oxford University Press; Linder, D. (2000). "The Amistad Case." Available at http://www.law.umkc.edu/faculty/projects/ftrials/amistad/AMISTD.HTM; Osagie, I. F. (2003). *The Amistad Revolt.* Athens, GA: University of Georgia Press.

8. Linder, D. (2000). "The Amistad Case." Available at http://www.law.umkc.edu/faculty/projects/ftrials/amistad/AMISTD.HTM.

9. Linder, D. (2000). "The Amistad Case." Available at http://www.law.umkc.edu/faculty/projects/ftrials/amistad/AMISTD.HTM.

10. Abraham, A. (1998). *The Amistad Revolt: An Historical Legacy of Sierra Leone and the United States.* Washington, D.C.: U.S. Information Agency; Barber, John W. (1840). *A History of the Amistad Captives.* New Haven, Connecticut: E.L. & J.W. Barber; Kohn, Bernice. (1971). *The Amistad Mutiny.* New York: McCall; Kromer, Helen. (1973). *The Amistad Revolt, 1839: The Slave Uprising Aboard the Spanish Schooner.* New York: Franklin Watts; Martin, Christopher. (1970). *The Amistad Affair.* New York: Abelard-Schuman; Niles, Blair. (1941). *East by Day.* New York: Farrar & Rinehart; Osagie, I. F. (2003). *The Amistad Revolt.* Athens, GA: University of Georgia Press; Owens, William A. (1953). *Black Mutiny: The Revolt on the Schooner Amistad.* Philadelphia: Pilgrim Press.

11. Owen, William A. (1997). *Black Mutiny: The Revolt on the Schooner.* New York: Black Classic Press.

12. Jones, H. (1997). *Mutiny on the Amistad.* New York: Oxford University Press; Linder, D. (2000). "The Amistad Case." Available at http://www.law.umkc.edu/faculty/projects/ftrials/amistad/AMISTD.HTM.

13. Abraham, Arthur. (1987). *The Amistad Revolt.* Freetown: USIS.

14. Osagie, I. F. (2003). *The Amistad Revolt.* Athens, GA: University of Georgia Press.

15. Linder, D. (2000). "The Amistad Case." Available at http://www.law.umkc.edu/faculty/projects/ftrials/amistad/AMISTD.HTM.

16. Linder, D. (2000). "The Amistad Case." Available at http://www.law.umkc.edu/faculty/projects/ftrials/amistad/AMISTD.HTM.

17. Linder, D. (2000). "The Amistad Case." Available at http://www.law.umkc.edu/faculty/projects/ftrials/amistad/AMISTD.HTM.

18. Linder, D. (2000). "The Amistad Case." Available at http://www.law.umkc.edu/faculty/projects/ftrials/amistad/AMISTD.HTM.

19. Jones, H. (1997). *Mutiny on the Amistad.* New York: Oxford University Press; Linder, D. (2000). "The Amistad Case." Available at http://www.law.umkc.edu/faculty/projects/ftrials/amistad/AMISTD.HTM; Osagie, I. F. (2003). *The Amistad Revolt.* Athens, GA: University of Georgia Press.

20. *Amistad* (Dreamworks, 1997)(Steven Spielberg, Director).

21. Osagie, I. F. (2003). *The Amistad Revolt.* Athens, GA: University of Georgia Press.

22. Osagie, I. F. (2003). *The Amistad Revolt.* Athens, GA: University of Georgia Press.

23. Hadden, Sally. (1998). "How Accurate is the Film?" *The History Teacher,* 31, 374–379.

24. Hadden, Sally. (1998). "How Accurate is the Film?" *The History Teacher,* 31, 374–379.

25. Connecticut State Library. (2011). "Roger Sherman Baldwin, Governor of Connecticut 1844–1846." *Connecticut State Library.* Available online at http://www.cslib.org/gov/baldwinrs.htm.

26. Hadden, Sally. (1998). "How Accurate is the Film?" *The History Teacher,* 31, 374–379.

27. Hadden, Sally. (1998). "How Accurate is the Film?" *The History Teacher,* 31, 374–379.

28. Hadden, Sally. (1998). "How Accurate is the Film?" *The History Teacher,* 31, p. 378.

29. Foner, E. (2010). "The Amistad Case in Fact and Film." *History Matters.* Available online at http://historymatters.gmu.edu/d/74.

30. Foner, E. (2010). "The Amistad Case in Fact and Film." *History Matters.* Available online at www.historymatters.gmu.edu.

31. Lemisch, J. (1999). Black agency in the *Amistad* uprising: Or, you've taken our Cinque and gone." *Souls: A Critical Journal of Black Politics, Culture, and Society,* 1, 57–70.

32. Foner, E. (2010). "The Amistad Case in Fact and Film." *History Matters.* Available online at www.historymatters.gmu.edu.

33. Osagie, I. F. (2003). *The Amistad Revolt.* Athens, GA: University of Georgia Press.

34. Foner, E. (2010). "The Amistad Case in Fact and Film." Available online at www.historymatters.gmu.edu.

35. Dalzell, F. (1998). "Dreamworking Amistad: Representing Slavery, Revolt and Freedom in America, 1839 and 1997." *The New England Quarterly,* 71, p. 132.

36. Schneider, A. (1998). Advising Spielberg: A career studying the *Amistad* Rebellion. *The Chronicle of Higher Education,* p. A12.

37. Schneider, A. (1998). Advising Spielberg: A career studying the *Amistad* Rebellion. *The Chronicle of Higher Education,* p. A12.

CHAPTER 2

SEPTEMBER DAWN AND THE MOUNTAIN MEADOWS MASSACRE (1857)

A lithograph of Mountains Meadows created by S. H. Redmond in 1877, featuring the Fancher-Party wagon train in the middle left and "Indians" hiding behind the rocks to the lower right. The print is courtesy of the Library of Congress Prints and Photographs Division, Washington, D.C.

The scene was one too horrible and sickening for language to describe. Human skeletons, disjointed bones, ghastly skulls and the hair of women were scattered in frightful profusion over a distance of two miles.
Harper's Weekly, August 13, 1859

Introduction

On September 11, 1857, 120 men, women, and children of the Fancher-Baker emigrant wagon train traveling through the Utah Territory were slaughtered at a place called Mountain Meadows.[1] They were killed by what appeared to be local Paiute Indians, but turned out to be local Mormons under orders to annihilate the members of the wagon train, leaving no witnesses behind. Seventeen children, all under the age of seven, were spared, many later becoming the witnesses the Mormons had so feared. The story they told, and the story visitors, both civilian and military, later shared, caused many to label the massacre at Mountain Meadows as "the darkest deed of the nineteenth century."[2]

The events that led up to the massacre centered on the Mormon Church, the most significant of all American-established religions. Brigham Young had established himself as both head of the Mormon Church in Salt Lake City and as the territorial governor. In a sense, he had established a theocracy with a religion that included such tenets as polygamy and *blood atonement,* the murder of men who committed heinous sins in order that their soul might be saved. These religious practices, along with other conflicts in the management of the territory, reached their zenith in early 1857, so much so that the few federal officials in Utah fled the territory. Word of the insurrection reached Washington and President James Buchanan ordered military troops west to regain federal control of the territory. The Mormons, in the meantime, began preparing for armed conflict.

Arriving in Utah as these tensions flared was the Fancher-Baker emigrant wagon train, most of the people coming from Arkansas and heading to California to seek a better life. As they entered the Utah Territory they were in need of rest and resupply, and the cattle needed to graze to regain much of the weight they had lost on the arduous trip west. They encamped at Mountain Meadows. Meanwhile, local militia leaders Isaac C. Haight and John D. Lee organized both the militia and the Southern Paiute Indians to attack the wagon train. The Indians were told the emigrants were a threat to them and that they would earn all of the spoils of the conflict. The Indians, with many of the militia in support, attacked the wagon train, but the Fancher-Baker party defended themselves and a five-day siege ensued.

The Indians, suffering many wounded and killed, left the fight, but the Fancher-Baker Party was quickly running out of supplies, specifically food, water, and ammunition. The militia leaders appeared under a flag of truce, promising to escort the wagon train safely through the Indians to safety if, and only if, they were willing to give up their weapons. A four-hour debate ensued, but finally the emigrants did as they were told. Weaponless, they followed the Mormon militia members to what would become the greatest massacre to date in American history.

At the time of the Mountain Meadows Massacre, the focus was on the potential armed conflict between the North and the South, and there was little information about the massacre itself. That changed in August of 1859, when one of the most popular magazines, *Harper's Weekly,* published an article by U.S. Army surgeon Charles Brewer in which he described not only the massacre but what he found when he visited Mountain Meadows. "To-day ... I ride by them, but no word of friendly greeting falls upon my ear, no face meets me with a smile of recognition," Brewer wrote.[3] He told of witnessing, "On every side around me for the space of a mile lie the remains of carcasses dismembered by wild beasts; bones, left for nearly two years unburied, bleached in the elements of the mountain wilds, gnawed by the hungry wolf, broken and hardly to be recognized. Garments of babes and little ones, faded and torn, fluttering from each ragged bush, from which the warble of the songster of the desert sounds as mockery. Human hair, once falling in glossy ringlets around childhoods brow or virtues form, now strewing the plain in masses, matted, and mingling with the musty mould. To-day, in one grave, I have buried the bones and skulls of twelve women and children, pierced with the fatal ball or shattered with the axe. In another the shattered relics of eighteen men, and yet many more await their gloomy resting-place."[4]

While the shocking account motivated the call for prosecution, the Civil War would interfere, and not until the mid 1870s were some of those involved in the massacre put on trial. Only one, John D. Lee, would be sentenced to death and executed by firing squad in 1877. From then on, the story of the Mountain Meadows Massacre continued to be shared in oral tradition and in various publications, becoming centered on the controversy of how high up the orders for the massacre went within the government/Mormon Church. Did Brigham Young himself order the massacre as a diversion for the U.S. military troops coming from Washington? History does not answer that question directly, which is why the Mountain Meadows Massacre remains so controversial today.

In 2008, director Christopher Cain decided to take on the Mountain Meadows tragedy with a film titled *September Dawn*. The film, considered a failure at the box office, centered on a love story between one of the Mormons, Jonathan (played by Trent Ford), and one of the members of the Fancher-Baker party, Emily (played by Tamara Hope). The mere fact that the love interest of Jonathan and Emily never occurred, for Jonathan was a fictional character and Emily Hudson left the wagon train prior to it entering the Utah territory, it is very clear that any historical accuracy in the film *September Dawn* was never intended by the motion picture director. Despite being based upon true events, the film does a very poor job of presenting the true tragedy that became known as the Mountain Meadows Massacre. Articulating the numerous historical errors of the film *September Dawn* is the focus of this chapter.

September Dawn: The History

Joseph Smith, Jr., the founder of the Mormon Church, was born on December 23, 1805.[5] He grew up in western New York during a time period of significant religious fervor. In his early twenties, in the late 1820s, Smith claimed that an angel bequeathed upon him golden plates that formed additional testaments to the Bible. After translating them into English, he destroyed the plates as instructed by the angel. Smith then moved to Kirtland, Ohio, in 1831, where he intended to establish a religious city, the City of Zion, in Missouri.

Smith's Church of Christ, later the Church of the Latter Day Saints or Mormon Church, was not well received in Missouri and the local settlers ran the Mormons out in 1833. Smith tried to lead a paramilitary expedition to retake the lands, but was unsuccessful. He then decided to establish a temple in Kirtland, which suffered a financial setback in 1837, thus causing him to join other Mormons in northern Missouri. Once again, conflict arose and Smith was imprisoned on capital charges of insurrection.

In 1839, after being allowed to escape, Smith led the Mormons to Nauvoo, Illinois, where once again he attempted to establish a religious city.[6] And, once again, as the teachings of the Church began to spread amongst the other citizens of Nauvoo, who learned that the Mormons advocated polygamy, and a confrontation ensued. Smith tried to declare martial law, but ultimately surrendered to the Governor of Illinois, who promised his safety. While awaiting trial in Carthage, Illinois, for treason, on June 27, 1844, an armed mob entered his room. They shot and killed his brother Hyrum, who was also held in the Carthage Jail on charges of treason, and they fired at Smith. Smith had a pepper-box pistol that had been smuggled into the jail and he fired it before turning to leap from the window. Shot several times, he fell to the ground and died.

Brigham Young became the successor to Joseph Smith, Jr., and he was ordained president of the Church of the Latter Day Saints on December 27, 1847.[7] Young faced the same problems that Smith had faced, repeated conflicts by locals who did not agree with the tenets of the Mormon Church at the time. Young decided to head west with his religious followers, into what at the time was part of Mexico, but would soon become the Utah Territory. Young arrived in the Salt Lake Valley on July 24, 1847, and established Salt Lake City as both home to the Mormon Church and the seat of the Utah government.

In the wake of the Mexican-American War, the land came under the possession of the United States government. Young petitioned Congress to create the State of Deseret, but instead the land was made into the Utah Territory and Young was seated as the territorial governor.[8] As Young was now both governor and head of the church, Utah became a theocratic government, with Young as its autocratic leader. This would ultimately give birth to the conflict between Young and the United States government.

While rumors and talk about the Church's teachings of polygamy continued to circulate, this did not create conflict as it had in the past, for those living in and around Salt Lake City were mostly Mormon. Young, however, found himself running into conflicts with the various federal officials, including the territorial chief justice located in his territory.[9] The tensions grew as Young refused to implement the U.S. government policies and as he became more confrontational; some of these officials, fearing for their lives, fled the territory. Word of the conflict made its way to President Buchanan, who decided to install a non-Mormon as territorial governor. He ordered a military detachment to travel west to the Utah Territory to ensure this change in leadership occurred without incident.

As the troops traveled west, word reached Brigham Young, who decided to declare martial law and defend Deseret, launching what would became known as the Utah War.[10] Young prepared a document notifying his followers throughout the territory that martial law had been declared. This first proclamation was dated August 5, 1857. The central issue regarding the proclamation of martial law centered on its meaning. Many of the territorial leaders began debating whether or not it meant armed conflict was authorized, or mandated, by the order. Realizing the dilemma, a second proclamation was issued on August 29, 1857, but it did not necessarily clear up the matter and it would take a week to reach many of the various territorial militia leaders. It took three days to reach Cedar City, arriving in early September.

As these events were occurring, a large wagon train of families from Arkansas began the arduous journey west to California in the hopes of starting a new and more prosperous life. Two key wagon trains, the Baker train and the Perkins train, merged together and called upon "Captain" Alexander Fancher, who had previously made two journeys to California, to lead them.[11] Thus the wagon train became known as the Fancher-Baker Party. This particular wagon train did not consist of destitute families, but was rather financially well-off, had an ample supply of stock, and were exceptionally organized for the journey. Now united under the leadership of Fancher and Baker, they departed for California in early May of 1857.

About this same time, sheerly by coincidence, one of the Mormon apostles was murdered in Arkansas, where most of the members of the wagon train originated.[12] Parley Pratt (the great-great-grandfather of Mitt Romney) was one of the original apostles in the Latter Day Saints Church, and had acquired, over time, 12 wives. The last of these wives was Eleanor McLean, the legal wife of Hector McLean. Eleanor had converted to Mormonism against the wishes of her husband. She absconded with her children to Utah and gained employment as a schoolteacher for Pratt's children. She then became Pratt's twelfth wife, despite that fact she was still legally married. Hector filed charges and Pratt was arrested, but was released for insufficient evidence. Hector hunted down Parley Pratt and shot and stabbed him in western Arkansas, leaving him to die from a loss of blood. Word of the Pratt killing reached the Utah Territory that summer, inciting hostility on the part of Mormons toward any and all non-Mormons.

The Fancher-Baker Party entered the Utah Territory in mid-August, passing by Salt Lake City and heading south.[13] On August 25, they camped near Corn Creek, having traveled 165 miles south from Salt Lake City. On September 4, they reached Cedar City, Utah, and continued south, arriving at Mountain Meadows late September 6, where they encamped. They had decided to spend several days there by the creek, allowing the livestock to graze and resting before traveling the last 40 miles that would take them out of Utah. The area was a well-known resting place; grassy and mountain-ringed, it had been a common stopover on the old Spanish Trail.

A second coincidence occurred shortly after the Fancher-Baker Party had left Corn Creek. Word began to circulate that the spring located at Corn Creek, which the wagon train had used to resupply its water, had been poisoned. Allegedly, several people and 18 head of cattle died after drinking from the spring.[14] A rumor that the emigrants had poisoned the spring, along with the fact that these people from Arkansas may have murdered Parley Pratt, began to circulate widely. Tensions were running high and it was at this same time that William H. Dame and Isaac C. Haight held the weekly Stake High Council meeting after church services. They discussed the Corn Creek poisoning, the emigrants from Arkansas, and the fact that Parley Pratt had been murdered in Arkansas about the time the wagon train would have left that state. They further discussed the declaration of martial law and what to do about the emigrants. One suggestion was to plan an Indian massacre, but not everyone on the council agreed. Haight sent a messenger, James Haslam, with a message to Brigham Young seeking advice, but it would take him three days to reach Salt Lake City and three days to return. In addition, Haight sent a message, its contents unknown, to John D. Lee, a prominent leader in the Church, territorial government, and a member of the local militia.[15]

On the morning of September 7, 1857, the Fancher-Baker Party, encamped at Mountain Meadows, awoke to the sound of gunfire as an estimated 50 Paiute Indians, along with Mormons dressed as Indians, attacked the wagon train.[16] Fancher and Baker took charge, circled the wagons and put up a strong resistance. They lowered the wagons to prevent being shot from underneath the wagons and chained the wagon wheels together to create a defensive barrier. As many of the younger men defended the wagon train with their rifles, others began piling dirt both in and behind the wagons to create a stronger barrier. Seven of the emigrants were killed in the opening confrontation, the first, a young girl. They were buried in the center of the wagon encirclement. Sixteen others were wounded. The Indians and Mormons, unable to get through the wagon's defenses, laid siege for the next five days.

The Mormons brought in more reinforcements and began discussing what to do with the emigrants. The Paiute Indians, disgusted with the senseless loss of life, had abandoned the Mormons. One hundred additional Mormon reinforcements were brought in and Isaac C. Haight and Colonel William Dame held a meeting.[17] Others present included Major John H. Higbee, William C. Stewart, Samuel Jukes, and John D. Lee. It is believed that here they devised a plan to end the siege by presenting a flag of peace and offering to give safe passage to the emigrants, then to do away with all of them except the youngest children. On the morning of September 11, 1857, that plan was put into motion.

That morning, two Mormon militia men approached the Fancher-Baker Party carrying a white flag. Arriving safely before the emigrants, they were then followed by Indian agent and militia officer John D. Lee. He explained that he had negotiated a truce with the Paiute Indians allowing him to escort the wagon train to Cedar City. The Indians, however, would get all of the party's supplies and livestock in exchange for their lives. One other thing was added: as a sign of good faith, they would have to turn over all of the weapons, placing them in one of the wagons. A dispute amongst the leaders of the wagon train ensued and after several hours of debate, they agreed. With little access to water, running low on food, and being almost out of ammunition, they had little choice.

The wounded and young children were placed in the wagons, and the older children and women were ordered to walk behind. The men followed, marching single file with the Mormons, mostly on foot, walking beside them. As the procession took off, the wagons, women and children stretched approximately a quarter of a mile ahead of the men and disappeared from sight. Major John H. Higbee then shouted to the Mormon guards, "Halt! Do your duty," and the men were all killed, most of them shot at point blank range.[18]

Major John D. Lee, still with the wagons, reached a point where he too called a halt. Mormon Nelphi Johnson then ordered the slaughter of the women and older children. Mormons rushed at the party from both sides and began to scream and yell as they shot and butchered all but 17 of the youngest children. In all, 120 men, women, and the older children were slaughtered in the massacre.

The various Mormons involved then began the process of denying their involvement in the massacre. Allegedly the letter from Brigham Young reached Haight on September 13, advising him to let the emigrants pass. No record of this letter was preserved. John D. Lee soon visited Young to advise him on the massacre. Lee reported that at first Young was dismayed, but then stated that the Lord had advised it would happen. Later that year, Lee wrote a fictionalized account of the massacre, blaming the Pauite Indians for the deaths.[19]

In June of 1858, the federal troops arrived and Young was forced to step down as territorial governor. An investigation into the massacre ensued and the information was widely disseminated to the American people in August of 1859, when the report of the massacre appeared in *Harper's Weekly*. Despite calls for justice, as the Civil War rose in the American conscience, the Mountain Meadows Massacre subsided. It was not until the early 1870s that the case would be revisited, when Philip Klingensmith, a former bishop in the church, swore in an affidavit about the true nature of the massacre. Eventually nine arrest warrants were issued for members of the militia, but only one would ultimately be prosecuted, John D. Lee. After two trials he was sentenced to death by firing squad. On March 23, 1877, sitting on the end of his coffin and shouting, "Center my heart, boys!"—defiant to the end—he was executed.[20] Lee was the only person ever held accountable for the murder of 120 men, women, and children at Mountain Meadows.

September Dawn: The Film

The film *September Dawn*, directed by Christopher Cain, was filmed entirely in Canada. It was released by Black Diamond Pictures on August 24, 2007.[21] The film starred Terence Stamp in the role of Brigham Young and Jon Voight as Jacob Samuelson, otherwise known throughout the film as "the Bishop." The two young lovers that are the center of the film, Jonathan Samuelson and Emily Hudson, are played by Trent Ford and Tamara Hope. The movie had an estimated budget of $11 million and is said to have grossed only slightly over $1 million dollars, hence losing between $9 and $10 million. The loss is explained in part by the fact it only remained in theaters for several weeks and that the majority of reviews when it was released were highly critical of the film.

The film opens with the deposition of Brigham Young on July 30, 1875, questioning his knowledge about the events surrounding the September 11, 1857 massacre of the Fancher-Baker Party.[22] As the title of the movie is displayed, there is a note that the film was "Inspired by true events." The movie then cuts to a meadow scene with lush green forests in the distance and a subtitle denotes that it is "March 23, 1877." A narrator begins to speaks and it is the voice of the young woman who is shown visiting Mountain Meadows with one of the Mormons, who would later be identified as Jonathan Samuelson. She recounts the time when she was six years old and riding in the wagon train through the Utah Territory as the scene begins to shift back in time.

The wagon train is then shown moving along as another date is displayed on screen: "September 1857." The wagon train stops as it sees several men on horseback in the distance and both Fancher and Baker ride to meet them. The riders consist of John D. Lee and several other Mormons, who tell them to move on, while Fancher and Baker plead for a place to graze their livestock and purchase supplies. Nancy Dunlap arrives to ask if there is a problem in order to help resolve the issue when a man and his two sons arrive on the scene in a horse-drawn wagon. He identifies himself as the local bishop, general, and mayor, Jacob Samuelson, along with his two sons, Jonathan and Micah. The Bishop agrees to check out the wagon train by riding by the men, women, and children. It is here that one of the sons, Jonathan, and one of the young ladies of the wagon train, Emily Hudson, see each other and fall in love at first sight. The Bishop, finished with reviewing the Fancher-Baker Party, agrees to allow them to camp at Mountain Meadows for two weeks.

The scene then shifts between the Bishop and his family and the Fancher-Baker Party. The Bishop criticizes Nancy Dunlop as an *abomination* for she dresses like a man, curses these people from *Missouri*, and condemns them by praying "may they all go to hell." At the camp, the members of the wagon train appear content, although Nancy Dunlop is worried and she voices her fear of the Mormons because she is alone without her husband Lorenzo and she is concerned for her children. The rest of the members are shown praying for the blessings bestowed upon them by "The Bishop."

The next day, after Jonathan is instructed to go amongst the heathens to see what they are plotting by his father, he rides out to Mountain Meadows. Micah, his brother, is told by the Bishop to go and watch Jonathan. They arrive at Mountain Meadows, greet Captain Fancher, and speak admiringly of their horses. Fancher explains they are taking the horses to California because they "plan to start horse racing," at which point Jonathan and Micah flinch. Their reaction is quickly overshadowed by a wild horse rearing up, at which point Jonathan *talks* to the horse and calms it down. Emily looks upon lovingly, while the men look on approvingly. There is talk about him breaking the horse by riding him, and Jonathan agrees, saying he needs a corral set up. Fancher says that can be arranged and for Jonathan to return tomorrow.

The scene shifts to the Bishop as he remembers the assassination of Joseph Smith. In a dream sequence, Smith is shown in a room being overtaken by a mob. One of the Mormons is shot and Smith is shown firing one shot before being shot himself and falling through a second story window to his death below. The belief is that Smith was killed by the people of Missouri, the evil Missourians.

The scene shifts to the next morning as Jonathan arrives to find a well-built, circular corral, perfectly constructed, with the wild horse blind-folded. A very long and drawn-out scene shows Jonathan talking and eventually riding the horse. During this fanciful scene, there is a cut away to Brigham Young talking about "blood atonement," a notion that when a person is so far removed from God and is a sinner, it is the requirement of other good Christians to atone for their sins by killing them. The film depicts various scenes of a rider being killed, another man having his testicles cut off and attached to the side of a wooden building by the knife. Another person has their throat slit. As this scene fades away, the film returns to the corral where Emily walks up to Jonathan with a baby and he believes it is hers, which she realizes and quickly affirms it is not. Again the film shifts to a dark scene with Brigham Young talking about how President Buchanan had sent soldiers to come kill the Mormons. Young talks about taking care of his own people, that he rules his own people, and they will fight the soldiers; for, he says, "I am the voice of God." He calls down curses upon the "gentiles," as the scene fades back to the corral, where Fancher is shown giving the horse to Jonathan.

The scene progresses to Emily and Jonathan speaking alone together. They talk about love at first sight, and how it happened to her parents. She speaks of her destiny to be a pastor's daughter. Jonathan makes the mistake of saying he had never been around "you people" before, meaning gentiles. He covers by saying she is the "prettiest girl" and that he is surprised at how she tells people what she thinks. They have a discussion over her being a "free woman," and further along, they discuss sin and Jonathan wants to know how they (the gentiles) punish sinners. He explains they have the Bishop.

The scene then switches to the Bishop talking about the "Missouri wildcats" and how they have lots of money and goods. The Bishop then talks about how they killed Smith and that they will not only kill Brigham Young, but all the Mormons. Thus they are plotting about what to do with the Fancher-Baker Party. Brigham Young is in attendance at this meeting, suggesting that the Bishop traveled to meet with Young. The scene also leaves an ominous overtone that the Francher-Baker Party is in trouble, but they do not know it.

The scene then shifts to a night scene with the wagon train. Nancy tells Emily she should be careful, then proceeds to the river, by herself, to bathe. The scene then cuts to Jonathan riding his horse at night and being pursued by an unknown rider, before discovering it is his brother spying on him. Micah tells him to watch himself as he is getting too close to the gentile woman. They return home and Jonathan puts up the horses, at which point the Bishop enters the stable. He argues with Jonathan that he is getting too close to the gentiles and that he should be married. The conversation switches to the talk about his mother and how the Bishop allowed the Church elders to steal her away from them because one of the Apostles wanted her for his wife. Jonathan then reveals that he knew his mother had come back for him and Micah and that she was killed for this reason. Jonathan begins to choke his father, the Bishop, when Micah appears out of nowhere and tells Jonathan that "he didn't kill her."

The scene shifts to the following morning when the Bishop, Micah, and other men come for Jonathan to take him to "'Temple." Jonathan says he has not taken the test yet, but he is escorted there anyway to receive his "endowment." Brigham Young is present for the nude baptism of Jonathan and several women stand in a circle around Jonathan, as they chant some form of prayer. Blood atonement is once again mentioned.

The film then shows Emily in the river, bathing sensually in the water. Jonathan shows up and spies on her. She sees him and briefly feigns contempt for his spying, but quickly climbs up on the horse and kisses him. They talk about his father having more than one wife, claiming he had 18, and that Brigham Young had 27 wives, but he only needed one. At that point, Emily screams, for she catches sight of a body floating in the river. They discover it is Nancy Dunlop. Jonathan carries the body to the wagon train's campsite and he is told to leave. The parson begins to pray and the others join him, while Emily goes to the rock upon the hill and visits Jonathan, who is distraught. He tells her he will go to California with her.

The scene then cuts to a meeting where the Bishop is in front of a group of Mormons and he is telling them how Joseph Smith came to him and told him the emigrants must die. He calls for blood atonement against the Fancher-Baker Party. Jonathan shows up and argues against this and finds himself quickly chained to his bed. He and the Bishop argue. In the meantime, John D. Lee speaks with the Paiute and gets them to agree to assist the Mormons in attacking the wagon train, for they were promised not to be harmed and they would be allowed to collect all supplies and livestock after the massacre. The Mormons are dressed to look like Indians and they are blessed as they prepare to kill the Fancher-Baker Party.

The film then shows a little blond girl standing in the middle of the circled wagons. She sees a glint of sunlight shining off of something on the hill and she watches. A shot is then heard, the little girl begins to bleed from the chest, and she falls. The wagon train finds itself under attack. The Paiute attack with rifles and arrows and several on both sides die, including Baker, who is hit with an arrow. As the Fancher Party defends itself and more Paiute die, they retreat from the field. A siege is now laid upon the circled wagons. It lasts for five days. The party begins to run out of water, food, and ammunition. At one point, Emily tells her father, the parson, that Jonathan was going to go with them to California and they were to be married. She asks if he would marry her to Jonathan. The parson says it has "always been my greatest desire." Later, he prays Psalm 23.

A flurry of rapid scenes then unfold. Mormon John D. Lee receives a message from President Haight, who says the orders come from the highest authorities, that Lee is to kill all those over the age of eight in the wagon train. At first he refuses, but quickly acquiesces. The next scene shows a member of the Fancher Party going for help, but he is shot and killed. Then Micah visits Jonathan with great remorse, at first, but then decides he will join the attack and "do his duty."

The scene is now set and a subtitle shows the date of the Mountain Meadows Massacre: September 11, 1857. John D. Lee is shown leading several Mormons on horseback displaying a white flag of truce. Lee explains that they have spoken with the Paiute and they can guarantee safe passage if the wagon train is willing to give up their weapons by loading them all into one wagon. They at first resist the request, but quickly give in. They place all their weapons in one wagon and all the children eight years and younger are also placed into the wagons. While this scene is being played out, the "blood atonement" speech is overlaid with the wagon train moving out under Mormon guard.

The women are marched ahead of the men, and Mormons on horseback surround the men who are walking. Lee then halts the men, while there are Indians (Mormons dressed in Paiute clothing and face-paint) waiting in the woods. Lee then turns and yells, "Mormons, do your duty!" In slow motion the killing scene begins. The men are shot and killed, the women are chased across a field and either killed with guns, arrows, or tomahawks by the Mormons. The entire scene is shown in slow motion with both close-ups and wide angle shots of the killing.

Emily is shown chasing after a young child, who ran. She catches up with her and tries to hide. Micah finds Emily, but Jonathan, who escaped his bonds, arrives to protect Emily. Everyone cries and Micah begs to be shot. Jonathan shoots and kills his brother, having saved Emily. The Bishop, however, from a great distance, pulls out a rifle and shoots Emily. Jonathan watches Emily die, then distraught, goes to shoot himself, but stops, for he hears the baby cry.

The scene then shifts back to the beginning of the movie with the deposition of Brigham Young, intermixed with a young woman and Jonathan arriving in a field. Young says he only heard of the massacre after it occurred, that it had been committed by Indians, and that he had ordered the wagon train to proceed through the Utah Territory unmolested. Meanwhile, the young girl (the baby Emily had chased) watches on as John D. Lee is executed while standing and cowering before a firing squad. The movie then closes with the captions that Lee was the only one held responsible for the Mountain Meadows Massacre and that the Mormon Church disavows any involvement.

September Dawn: Hollywood's Rendering

From the opening scenes to the closing scenes, the film *September Dawn* is rife with historical errors, many so egregious it is very clear that the director had no intent of trying to create a historically accurate movie. Despite the claims by Christopher Cain that there was "some fiction" in the film, he argued they created a film that was "fairly accurate in terms of the real story."[23] This could not have been further from the truth.

The film commences with the deposition of Brigham Young and quickly moves to the title of the film and then a short statement, "inspired by true events."[24] From there, it depicts the date (March 23, 1877) and shows a young woman who begins to narrate the movie. She will return at the end. The viewer learns that she was one of the surviving children of the Mountain Meadows Massacre and was taken in by Jonathan Samuelson, the Mormon who is at the center of the story. He brought her there to witness the execution of the one individual who would be held responsible for the massacre, John D. Lee. The area they depict is a beautiful grasslands surrounded by forests dense with trees. This error stands out for Mountain Meadows was a hilly grasslands, but had no extensive forests surrounding it.[25] This mistake is caused by the fact the entire production was filmed in Canada and the vistas are not the same as the Mountain Meadows of today, nor of the nineteenth century. Additionally, the Jonathan Samuelson character never existed, so he would not have been present at the execution of John D. Lee, nor would the young lady, whom we learn was one of the surviving children. All of the children that survived the massacre were taken in by Mormon families, but within months they were all turned over to the United States Military who returned them to relatives. The young child would not have grown up under the care of one of the Mormons, in this case, the fictitious Jonathan Samuelson.

The film then progresses to show the past (September 1857), and the Fancher-Baker Party approaching Mountain Meadows. A filming issue that strikes the viewer is the fact that all of the people are very clean, despite the dust being kicked up by the wagon train, and they never appear to get dirty throughout the movie. Further, they had traveled all the way from Arkansas (not Missouri, as they claim in the film) and the arduous trek would have left them even more grimy and tired. Yet, everyone in the film is perfectly clean and very, very happy.

They are then confronted by six riders, which never occurred, and Fancher and Baker go to converse with them. As they negotiate to stay at Mountain Meadows to rest their livestock and purchase supplies, Nancy Dunlap (later identified as the "woman who wears pants") rides up and attempts to resolve the conflict. The concept that a woman in the wagon train would be equal to either Fancher or Baker is not befitting of the times, nor is it historically accurate in any way. Further, if a Dunlap would have come to inquire, it would have been Nancy's husband, Lorenzo Dunlap, who was in the wagon train, although it is quickly revealed in the film that her husband was killed before they left Arkansas and she is a widow. That is wholly incorrect, for Lorenzo Dunlap died beside his wife in the Mountain Meadows massacre.

The next individual that rides up to resolve the dispute is a character played by Jon Voight, who goes by the name Jacob Samuelson. He states he is the bishop, the general, and the mayor. All of this is incorrect, for the character Jacob Samuelson never existed, nor did his two sons, Jonathan and Micah. The character is possibly based upon the mayor, an ecclesiastical leader and head of the local militia in Cedar City, Isaac C. Haight. Despite this similarity, the activities of the film's Bishop and Isaac Haight are so poorly rendered that it is a weak connection.

As the film's Bishop reviews the Fancher-Baker Party to see if they are "acceptable," they drive by a wagon and one of the sons, Jonathan, catches the eye of one of the emigrants, Emily Hudson. They are seen to be falling in love at first sight, and later we learn that Emily's father, the Parson, is also in the wagon train. The scene of love-at-first-sight could not have happened for a number of reasons. First, the Fancher-Baker Party was not at Mountain Meadows but one evening, so the several days of Jonathan and Emily meeting each other to talk about how much they love each other is false. After the emigrants arrived at Mountain Meadows two days later, they were attacked. Further, Emily Hudson and her father, the parson, left the wagon train before it even entered the Utah Territory, so there exists another reason the love story could not have happened. And, finally, to reiterate, the Jonathan Samuelson character was entirely fictitious.

When the Fancher-Baker Party moves into Mountain Meadows, again, many of the mistakes become clear. The forests and lake nearby were not truly present, for all that Mountain Meadows had was a small stream, the Magotsu Creek, and at best scrub oak with hills that were simply grassland. When Jonathan and Micah then come to visit them at Mountain Meadows, the film portrays them as living nearby, when it would have been a full day's ride from Cedar City, where they lived, as the emigrants had just come from Cedar City, taking several days to make their way to Mountain Meadow.

Jonathan is then seen calming a wild horse, a long, played-out scene, and he says he will fully break the horse the next day if the emigrants set up a circular corral. The following day he returns and a very fancy split rail fence corral is already set up. The emigrants would neither have had the time to split the logs to create it, or been able to create it for there were no trees at Mountain Meadows. Nor would they have carried the fencing with them, for it would have been too heavy and only necessities were carried in a wagon train. Hence, the whole long, drawn-out scene of Jonathan breaking the horse was fictitious and played most likely because the director loved (or someone loved) horses. One other horse-related error came when Jonathan is admiring the horses and Captain Fancher tells him they plan to use them to start horse racing in California. Jonathan, the Mormon, is stunned by this revelation, but that was not true, there is no evidence to suggest the emigrants were migrating from Arkansas for that purpose.

Interspersed among these fictitious horse scenes is a flashback, as the Bishop remembers the assassination of his leader, Joseph Smith. A reference is made that Smith was killed by Missourians in Missouri, when in fact he was killed in Illinois in the Carthage Jail. As the mob enters his room, Smith is shown fighting back by shooting a single-shot pistol. In reality, he had had a six-shooter pistol that had been smuggled into the jail, and he shot three of his attackers before being struck himself and jumping/falling out of the window.[26]

A follow-up scene shows Brigham Young talking about the nineteenth century Mormon tenet of blood atonement. The concept is greatly overplayed in the movie for effect. The film makes death by blood atonement appear to be very common, which it was not. The film also depicts a woman being killed, but there is no evidence that blood atonement was ever enacted upon a female. Still further, in one of the scenes, a man's scrotum is cut off and it is hung on the side of a wooden building by a knife. Blood atonement called for the killing of a Mormon who had strayed too far from the Church if there was not hope for his salvation; thus, other Mormon's were called upon to commit murder, but not mutilation. It was also only directed toward Mormons and carried out by Mormons, hence for blood atonement to be enacted upon the emigrants of the wagon train is a falsehood. In addition to this, Young's words are taken both out of context and his words are lifted not from a specific speech, but piecemeal from a number of speeches he had given. For instance, in the film Young is quoted as saying "I am the voice of God." He never stated that, but many Mormons claimed he was the "voice of God."[27]

A number of other Mormon-centric issues arise in the film as well. When the Bishop, disgruntled with Jonathan, orders him to go to Temple for his endowment, this would have been impossible. This was 1857, and the first Temple was not built until 1890.[28] Still further, in 1857, there were no temples in all of Utah, so he could not have gone to one in Cedar City either, nor was a temple ever built in Cedar City. In addition, as Jonathan is immersed in water naked, there are women present in the background with towels, which, especially in the nineteenth century, would not have happened. Then the men and women stand around Jonathan and begin chanting. Although going to Temple was a private ceremony, there is no evidence that the rituals displayed in the film are the ones actually practiced.

Amongst all of this, the Bishop is shown going to visit Brigham Young in Salt Lake City, for he tells his son as he departs in a horse-drawn carriage that he will be gone two days or more. This would have been impossible, for it was a three day's ride from Cedar City to Salt Lake City, and therefore three days back, so had the Bishop really existed, there is no way he could have made this trip in the alleged time.

More specifically, and with greater nitpicking perhaps, the film claims that Young transported all of the people in one wagon train to the Rocky Mountains, but in reality he helped people emigrate from 1847 to 1851. They also described the first presidency as that level below the office of the prophet, but the prophet was actually part of the first presidency.[29]

Other scenes with additional historical errors show Emily and Jonathan talking and Jonathan being perplexed at how a woman could be so outspoken. It is unlikely a girl like Emily would have been outspoken in 1857, but it is again a moot point for she was never at Mountain Meadows and Jonathan's character was fictitious. This again occurs when Jonathan spies Emily bathing in the river (it was only a stream in real life), and then she climbs up on the horse with Jonathan as they go to kiss. She then screams as Nancy Dunlap's body floats by. No one in the Fancher-Baker Party died before the massacre, and Nancy Dunlap, again, died in the massacre itself.

This scene then creates another chain of events that is disgraceful to the memory of those who suffered the massacre. Because of Nancy Dunlap's body being discovered, the Fancher-Baker Party, in the film, was forewarned and so Captain Fancher orders the wagons to be circled and the number of outriders doubled. In reality, the emigrants were caught totally unaware and did not have the wagons circled at the time, for they thought they were in a safe location. As they were attacked, they circled the wagons and began building up their defenses while putting off the Indians and Mormons attacking; a very noble act in the face of such danger.[30]

As the film moves closer to the massacre itself, it depicts the Bishop saying that Joseph Smith came to him in a dream, and he told them to use blood atonement on the emigrants. The real life person who called for the massacre was Isaac Haight, but there is no evidence that he had a dream, nor was the call to massacre for blood atonement. The order came from a higher authority, which has been the central debate as to who this was—with most suggesting Brigham Young himself. In the end, the Mormons team up with the Paiute to attack the wagon train. Humorously, the scene shows the Mormons receiving a blessing as they put on war paint, despite still being in the dress of the Mormons, as if the war paint alone would fool the emigrants.

After the Mormons are attacked and the Paiute Indians leave, disgruntled, the siege begins. The Mormons then devise the plan to negotiate safe passage to the wagon train, but the emigrants have to give up their weapons. The debate in real life took nearly four hours, but in the film it appears to take about four seconds. When the Mormons then escort the wagon train toward the massacre site, they are all on horseback. In reality, most of the Mormons walked their horses beside the emigrants. Next, the film shows John D. Lee giving the orders to "Do your duty," when in reality it was John Higbee who issued that command.[31]

The film then follows with an odd slow motion depiction of the massacre using wide angles and close-ups, and showing (interestingly for Hollywood) less carnage then there actually was. In real life, 120 people were killed, but Hollywood depicts only a couple of dozen, at best. Yet, the filmmaker also adds in a rape scene occurring during the massacre and there is no evidence that any of the victims were ever raped. As one historian of the massacre has noted, "the whole suggestion of rape in this incident seems to be another example of how repeated suggestion and whisperings may grow into more and more impossible tales, which are then passed on as fact."[32]

The survivors were 17 children, but as mentioned before, while Mormon families did take them in temporarily, they were all handed over to the military upon their arrival. The one little girl, who becomes the female narrator, would never have been raised by Mormons. Additionally, the entire of scene of Jonathan killing his brother Micah to save Emily, only to have her shot by the Bishop (from a great distance with a smooth bore rifle!), would not have happened. Further, at the end, they show many of the massacre victims being buried. The Mormons never buried any of the dead; they left them exposed for the animals to drag them away.

When they finally switch to the year 1877, to show the execution of John D. Lee, the movie depicts him as a sniveling coward standing by his coffin before he was shot. In reality, he was seated at the end of the coffin so his body would fall back into it, and his last words to the executioners was "Center my heart boys!"[33] He was defiant to the end.

Conclusion

Once again, it is evident that Hollywood has presented a historic tragedy and true tale of one of the most horrific massacres in American history, in such a way as to diminish the true story of the Fancher-Baker Party and the realities of what happened on the first 9/11 tragedy. Still further, because of the misrepresentation of the nineteenth century Mormon teaching of blood atonement and its misapplication for why the Mormons attacked the wagon train, it curiously raises the possibility that the movie was intended to be an anti-Mormon screed. And finally, the wholly unrealistic story arc of a Mormon boy falling in love with one of the young ladies of the Fancher-Baker wagon train, something that is absolutely ludicrous knowing the true history of the Mountain Meadows Massacre, results in the diminishing of the factual history and the valiant story of those who died that day. As one critic summed it up best, *September Dawn* "is a bit of salacious trash, designed to sensationalize a terribly tragic event and horrible atrocity as well as to exploit current anti-Mormon and anti-Religious sentiment that seems to be sweeping through popular culture."[34] Perhaps it is fortunate that this particular movie failed at the box office, for otherwise, too many viewers would have the wrong impression and a poor understanding of the Mountain Meadows Massacre.

Further Reading

Abanes, Richard. (2003). *One Nation Under Gods: A History of the Mormon Church.* New York: Basic Books.

Arrington, Leonard J. (1986). *Brigham Young: American Moses.* Champaign, IL: University of Illinois Press.

Bagley, Will. (2002). *Blood of the Prophets: Brigham Young and the Massacre at Mountain Meadows.* Norman, OK: University of Oklahoma Press.

Brodie, Fawn. (1995). *No Man Knows my History: The Life of Joseph Smith.* 2nd Ed. New York: Vintage.

Brooks, Juanita. (1950). *The Mountain Meadows Massacre.* Norman, OK: University of Oklahoma Press.

Brooks, Juanita. (1991). *The Mountain Meadows Massacre.* 3rd Ed. Norman, OK: University of Oklahoma Press.

Denton, Sally. (2004). *American Massacre: The Tragedy at Mountain Meadows, September 1857.* New York: Vintage.

Fancher, Burr. (2006). *Captain Alexander Fancher.* Portland, OR: Inkwater Press.

Gibbs, Josiah F. (1910). *The Mountain Meadows Massacre.* Salt Lake, UT: Salt Lake Tribune.

Lee, John Doyle. (1877). *Mormonism Unveiled: The Life and Confession of John D. Lee and the Complete Life of Brigham Young.* New York: W. H. Stelle & Co.

Linder, Doug. (2011). Famous Trials webpage. "Mountain Meadows Massacre Trial." Available online at http://law2.umkc.edu/faculty/projects/ftrials/ftrials.htm.

Walker, Ronald W., Richard E. Turley, & Glen M. Leonard. (2011). *Massacre at Mountain Meadows*. New York: Oxford University Press.

Endnotes

1. Bagley, Will. (2002). *Blood of the Prophets: Brigham Young and the Massacre at Mountain Meadows*. Norman, OK: University of Oklahoma Press.

2. Bagley, Will. (2002). *Blood of the Prophets: Brigham Young and the Massacre at Mountain Meadows*. Norman, OK: University of Oklahoma Press, p. xiii.

3. Brewer, Charles. (1859). "The Massacre at Mountain Meadows, Utah Territory." *Harper's Weekly*. August 13.

4. Brewer, Charles. (1859). "The Massacre at Mountain Meadows, Utah Territory." *Harper's Weekly*. August 13.

5. Brodie, Fawn. (1995). *No Man Knows My History: The Life of Joseph Smith*. New York: Vintage.

6. Abanes, Richard. (2003). One Nation Under Gods: A History of the Mormon Church. New York: Basic Books.

7. Arrington, Leonard J. (1986). *Brigham Young: American Moses*. Champaign, IL: University of Illinois Press.

8. Abanes, Richard. (2003). One Nation Under Gods: A History of the Mormon Church. New York: Basic Books.

9. Linder, Doug. (2011). Famous Trials webpage. "Mountain Meadows Massacre Trial." Available online at http://law2.umkc.edu/faculty/projects/ftrials/ftrials.htm.

10. Bigler, David L. and Will Bagley. (2011). *The Mormon Rebellion: America's First Civil War, 1857–1858*. Norman, OK: University of Oklahoma Press.

11. Fancher, Burr. (2006). *Captain Alexander Fancher*. Portland, OR: Inkwater Press.

12. Givens, Terry L. and Matthew J. Grow. (2011). *Parley P. Pratt: The Apostle Paul of Mormonism*. New York: Oxford University Press.

13. Brooks, Juanita. (1950). *The Mountain Meadows Massacre*. Norman, OK: University of Oklahoma Press.

14. Linder, Doug. (2011). Famous Trials webpage. "Mountain Meadows Massacre Trial." Available online at http://law2.umkc.edu/faculty/projects/ftrials/ftrials.htm.

15. Walker, Ronald W., Richard E. Turley, & Glen M. Leonard. (2011). *Massacre at Mountain Meadows*. New York: Oxford University Press.

16. Brooks, Juanita. (1950). *The Mountain Meadows Massacre*. Norman, OK: University of Oklahoma Press.

17. Linder, Doug. (2011). Famous Trials webpage. "Mountain Meadows Massacre Trial." Available online at http://law2.umkc.edu/faculty/projects/ftrials/ftrials.htm.

18. Bagley, Will. (2002). *Blood of the Prophets: Brigham Young and the Massacre at Mountain Meadows*. Norman, OK: University of Oklahoma Press, p. 146.

19. Lee, John Doyle. (1877). Mormonism Unveiled: The Life and Confession of John D. Lee and the Complete Life of Brigham Young. New York: W. H. Stelle & Co.

20. Bagley, Will. (2002). *Blood of the Prophets: Brigham Young and the Massacre at Mountain Meadows*. Norman, OK: University of Oklahoma Press, p. 316.

21. Internet Movie Database (IMDB). (2011). *September Dawn (2007)*. Available online at http://www.imdb.com/title/tt0473700/.

22. This section is based on the film *September Dawn* (2007). Directed by Christopher Cain. Hollywood, CA: Black Diamond Pictures.

23. Foster, Craig L. (2007). "Massacring the Truth." *FARMS Review, 19*. Available online at http://maxwellinstitute.byu.edu/publications/review/?vol=19&num=2&id=665.

24. *September Dawn* (2007). Directed by Christopher Cain. Hollywood, CA: Black Diamond Pictures.

25. Novak, Shannon A. (2008). House of Mourning: A Biocultural History of the Mountain Meadows Massacre. Salt Lake City, UT: University of Utah Press.

26. Brodie, Fawn. (1995). *No Man Knows my History: The Life of Joseph Smith*. 2nd Ed. New York: Vintage.

27. Linder, Doug. (2011). Famous Trials webpage. "Mountain Meadows Massacre Trial." Available online at http://law2.umkc.edu/faculty/projects/ftrials/ftrials.htm.

28. Abanes, Richard. (2003). One Nation Under Gods: A History of the Mormon Church. New York: Basic Books.

29. Arrington, Leonard J. (1986). *Brigham Young: American Moses*. Champaign, IL: University of Illinois Press.

30. Fancher, Burr. (2006). *Captain Alexander Fancher*. Portland, OR: Inkwater Press.

31. Walker, Ronald W., Richard E. Turley, & Glen M. Leonard. (2011). *Massacre at Mountain Meadows*. New York: Oxford University Press.

32. Brooks, Juanita. (1991). *The Mountain Meadows Massacre*. 3rd Ed. Norman, OK: University of Oklahoma Press, pp. 105–106.

33. Bagley, Will. (2002). Blood of the Prophets: Brigham Young and the Massacre at Mountain Meadows. Norman, OK: University of Oklahoma Press, p. 316.

34. Paulson, Michael. (2007). "Religious Violence Stirs a Western." *The Boston Globe*, August 19.

CHAPTER 3

TOMBSTONE AND THE SHOOTOUT AT THE O.K. CORRAL (1881)

A replica of the original Tombstone of Tom McLaury, Frank McLaury, and Billie Clanton in Boot Hill Cemetery, Tombstone, Arizona. Photo courtesy of the Library of Congress.

William Clanton, Frank and Thomas McLaury, came to their deaths in the town of Tombstone on October 26, 1881, from the effects of pistol and gunshot wounds inflicted by Virgil Earp, Morgan Earp, Wyatt Earp, and one—Holliday, commonly called 'Doc Holliday'.
—Tombstone Coroner Henry Matthews, 1881

Introduction

On October 26, 1881, in Tombstone, Arizona, four men met at the O.K. Corral and were heatedly discussing what to do next.[1] Billy Clanton and Frank McLaury had just arrived in town and learned that their brothers, Ike Clanton and Tom McLaury, had just had a confrontation with the Earp brothers. Virgil Earp had grabbed Ike Clanton's rifle and clubbed him with his pistol. Then Virgil and his brother Morgan proceeded to drag Ike to the Tombstone Courthouse, where they charged him with violating the local town ordinance which prohibited anyone other than law enforcement officials from carrying firearms in public places. Ike was allowed to leave the courthouse after paying a $25 fine, sans rifle. Tom McLaury, disturbed by the treatment of his brother, confronted Wyatt Earp upon leaving the courthouse. Words were exchanged and this time, Wyatt Earp pistol-whipped Tom McLaury twice, once on the head and once on the shoulder. Ike and Tom, both suffering from bruised heads and egos, were looking for a fight.[2]

The two men met up with their respective brothers, Billy Clanton and Frank McLaury, in the O.K. Corral. They then moved next door to a vacant lot that was situated between Fly's Rooming House and the Harwood house on Freemont Street. While there, Sheriff Behan, who was made aware of their location and the fact they were armed, confronted them. He tried to disarm Frank McLaury, but he refused. When he noticed Billy Clanton was also carrying, he asked for his weapons, but Billy claimed he was leaving town and would not need to check his weapons. Behan left, walked up Freemont, and alerted the Earps; it was, after all, a town matter, not a county one. The Earp brothers and Doc Holliday headed down the street.

In less than a minute, they had arrived at the empty lot, a narrow 15 feet across, all four men standing in a row.[3] Wyatt Earp was on the left, followed by Virgil, Morgan, and Doc Holliday. Billy Clanton, and both Tom and Frank McLaury, were said to also be in a row in front of the wall that was the Harwood House, possibly along with Billy Claiborne. Behind them were two horses belonging to Billy and Frank. Ike Clanton was nearly in front of Wyatt. As they stood facing each other, it is believed one of the Clantons or McLaurys made a motion for their gun, and town Marshal Virgil Earp was reported to have said, "Hold on, I don't want that."[4]

It was too late.

The Earps and Doc Holliday all drew their guns, then Doc and Morgan fired, hitting Frank McLaury and Billy Clanton. Billy, despite being shot, drew his gun and started to fire. His brother, Ike, did not draw his gun; instead, he began to beg Wyatt Earp not to shoot him. Doc and Morgan continued to fire at Frank McLaury, while he and his brother Tom tried to hide behind their horses. At this point, Ike cut and ran from the gunfight. Doc turned to fire at him, while Morgan continued to fire at the, now wounded, Frank McLaury. Frank managed to get behind his horse and moved onto Freemont Street using the animal as a shield. Doc then pulled out a sawed-off shotgun from underneath his coat.

Frank fired off a round from underneath the head of his horse, striking Virgil Earp in the right leg. Tom McLaury fired his pistol over the saddle of his horse, and managed to hit Morgan Earp in the shoulder. He slumped to the ground. Wyatt fired his gun and grazed Tom McLaury's horse, which bolted, leaving Tom exposed to Doc Holliday's shotgun. Struck by the blast, he was killed instantly.[5]

Meanwhile, Billy Clanton, despite having slid down the wall of the Harwood house, continued to fire his pistol, running out of ammunition before expiring. The only one left in the fight was Frank. His horse finally broke free, leaving him exposed to gunfire, but with an open field he was able to take a shot. He fired at Doc Holliday, striking him in the holster. Morgan, seriously wounded, turned and fired a shot toward Frank's head. The bullet hit and Frank crumpled to the ground, dead.[6]

From the first shot to the last, it has been estimated that only 30 seconds elapsed. Thirty seconds for an insignificant local gunfight to occur, over an insignificant matter, in a small, insignificant desert town in the American Southwest. No one knew at the time that those 30 seconds would become a legend so big that the story would be retold over and over again, through dozens of books and eight Hollywood films. One of those films, *Tombstone*,[7] starring Kurt Russell as Wyatt Earp and Val Kilmer as Doc Holliday, became a box office success and is generally considered the quintessential movie on the gunfight at the O.K. Corral.[8] Despite the notoriety of the film, not only did they get the 30-second gunfight wrong (it lasts well over a minute on film), they made numerous historical mistakes in regard to the events that transpired before and after the gunfight.

Tombstone: The History

The town of Tombstone is located in the San Pedro Valley, which looks up toward the Huachuca Mountains in southern Arizona.[9] In those dry washes just 30 miles from the Mexican border, a prospector discovered a vein of silver in a rocky outcropping. Later that summer of 1877, another prospector by the name of Ed Schieffelin decided to venture into that desolate country from nearby Camp Huachuca, a military fort that was established earlier that same year.[10] One of the soldiers is alleged to have told Schieffelin not to go into that territory for it was not only hot and desolate, it was Apache country. Schieffelin explained he was looking for valuable rocks. The soldier reportedly said, "The only rock you'll find out there will be your own tombstone!"[11] Schieffelin found his rock—silver—and after laying claim to much of the land, he established a town inspired by the soldier's comment: Tombstone, Arizona.

Established in 1879, Tombstone had a population of 100. Two years later, with the silver rush on, the population swelled to 7,000.[12] It was a very typical western boomtown, with wooden buildings thrown up over night with fancy facades, and more saloons, gambling houses, and brothels than actual homes. In addition to immoral behavior, criminal behavior was rampant, and according to one citizen, the local town marshal's office was lacking in its ability to provide protection: "The law must be carried out by the citizens, or should be, when it [the marshal's office] fails in its performance as it has lately done."[13]

It was at this time, late in 1879, that Wyatt Earp and his brothers arrived in Tombstone, Arizona.[14] Although Wyatt had been a lawman in Dodge City, Kansas for four years, he was not heading to Tombstone to serve in that capacity. Rather, he, like so many others, was heading to Tombstone because of the silver rush in the hopes of making a lucrative profit. Wyatt arrived along with his brothers James and Virgil, and they would be joined the following summer by Morgan (the youngest brother) and their friend Doc Holliday.

During 1879 and 1880, the Earp brothers laid claim to several mining stakes and made some other property deals in town. Wyatt also obtained a 25% interest in the stakes of a faro table at the Oriental Saloon, where he provided protection for the games. James served as both a bartender and a faro dealer at the Oriental, working alongside his brother Wyatt. Meanwhile, Virgil, and soon Morgan, found employment guarding shipments made by the famous Well's Fargo stagecoach company. In early 1880, Virgil added Deputy U.S. Marshal to his name, and in July of that year, Wyatt became a deputy sheriff for Pima County (which included Tombstone).[15]

It was actually Virgil, in his role as Deputy U.S. Marshal, that brought the Earp brothers in conflict with the Clantons and McLaurys, sometimes loosely referred to as *cowboys*. The same gentleman who commented on the lack of law enforcement in Tombstone noted that "A cowboy is a rustler at times, and rustler is a synonym for desperado—bandit, outlaw, and horse thief."[16] The Clantons and McLaurys were sometimes referred to as *cowboys* in the pejorative.

It was July 25, 1880, and Virgil and his posse tracked six stolen U.S. Army mules to McLaury's Ranch.[17] A brand had been used to change the existing "US" brand to "D8." When confronted, the McLaurys promised to return the mules to the U.S. Army at Camp Rucker, but they never did. A captain from the camp created a handbill naming some of the Clantons and McLaurys as thieves, and these were given to Virgil to post. Word was relayed to Virgil that if he posted the bills, Frank McLaury would kill him. This was the first confrontation that would eventually lead to the famous gunfight.

The second encounter occurred on October 28, 1880, when Tombstone Marshal Fred White tried to disarm Curly Brocius and Curly's gun went off. It was disputed whether the gun firing was intentional and, hence, murder, or whether it was an accident. White lingered for several days, but while he lay dying in bed he stated it was purely an accident. Regardless, Tombstone needed a new marshal and Virgil was appointed as the acting marshal. In addition, Wyatt was competing at this time with the local sheriff, Johnny Behan, to not only become the next Pima County sheriff, but they were also competing for the same woman, Josephine Marcus. Behan was known to be associates with many of the cowboys, hence the Earps were finding themselves, at least subtly, in opposition to the outlaws.

The next major confrontation occurred on March 15, 1881, when a stagecoach robbery ended with the driver and one of his passengers dead.[18] The bandits made off with the Wells Fargo shipment—$26,000 in cash. Two posses were formed to hunt down the outlaws. The first was headed by Virgil and included Wyatt, Morgan, Doc Holliday, and Bat Masterson. The second was led by Sheriff Behan. The Earp posse tracked down one of the members of the gang whom they turned over to Sheriff Behan. Within 24 hours the outlaw managed to *escape* by walking out of his unlocked jail cell. Behan seemed unconcerned. He also refused to pay the Earps for their work in capturing the murderer and robber.

Wyatt, infuriated over Behan's dishonest behavior, was determined to take the position of sheriff from Behan. Wyatt decided to strike a deal with Ike Clanton by promising him the $6,000 in reward money put up by Wells Fargo if he would secretly give Wyatt information leading to the criminals responsible for the murders. Wyatt believed that if he made the arrest, his election over Behan would be guaranteed. Ike Clanton readily agreed, but the deal fell through when the same *cowboys* responsible were gunned down in a New Mexico gunfight.[19]

Any dealings between Wyatt and Ike Clanton were also ended by the events that transpired from the September 8, 1881 Brisbee stagecoach robbery.[20] Virgil arrested two of Ike's *cowboy* friends for the robbery and Ike believed the Earps were simply trying to persecute all of the *cowboys*. He began making repeated threats toward all of the Earp brothers. This culminated with the October 25, 1881 threat that led directly to the famous gunfight.

That evening, Tom McLaury and Ike Clanton arrived in Tombstone to sell their beef stock. Ike ran into Doc Holliday and Morgan had to intervene in the confrontation. Ike had once again threatened the Earp brothers. The next morning, Virgil confronted Ike Clanton, who was carrying a pistol in defiance of the town ordinance against carrying guns inside the town limits. Virgil pistol-whipped Ike Clanton and hauled him off to court. When they exited the courthouse later, Tom McLaury was there and began to threaten the Earps, whereupon Wyatt pistol-whipped Tom McLaury, as he too was carrying against the ordinance.[21]

A short while later, Billy Clanton and Frank McLaury arrived in Tombstone. Citizens reported to Marshal Virgil Earp that they were armed in violation of the ordinance and that they were located just off Freemont Street. They were meeting with Ike and Tom and learning of the events that had transpired earlier that day. Tensions were running high. Sheriff Behan tried to intervene and disarm the group, but they were not listening. He then proceeded up Freemont Street.

At this point, Behan ran into the Earps and Doc Holliday, who were walking down the street intent on disarming the Clanton and McLaury brothers themselves.[22] Behan told them not to go stating they would be murdered. The Earps and Doc ignored his pleas, whereupon Behan told them (falsely) that he had already disarmed them all. The Earps and Doc continued down the street, came within ten feet of the Clantons and McLaurys, and stopped. The events that next transpired were in dispute perhaps no sooner than the smoke had cleared, for both sides gave conflicting testimony and eyewitness accounts were mixed.

What is known is that Virgil Earp said something to the effect of wanting the boys to disarm, and then the shooting began. It was over in 30 seconds. Three of the so-called *cowboys* were dead. Frank McLaury was killed from a bullet to the head, Billy Clanton had been shot in the chest, and Tom McLaury had been blasted with buckshot from Doc's shotgun. Ike Clanton had run away. Virgil, Morgan, and Doc were all wounded—Virgil struck in the leg, Morgan hit in the shoulder, and Doc shot in the hip. Wyatt Earp was the only one to walk away from the gunfight without so much as a scratch.

Sheriff Behan arrived and notified the Earps and Doc that they were all under arrest. Wyatt replied, "I won't be arrested today. I am right here and am not going away."[23] Matters lingered for several days until the coroner released his report, which stated "William Clanton, Frank and Thomas McLaury, came to their deaths in the town of Tombstone on October 26, 1881, from the effects of pistol and gunshot wounds inflicted by Virgil Earp, Morgan Earp, Wyatt Earp, and one—Holliday, commonly called Doc Holliday."[24] The vagueness of the report caused Justice of the Peace Wells W. Spicer to have all four arrested. He then opened up a preliminary hearing in order to determine if there was enough evidence to move forward with the charges against the Earps and Holliday. After nearly a month of testimony, Judge Spicer ruled there was not enough evidence to move the case to trial.[25]

Neither the gunfight nor the trial ended the feud between the Earps and the *cowboys*. Two weeks after Judge Spicer's decision, Mayor John Clum (who was considered pro-Earp) narrowly escaped what was believed to be an assassination attempt while riding in a stagecoach. Two weeks after that, Virgil Earp was ambushed while walking home from a saloon. He was hit with buckshot so heavily that he lost nearly all mobility in his left arm for the remainder of his life. Then, on March 18, 1882, Morgan Earp was playing pool in a pool hall when a bullet was fired through the window. He was struck in the stomach and the bullet passed through his spine. He was dead within the hour.

The following day, Wyatt Earp, Doc Holliday, and others went on what became known as the *Vendetta Ride.*[26] Wyatt tracked down Frank Stilwell, who was believed to be responsible for the death of Morgan, and mercilessly gunned him down. A warrant was then issued for Wyatt's arrest and a posse, led by Sheriff Behan and featuring such people as Johnny Ringo, rode out in pursuit. Wyatt, meanwhile, tracked down another individual believed to be involved in Morgan's death, Florentino "Indian Charlie" Cruz, in the Dragoon Mountains and killed him. Wyatt's posse then ended up near Iron Springs, where they ran into a group of *cowboys* and Wyatt shot and killed Curly Bill Brocius.

At this point, Wyatt and Doc fled to New Mexico to avoid the pursuing posse and then traveled on to Colorado. Arizona requested the extradition of Wyatt and Doc from Colorado but the Colorado governor refused. A short time later, Johnny Ringo was found dead in Turkey Creek Canyon beside a tree. Josephine Marcus Earp would later write that Wyatt and Doc returned to Arizona to kill Ringo, but this is the only reference to this possibility and a number of circumstances suggest it to be false.[27]

Wyatt and Josephine married in 1887, and remained together until Wyatt's death in January of 1929. After his death, Josephine wrote a biography that she tried to have published, but no one was interested unless she was honest in her memoirs. She eventually gave up the idea, and after her death in 1944, the book lingered until it was published by the University of Arizona Press in 1976.[28]

The same year that Wyatt and Josephine were married, Doc Holliday died in the sanatorium located in Glenwood Springs, Colorado. The only people present were the nurses, who noted that his last words were, "Damn, this is funny."[29] The reference is believed to be in regard to the fact he died without his boots on; he always swore he would die with his boots on.

Tombstone: The Film

The film opens with what appears to be an old newsreel documentary giving the *factual* history of Wyatt Earp, Tombstone, and the reason that the Earps found their way to that desolate little town—a silver rush.[30] The film then cuts to a scene showing a mission church in the desert with a water fountain running in the front. Surrounding the courtyard area are tables set up for a banquet and the signs of a wedding are evident. Curly "Bill" Brocius and the *cowboys* show up and begin shooting up the wedding party. The groom is eventually shot and the bride is taken into the mission and raped off-camera. Johnny Ringo then shoots the Catholic Priest. This scene is an introduction to the bad guys in the film.

The scene shifts to their counterparts, the good guys, as Wyatt Earp arrives at the train station in Tucson, Arizona. The local authorities seek out Wyatt to become the town marshal, but he refuses. Virgil and Morgan Earp arrive next, along with their wives, Allie and Louisa. Mattie joins Wyatt and the three couples admire themselves in a storefront window. As they head to the stagecoach for their trip south to Tombstone, Mattie is shown needing a bit of laudanum, a liquid opiate prescribed during that time period for headaches and other ailments.

The final introduction scene then presents Doc Holliday and "Big Nose" Kate sitting in a saloon while Doc gambles. Doc wins his hand and is accused by another card player of cheating. Doc gets the drop on the other player and then takes all of the money from the pot, as well as the money from the saloon's cash register on the way out. Doc and Kate then plan to quickly leave town.

Wyatt and his entourage are then shown arriving in Tombstone. As they drive down the road they see the town still under construction and people moving along the raised city sidewalks. They pass by the Bird Cage Theater and arrive at the Grand Hotel. A dapper looking man in a bowler watches the new arrivals and comes over to introduce himself as Johnny Behan, the Conchise County sheriff. He also says he is the tax collector, head of the anti-Chinese committee, and a local realtor. Upon finding out that the man he is talking to is Wyatt Earp, he offers him a free place to stay just down the street.

Wyatt and his brothers, wasting no time in getting familiar with Tombstone, are shown talking to Fred White, the town marshal. He is a short, older white-haired man who talks about the cowboys and the trouble they cause and that the way to recognize a cowboy is by their red sashes. He points out a few of the places along the main street in Tombstone and particularly points out the saloon called the Oriental, which he refers to as a slaughterhouse. With that statement, Wyatt decides to go into the Oriental, leaving Virgil, Morgan, and Fred White on the street.

Wyatt walks into the Oriental and introduces himself to the bartender and inquires as to the owner. He points out an abusive looking card player by the name of Johnny, and Wyatt confronts him. After driving him out, Wyatt takes over control of the Oriental and promises a 50 percent split on the take of the house. Wyatt then goes back outside to tell his brothers the good news, but Johnny returns armed and is ready to shoot Wyatt. An individual nearby intervenes, telling Johnny it would not be a good idea to shoot his friend. Realizing it is Doc, the Earps celebrate being back together again. In their discussion, Doc praises the game of poker, when several *cowboys* in their red sashes come out of a saloon shooting. These two turn out to be Creek Johnson and Texas Jack, who know Doc Holliday. Fred White, the town marshal, takes their guns from them and turns them over to Judge Spicer.

An arriving carriage catches Wyatt's attention and he watches as the actor and actress of a small troupe arrive. One in particular, Josephine, not only catches Wyatt's eye, but he catches hers as well. The scene then shifts to the Bird Cage Theater where the acting troupe is putting on a variety show with the cowboys in attendance, including Curly Bill, all wearing their red sashes. Wyatt and his clan are present that evening in a box seat. A juggler comes out, but the *cowboys* shoot at the items he is juggling. An actor comes out and gives Shakespeare's Henry V Speech and the cowboys try to drive him from the stage. Then a scene from *Faust* is played out and Josephine reveals she is the concealed *actor* in the play and there is much cheering. Wyatt pays more attention to Josephine, but leaves with his clan.

Outside of the theater there is small talk about the stars and Morgan asks Wyatt if he believes in God. Wyatt gives a non-committal answer. Morgan presses about what happens when you die, and again, Wyatt gives a non-committal answer. Virgil complains about Morgan's spiritualism talk and that breaks up the gathering. Wyatt has to "go to work" at the Oriental so he sends Mattie home alone and advises her to go easy on the laudanum.

The scene shifts to the inside of the Oriental where the Faro gaming tables are being run and Doc talks to Wyatt about Josephine. Josephine and the actor arrive and Wyatt observes Josephine. Curly Bill and Johnny Ringo have a minor confrontation with Wyatt, then Johnny Ringo and Doc have their own exchange in Latin. Ike Clanton is also present and acts like a crazy old man before leaving the Oriental. None are happy with the Earps or Doc being in Tombstone.

The next day Wyatt is seen riding a horse when he comes across Josephine. They then ride through the pine forests through the mountains. They end up relaxing under a tree and they discuss the relationship between Josephine and Sheriff Behan. Wyatt is smitten with Josephine and calls her "different." Wyatt then heads up to find Mattie consuming another bottle of laudanum. Wyatt confronts her and Mattie becomes enraged.

The scene returns to another night at the Oriental. Doc is playing music and Curly Bill gets up and starts shooting. Sheriff Behan says someone should do something, but not him, as it is town business. Curly Bill goes outside and continues shooting at the stars when Town Marshal Fred White confronts him and tells him to hand over the pistols. As he does so, Curly Bill shoots White, who then dies in the street. Curly Bill is taken into custody, but Ike Clanton demands his release. Wyatt, Doc, and Virgil drive him off and Ike Clanton threatens them as he leaves.

The scene then shows the Earps playing pool and talking real estate. Wyatt tells everyone that Judge Spicer let Curly Bill go. The mayor next arrives, asking for Wyatt to become the new town marshal, and he refuses. Wyatt tells him and his brothers that none of them are going to get involved. The next day, however, Virgil sees a child almost get killed by ruffians riding rampant through town and Virgil is next shown putting up bills announcing a "no-gun" ordinance.

The scene shifts again to the Oriental where Josephine is singing the song "*Red River Valley*." Doc is running a poker table and Ike Clanton is playing. Doc wins a hand and Ike thinks he was cheated. Doc then collapses due to his tuberculosis. Ike continues to complain and Virgil whacks him with his gun and puts him in jail. The red-sashed cowboys come to pick up Ike at the jail and as he leaves, he screams, "You got a fight coming today." The scene then shows Doc in bed recovering and Kate comes into the room. They have an exchange, she gives him a cigarette, and as she disappears off camera (apparently for purposes of oral sex), Doc says, without explanation, "You may be the Anti-Christ." The scene returns to Ike. Six others are coming into town with guns and Wyatt looks at his brothers and says, "You had better swear me in."

The Earp brothers are next seen walking down the streets of Tombstone with a building burning in the background. The camera pans to show the Clantons preparing for a showdown then returns to the Earp brothers walking down the street, but now there is no burning building. As they near the alley, they pass McFly's photography studio and the scene quickly cuts to the interior, showing Josephine having a semi-nude photo taken. It then returns outside and the Earps are joined by Doc Holliday before they face off with Ike Clanton, his brothers, and the Cowboys. The Clantons make a motion of going for their pistols when Virgil puts up a hand and says, "Hold it. It's not what I want." There is a long pause.

The film does not show who draws first, but rather focuses on one of the *cowboys'* eyes and Wyatt says, "Oh my God." Then everyone appears to open up at once. Three of the *cowboys* go down almost simultaneously, then a horse rears between Doc and the Clantons, whereupon Doc fires two blasts from his shotgun, hitting two. At this point Ike Clanton drops his weapon and begins begging not to be shot. He then flees into McFly's studio where Sheriff Behan is hiding. More shots are exchanged and Virgil goes down with a bullet to the lower leg. Morgan is then shot before another *cowboy* is shot multiple times by Wyatt and Doc. Ike Clanton then returns to the fight by grabbing Behan's pistol and firing multiple times out the window, before fleeing. Then the last of the *cowboys* is shot to death by Morgan and Doc. The gunfight lasts one minute and 38 seconds on-screen, and between 60 and 70 shots are fired.

As the smoke and dust clear from the shoot-out, Sheriff Behan arrives and notifies the Earps and Doc that they are under arrest. Wyatt explains not today, whereupon all the women arrive to take care of their men. The scene then shifts to the funeral procession, ostensibly that evening, heading to the cemetery (Boot Hill), which appears to be in town on flat ground.

The next morning as the sun rises, the Earps appear better. They come across Billy who does not want to talk to them. Next they encounter Ringo, who talks bad about the Earps, but Curly Bill arrives to stop Ringo. Then, what appears to be that evening, the ladies are sitting around Wyatt's house talking when a knock comes at the door. A man enters and fires a shotgun at the ladies, but no one is hurt. Then Virgil, walking to the bar where Wyatt and Morgan are located, is shot. He enters the bar bleeding and they move him to a couch. Morgan leaves the house in a rage and Virgil tells Wyatt to leave him alone. Wyatt then leaves and runs into McMasters, who throws down his red sash. Soon after, Morgan is shot while playing pool. He is lifted onto the pool table and a doctor tries to locate the bullet. Just before he dies he says, "You're right Wyatt, they got me good."

The next morning Wyatt and Doc are seen by the casket, and Virgil and the ladies take the casket via wagon and leave town for the train station. Wyatt rides alongside, passsing Curly Bill, Ringo, and Ike Clanton. Upon arriving at the train station, Wyatt shoots and kills Stilwell but lets Ike Clanton go after showing him that he is a certified U.S. Marshal. Wyatt tells Ike to run and explains hell is coming. Thus begins the *Vendetta Ride.*

Wyatt and his crew go after the *cowboys* and begin killing them. They first kill five in a bar, two in bed in a hotel, one on the plains, one riding a horse, one in an opium den, two are hung near a saloon, and then Curly and three others are shot and killed along a creek. Doc then explains to the other members of the Vendetta crew that it is not revenge Wyatt is after, but a "reckoning."

A stagecoach is next shown with the male actor murdered and Josephine holding him, while Billy is clearly upset at the loss of the actor. Behan is there with Billy and over 30 lawmen who are hunting Wyatt and his posse. Wyatt goes to Hooker's ranch, where he holes up and Josephine finds him there. While there, however, a horseman comes riding up, dragging a body, which they discover is McMasters, and the horseman yells that Ringo wants a solo fight. Wyatt talks to Doc, who is once again bedridden with his tuberculosis, and he tells Wyatt that he can't beat Ringo in a gunfight. Wyatt heads to the fight, but Doc gets out of bed, makes it to the meeting place and after both drawing, Doc kills Ringo. Wyatt then says it is time to finish it and the film shows another eight *cowboys* being killed.

Presumably the vendetta ride is over and Wyatt visits Doc in the Glenwood Sanatorium where he is bedridden, dying. Wyatt brings him a book titled *My Friend Doc Holliday,* written by Wyatt Earp. They play cards and Wyatt Earp leaves. Doc looks at his toes, says, "This is funny," and dies.

The next scene is a music hall where the *HMS Pinafore* is playing and Josephine is there. Wyatt shows up and Josephine is happy. Wyatt explains he has no money, they kiss, and Josephine tells Wyatt not to worry because "my family is rich." They dance in the snow as the narrator begins to speak. The voice talks as if concluding a documentary, explaining that Ike Clanton was later shot and killed, Mattie died from an overdose, Virgil became a town sheriff, and Wyatt and Josie had a series of adventures before he died in 1929. Cowboy stars were at his funeral and "Tom Mix wept."

Tombstone: Hollywood's Rendering

The story of the shootout at the O.K. Corral has long been a staple of the Hollywood film industry. One of the first motion pictures to feature the famous shoot-out was *Frontier Marshal* (1939), starring the famous Randolph Scott. The next film was a lesser known version, *Tombstone, The Town too Tough to Die* (1942), but it was soon followed by one of the most famous (although historically inaccurate) of the films, *My Darling Clementine* (1946). Another popular version was *Gunfight at the O.K. Corral* (1957), which starred Burt Lancaster as Wyatt Earp and Kirk Douglas as Doc Holliday. Two more lesser known films, *Hour of the Gun* (1967) and *Doc* (1971) appeared before a hiatus in Tombstone movies occurred, lasting 20 years.

Then, in 1993, Hollywood released a new version of the story, *Tombstone* (1993), starring Kurt Russell as Wyatt Earp, Val Kilmer as Doc Holliday, and Sam Elliott as Virgil Earp. The film, directed by George P. Cosmatos, opened on Christmas Day and made $6.5 million the first weekend. The total gross for the film was $56 million, with the estimated cost being $25 million to produce.[31] In all, it was considered a box office success and is considered by many to be the quintessential film on the shootout at the O.K. Corral.

The film opens with a documentary feel, as it presents the history of Wyatt Earp, Tombstone, and the silver rush. As the opening fades, a desert mission scene unfolds and the *cowboys* arrive for a wedding. The scene insinuates that Curly Bill Brocius is the leader of this gang of red sash wearing outlaws who go on to shoot the groom, rape the bride, and kill the priest. While the scene does a nice job of painting the *cowboys* as the antagonists of the film, it is historically inaccurate for there is no evidence the event ever took place. Curly Bill was not the leader of the gang, the *cowboys* were never an organized gang but rather were a loose group of shady outlaws and ranchers, and they did not wear red sashes. The red sashes is believed to have come from the culture at the time the film was released, where the news of the day was often filled with reports of the Los Angeles-based gang the *Bloods*, who wore red, particularly red bandanas. The red sashes were used to denote an outlaw gang, but was never a fixture of the *cowboys* or any western outlaw group.[32] And finally, it should be noted that it would have been impossible for the water fountain, running so pleasantly in the opening scene to have worked—there was no electricity in Southern Arizona or Northern Mexico at that time.

When the film introduces the protagonists of the story, the Earp brothers, it shows all three of them arriving together, along with their wives/girlfriends, in the train station in Tucson, Arizona. Wyatt and Mattie arrived in Tombstone first, but they traveled west by wagon, not train. James and Virgil Earp did not arrive until a month later, so they would not have been able to meet in Tucson. Also, James Earp is entirely erased from the film. Morgan Earp and his wife Lou also could not have been at the train station for they did not arrive until the following summer, and Warren Earp, who was also removed from the film, arrived one month after Morgan.[33]

When Wyatt arrives in Tombstone, the camera passes through Boot Hill and focuses on the famous epitaph on Lester Moore's grave: "Here lies Lester Moore, four slugs from a .44, no Les, No more." This is an anachronism for Lester Moore was killed and buried in 1884, three years after the gunfight. Also, when Wyatt pulls up to the Grand Hotel, he is greeted by Sheriff Behan. The issue here is that Behan was not the sheriff when Wyatt arrived, but only became the sheriff later.

The film transitions to introduce the other key protagonist in the film, Doc Holliday. Doc is shown playing cards and Ed Bailey accuses him of cheating and pulls a gun. Doc ends up stabbing Bailey, which was true. Doc is then seen leaving with Kate Elder; however, on the way out he is shown stealing from the cash register. There is no evidence that Doc ever stole in so blatant a manner.[34] Also, Kate Elder was nicknamed "Big Nose Kate" for the obvious fact she had a big nose. In the movie, Kate is played by the attractive Joanna Pacula, who has a very slim nose—clearly an inaccurate casting issue.

Another inaccuracy in casting comes with the character of town marshal, Fred White. Shortly after arriving in town, Wyatt and his brothers are given a tour of the town by Fred White, who was played by Harry Carey, Jr. Carey had long been a fixture in western movies in the 1940s and 1950s and so was brought in to play the town marshal. At the time of the film, Carey was a little over 70 years old. The real Fred White was just over 30. Also, when White shows the Earps around town he mentions being able to tell a *cowboy* by the red sash, again, a gang symbol that was entirely fictitious for the real *cowboys*.

Wyatt then enters the Oriental and after an amusing scene of running out the fake tough guy, Johnny Tyler, who was dealing at the gambling table, he takes over a 50% stake in the gambling receipts. In reality, it is doubtful Wyatt had such an entertaining encounter, but rather he had gained a 25% stake in the gambling receipts in return for protection of the gaming tables because of his notoriety. He obtained this position by running out Johnny Tyler, who was a customer, not a dealer. When Wyatt steps outside and Johnny Tyler returns with a shotgun, Doc Holliday appears to prevent him from shooting. Doc did not appear in Tombstone until a year later, and Johnny Tyler did not confront Wyatt after his removal, in real life he confronted Doc Holliday. This also means that this event did not take place until late 1880, not after Wyatt arrived in town, as shown in the film.

One other aspect related to gambling in the movie was Doc's disdain for Faro and his love for poker. In real life, it was the other way around. Doc was addicted to the game of Faro, not poker.[35] Still further, there were times where Doc is shown in the Oriental watching the play at the Faro table as a bystander, but in real life, when Doc came into Tombstone, he became *the* Faro dealer at the Oriental. Finally, it should be noted that the Faro table, as shown in the film, is not set up correctly.[36]

It should also be noted that the film comes across historically inaccurate not so much for what it shows, but for what it leaves out. The film never shows two of the Earp brothers, it does not show the stagecoach robbery or the theft of the U.S. Army mules. It does not show Virgil accepting the position of U.S. Deputy Marshal, only town marshal. It also plays to this notion that Wyatt was out of the law enforcement business and refused to allow himself or his brothers to be roped into any such position. This is an entirely false notion for the fact Wyatt become deputy sheriff under the Pima County Sheriff Shibell, demonstrating Wyatt was not against taking any such position.

The confrontation of the *cowboys* in the Oriental is often considered one of the best scenes in the movie for Val Kilmer's portrayal of Doc Holliday. At one point, Johnny Ringo and Doc Holliday square off and have a verbal exchange in Latin. There is no evidence Doc Holliday or Johnny Ringo knew Latin and with their level of education and background, it is not likely. Further, the twirling of the pistol by Johnny Ringo and the hilarious twirling of the tin cup by Doc never occurred. In fact, during that time period, one did not twirl a gun. They were not for show, they were for shooting. The twirling of six-shooters was created for entertainment purposes, using prop guns, by the old wild west traveling shows and then by Hollywood.

In another scene in the film, Curly Bill Brocius appears to be very high on something (opium?) and begins hallucinating. He pulls out his pistols and starts shooting at windows, street lamps, and the stars. Town Marshal Fred White confronts him and demands Curly Bill's pistols. As Curly Bill hands them over, he shoots and kills Fred White on the street. In reality, Curly Bill did not go on a shooting rampage. There were other cowboys firing their pistols, Fred White just happened to confront Curly Bill for his. As Curly Bill handed them over, once gun fired once, striking White. In the film he is struck in the chest; in real life he was struck in the groin.[17] The pistols were recovered and found to have only been fired once, further indication that Brocius was not firing his guns prior to shooting White. Further, White did not die on the street, but rather lingered for several days before dying. During that time he stated that it was not an intentional shooting, it was an accident.

In the film, there is a lot of play between Wyatt and Josephine (Josie) that is supposed to demonstrate their love interest in each other. The first scene, where Josie steps out of the stagecoach and they lock eyes, could not have happened, for Josie did not meet Wyatt when she was first playing in Tombstone. Josie met Behan when she was playing in the *H.M.S. Pinafore* in Tombstone, but she returned to San Francisco. Behan then proposed to Josephine and asked her to come back, so it was upon her return that she met Wyatt. The love interest did developed, mainly because Behan was noncommittal about getting married. The other issue with Josie appearing in town as she did in the film was the fact she played the leading actress at the Bird Cage Theater. Josie was never a leading actress and the Bird Cage Theater was being built at the time of the shootout and did not open until December of 1881, two months after. Therefore, it would have been impossible for the acting troupe to play at the Bird Cage before the shoot-out as they did in the film. One other minor aspect regarding Josie was the fact in one scene in the film she was singing the song "*Red River Valley.*" The song was written and published in 1879, but it is doubtful that it had made it that far west by the year 1881.

On the day of the actual gunfight at the O.K. Corral, it was still cold. The characters are shown wearing heavy clothes, but they are sweating as if the temperatures were extremely hot. As they begin their walk down Freemont Street there is a building ablaze in the background. Within seconds, after the scene pans away and back to them, there is no longer a building burning. No building was on fire that day in Tombstone, Arizona, and it is most likely that had there been one on fire, Virgil, as the town marshal would have been more concerned about the fire than the Clantons and McLaurys.

As they continue their march to the gunfight, the scene moves to inside of Fly's Photography Studio and shows Josie having a semi-nude photograph taken. Although there is some controversy over the semi-nude photo that does exist, it was not taken on the day of the gunfight. In fact, the photo is largely believed to have actually been taken in 1914, in San Francisco, California.

When the Earps and Holliday arrive, the *cowboys* go for their pistols and Virgil is shown throwing up a hand and saying, "Hold on, we don't want that."

That is largely accurate, but then the film has a long pause that looks at the hands on pistols and the eyes of each of the Earps, Doc, and the *cowboys*. There was no pause. Immediately after Virgil threw up his hand, gunfire was exchanged. The film then shows the opening shots several times repeatedly, so it is difficult to determine how many shots are exchanged during the entire shoot out scene. However, a rough estimate is 50–60 shots being fired and the entire gunfight lasts one-and-a-half minutes of film time. In reality, the shoot out lasted 30 seconds and just over 30 bullets were fired.

Other issues with the gunfight included the wide lot onscreen, versus the narrow 18 foot lot in real life. Doc also fires his shotgun late in the fight to move the horse and he only had one pistol, not two as displayed in the movie; and somehow, Doc manages to fire three blasts from his double-barrel shotgun. Morgan Earp was not struck in the right shoulder; the bullet that struck him was in his left shoulder and it entered from behind. Also, Frank McLaury, despite the dramatic end to the shootout in the film, was not shot in the forehead. And further, when Ike Clanton fled the gunfight, he did not take Sheriff Behan's gun and begin shooting from Fly's House. The truth is, Ike ran straight through the stables and kept on running. The individual who ran through Fly's studio was Billy Claiborne, and he too never bothered to stop and take Behan's gun and shoot through the window. He simply fled out the back door.

After the shootout, on what appears to be that same evening as the sun is setting, Wyatt and the others watch a funeral procession travel past Wyatt's house. The three killed in the gunfight are in caskets traveling on a carriage to Boot Hill. The procession is seen entering a cemetery that appears to be in town on level terrain. Anyone having been to Tombstone, Arizona, would know that Boot Hill, the famous cemetery, is located outside of Tombstone, on top of a hill, hence the name.

The film moves quickly to a scene that appears to be only a short time later, when Virgil is ambushed by shotgun blasts. This is a case of time compression, where Hollywood makes the revenge shooting appear to happen soon after the gunfight. In actuality, the assassination attempt on Virgil's life did not occur until December 28, two months later. Shortly after that, in the film, Morgan is shot. Yet, he was not shot while playing pool until March 18, 1882, nearly five months after the gunfight. In the film, Wyatt is not present when Morgan is shot, yet in reality Wyatt and a number of others, including Sherman McMasters, were there.[38] After Morgan was shot, he was on the floor and it was there he was examined by the doctor, but the doctor did not try to remove the bullet. He was then moved to a couch, not the pool table, where he would die 40 minutes later. His last words were not those spoken in the movie, but rather, "Are my legs stretched out straight and my boots off?"[39]

The following day, the ladies and Virgil are shown accompanying Morgan's body back to California, leaving Wyatt behind. In reality, James Earp accompanied Morgan's body and the ladies back to California. Virgil remained behind with Wyatt.

Perhaps the most historically inaccurate aspect of the entire movie comes at this point, when Wyatt Earp goes on his *Vendetta Ride*. It is true that Wyatt began hunting down those who were involved in the attack on Virgil and the killing of Morgan, but the movie over-inflates and sensationalizes what really happened. None of the vendetta killings were carried on in town. There were no chases. And no one was hung. Only four individuals were killed in the real *Vendetta Ride*: Stilwell, Florentino, Curly Bill, and Johnny Barnes. Stilwell was killed in a livery stable. The last three were killed in the same gunfight. So, two encounters and four killed. In the film, there were nearly a dozen incidents shown and approximately 26 individuals were killed. Also, the shoot-out where Curly Bill (and two others) were killed did not take place in a river as depicted in the film.

Other historical errors also show up during the Vendetta Ride portion of the film. At one point, Behan's posse comes across a stagecoach with Josephine and the actor. They had been robbed and the actor was killed. No actor was killed and Josie was never robbed. Further, when Wyatt hides out at the ranch to avoid Behan's posse, Josie arrives. This never occurred. Still further, a body is dragged behind a horse and left with the challenge for Wyatt to meet Ringo. Wyatt et al., discover it to be the body of Sherm McMasters. In reality, Sherm McMasters was not killed by dragging. In fact, he left Arizona with Wyatt and headed to Colorado to avoid the law. Wyatt also fled with Bat Masterson, but he was not depicted in the film at all.

After the Vendetta Ride, there is a scene where Wyatt goes to visit Doc in the sanatorium. In this scene, Wyatt brings him a book titled, "My Friend Doc," written by Wyatt Earp. This is historically inaccurate for Wyatt never visited Doc before he died, and he never wrote a book. Still further, Doc did not die in a sanatorium, he died at the Hotel Glenwood. Right before Doc dies in the movie, he says, "This is funny."[40] It is recorded that those were his last words, but the circumstances were different. First of all, there was a nurse present to hear Doc's last words, as opposed to in the film which had no one present at all. In reality, Doc had been delirious for several weeks, woke up, asked for whiskey, and then said his dying words, "Damn, this is funny." It is believed that the comment was in reference to dying without his boots on.

The ending scene in the film shows a theater playing the *HMS Pinafore* as Wyatt meets Josie there. Wyatt explains he has no money, but wants to be with Josie. Josie makes a comment that it is okay, her family is rich. This was incorrect; her family was not rich. Her father was a baker. They then dance in the snow as the film closes. As for the snow, it is unlikely: Josie had moved back to San Francisco and it does not snow there very often.

A few other anachronisms appear throughout the film and, while minor, are still historical inaccuracies. In one scene, a modern flag is shown flying over the buildings, but at that time the flag would have had 38 stars, not 50. In one scene in the Oriental, Wyatt and Morgan are shown eating Chinese noodles with broccoli. Eating broccoli did not become common until the 1920s in America. Finally, in the pool hall especially, there are electric lights with light bulbs shown. The light bulb had been invented prior to 1881, but only a short time before—1878. The biggest issue here is that Tombstone did not get electricity until 1902. Therefore, there could not have been electric lights in Tombstone as depicted in the film.

Conclusion

Tombstone is an interesting and highly entertaining film, but when it comes to the history of Wyatt Earp, his brothers, Doc Holliday, and the famous shoot-out at the O.K. Corral, it falls short. The film does portray many of the concepts related to the real history in that Wyatt et al., went to Tombstone, had some confrontations with the Clantons and those dubbed the *cowboys*, ended up in a shoot-out, one of the Earp brothers was then shot, another killed, and Wyatt went on a Vendetta Ride. The real reasons for the shoot-out, however, are inadequately portrayed in the film, the shoot-out has numerous mistakes, and the *Vendetta Ride* is entirely sensationalized and out of proportion with what really happened. When it comes to the basic historical facts, the film is rife with character elimination, composites of characters, time compression, fictitious characters and events, and anachronisms. Hence, while the film is enjoyable, it is grossly inaccurate historically and falls victim to the typical liberties that Hollywood takes with historical events in criminal justice history.

Further Reading

Barra, Allen. (2009). *Inventing Wyatt Earp: His Life and Many Legends*. Secaucus, NJ: Castle Books.

Blake, Michael F. (2006). *Hollywood and the O.K. Corral: Portrayals of the Gunfight and Wyatt Earp*. Jefferson, NC: McFarland & Company, Inc.

Burns, Walter Noble. (1929). *Tombstone: An Iliad of the Southwest*. New York: Doubleday, Doran, & Company, Inc.

Carmony, Neil B. (2000). *The Real Wyatt Earp: A Documentary Biography.* Silver City, NM: High Lonesome Books.

Guinn, Jeff. (2011). *The Last Gunfight: The Real Story of the Shootout at the O.K. Corral—And How it Changed the American West.* New York: Simon & Schuster.

Herda, D.J. (2010). *They Call Me Doc: The Story Behind the Legend of John Henry Holliday.* Guildford, CT: Lyons Press.

Linder, Doug. (2005). "The O.K. Corral Trial (Trial of Wyatt Earp) 1881." *Famous Trials Homepage.* Available online at http://law2.umkc.edu/faculty/projects/ftrials/ftrials.htm.

Lubet, Steven. (2006). *Murder in Tombstone: The Forgotten Trial of Wyatt Earp.* New Haven, CT: Yale University Press.

Marks, Paula Mitchell. (1989). *And Dies in the West: The Story of the O.K. Corral Gunfight.* Norman, OK: University of Oklahoma Press.

Roberts, Gary L. (2007). *Doc Holliday: The Life and Legend.* New York: Wiley.

Tefertiller, Casey. (1999). *Wyatt Earp: The Life Behind the Legend.* New York: Wiley.

Turner, Alford E. (1981). *The O.K. Corral Inquest.* College Station, TX: Creative Publishing Company.

Endnotes

1. Marks, Paula M. (1989). *And Die in the West: The Story of the O.K. Corral Gunfight.* Norman, OK: University of Oklahoma Press.

2. Linder, Doug. (2005). "The Earp-Holliday Trial: An Account." *Famous Trials Homepage. Available online at http://law2.umkc.edu/faculty/projects/ftrials/earp/earpaccount.html.*

3. Guinn, Jeff. (2011). The Last Gunfight: The Real Story of the Shootout at the O.K. Corral—And How it Changed the American West. New York: Simon & Schuster.

4. There is much dispute over what exactly was said and by whom. This specific reference comes from Marks, Paula M. (1989). *And Die in the West: The Story of the O.K. Corral Gunfight.* Norman, OK: University of Oklahoma Press, p. 223. See also http://law2.umkc.edu/faculty/projects/ftrials/earp/earphome.html.

5. Guinn, Jeff. (2011). *The Last Gunfight: The Real Story of the Shootout at the O.K. Corral—And How it Changed the American West.* New York: Simon & Schuster; Roberts, Gary L. (2007). *Doc Holliday: The Life and Legend.* New York: Wiley.

6. Marks, Paula M. (1989). *And Die in the West: The Story of the O.K. Corral Gunfight.* Norman, OK: University of Oklahoma Press.

7. *Tombstone* (1993). Hollywood Pictures.

8. Blake, Michael F. (2006). *Hollywood and the O.K. Corral: Portrayals of the Gunfight and Wyatt Earp.* Jefferson, NC: McFarland & Company, Inc.

9. Eppinga, Jane. (2003). *Tombstone.* Charleston, SC: Arcadia Publishing.

10. Marks, Paula Mitchell. (1989). *And Dies in the West: The Story of the O.K. Corral Gunfight.* Norman, OK: University of Oklahoma Press.

11. Linder, Doug. (2005). "The O.K. Corral Trial (Trial of Wyatt Earp) 1881." *Famous Trials Homepage.* Available online at http://law2.umkc.edu/faculty/projects/ftrials/ftrials.htm.

12. Linder, Doug. (2005). "The O.K. Corral Trial (Trial of Wyatt Earp) 1881." *Famous Trials Homepage.* Available online at http://law2.umkc.edu/faculty/projects/ftrials/ftrials.htm.

13. Parsons, George W. (2010). *A Tenderfoot in Tombstone, The Private Journal of George Whitwell Parsons: The Turbulent Years, 1880–1882.* Tucson, AZ: Westernlore Press.

14. Barra, Allen. (2009). *Inventing Wyatt Earp: His Life and Many Legends.* Secaucus, NJ: Castle Books; Carmony, Neil B. (2000). *The Real Wyatt Earp: A Documentary Biography.* Silver City, NM: High Lonesome Books.

15. Marks, Paula Mitchell. (1989). *And Dies in the West: The Story of the O.K. Corral Gunfight.* Norman, OK: University of Oklahoma Press.

16. Parsons, George W. (2010). *A Tenderfoot in Tombstone, The Private Journal of George Whitwell Parsons: The Turbulent Years, 1880–1882.* Tucson, AZ: Westernlore Press.

17. Guinn, Jeff. (2011). *The Last Gunfight: The Real Story of the Shootout at the O.K. Corral—And How it Changed the American West.* New York: Simon & Schuster.

18. Marks, Paula Mitchell. (1989). *And Dies in the West: The Story of the O.K. Corral Gunfight.* Norman, OK: University of Oklahoma Press.

19. Guinn, Jeff. (2011). *The Last Gunfight: The Real Story of the Shootout at the O.K. Corral—And How it Changed the American West.* New York: Simon & Schuster; Marks, Paula Mitchell. (1989). *And Dies in the West: The Story of the O.K. Corral Gunfight.* Norman, OK: University of Oklahoma Press.

20. Guinn, Jeff. (2011). *The Last Gunfight: The Real Story of the Shootout at the O.K. Corral—And How it Changed the American West.* New York: Simon & Schuster.

21. Linder, Doug. (2005). "The O.K. Corral Trial (Trial of Wyatt Earp) 1881." *Famous Trials Homepage.* Available online at http://law2.umkc.edu/faculty/projects/ftrials/ftrials.htm.

22. Marks, Paula Mitchell. (1989). *And Dies in the West: The Story of the O.K. Corral Gunfight.* Norman, OK: University of Oklahoma Press.

23. Linder, Doug. (2005). "The O.K. Corral Trial ("Trial of Wyatt Earp") 1881." *Famous Trials Homepage.* Available online at http://law2.umkc.edu/faculty/projects/ftrials/ftrials.htm.

24. Lubet, Steven. (2006). *Murder in Tombstone: The Forgotten Trial of Wyatt Earp.* New Haven, CT: Yale University Press, p. 66.

25. Lubet, Steven. (2006). *Murder in Tombstone: The Forgotten Trial of Wyatt Earp.* New Haven, CT: Yale University Press; Turner, Alford E. (1981). *The O.K. Corral Inquest.* College Station, TX: Creative Publishing Company.

26. Guinn, Jeff. (2011). *The Last Gunfight: The Real Story of the Shootout at the O.K. Corral—And How it Changed the American West.* New York: Simon & Schuster; Marks, Paula Mitchell. (1989). *And Dies in the West: The Story of the O.K. Corral Gunfight.* Norman, OK: University of Oklahoma Press.

27. Boyer, Glenn C. (1976). *I Married Wyatt Earp: The Recollections of Josephine Sarah Marcus Earp.* Tucson, AZ: University of Arizona Press; Roberts, Gary L. (2007). *Doc Holliday: The Life and Legend.* New York: Wiley; Tefertiller, Casey. (1999). *Wyatt Earp: The Life Behind the Legend.* New York: Wiley.

28. Boyer, Glenn C. (1976). *I Married Wyatt Earp: The Recollections of Josephine Sarah Marcus Earp.* Tucson, AZ: University of Arizona Press.

29. Roberts, Gary L. (2007). *Doc Holliday: The Life and Legend.* New York: Wiley, p. 319.

30. This section is based on the film *Tombstone* (1993). Hollywood Pictures.

31. Internet Movie Database. (2011). *Tombstone* (1993). Retrieved online at http://www.imdb.com/title/tt0108358/.

32. Stephens, J.R. (2008). "Historical Inaccuracies of the movie *Tombstone*." Retrieved online at www.ferncanyonpress.com/tobston/movie.shtml.

33. Marks, Paula Mitchell. (1989). *And Dies in the West: The Story of the O.K. Corral Gunfight*.

Norman, OK: University of Oklahoma Press; Stephens, J.R. (2008). "Historical Inaccuracies of the movie *Tombstone*." Retrieved online at www.ferncanyonpress.com/tobston/movie.s html.

34. Stephens, J.R. (2008). "Historical Inaccuracies of the movie *Tombstone*." Retrieved online at www.ferncanyonpress.com/tobston/movie.shtml.

35. Stephens, J.R. (2008). "Historical Inaccuracies of the movie *Tombstone*." Retrieved online at www.ferncanyonpress.com/tobston/movie.shtml.

36. This is based on a placard in the Tombstone Museum next to a Faro table. The placard explains the game of Faro, how the table should be set up, and how the game proceeds. It states that the Faro table in the movie *Tombstone* is set up incorrectly. See also Howard, Mark. (2009). "Mistakes in the Movie *Tombstone*." Retrieved online at www.bcvc.net; Turner, Nigel E, Barry Fritz, & Masood Zangeneh. (2007). "Images of Gambling in Film." *Journal of Gambling Issues, 20:* 117–143.

37. Stephens, J.R. (2008). "Historical Inaccuracies of the movie *Tombstone*." Retrieved online at www.ferncanyonpress.com/tobston/movie.shtml.

38. Marks, Paula Mitchell. (1989). *And Dies in the West: The Story of the O.K. Corral Gunfight*.

Norman, OK: University of Oklahoma Press.

39. Marks, Paula Mitchell. (1989). *And Dies in the West: The Story of the O.K. Corral Gunfight*.

Norman, OK: University of Oklahoma Press, p. 340.

40. Herda, D.J. (2010). *They Call Me Doc: The Story Behind the Legend of John Henry Holliday*

Guildford, CT: Lyons Press; Marks, Paula Mitchell. (1989). *And Dies in the West: The Story of the O.K. Corral Gunfight*. Norman, OK: University of Oklahoma Press.

CHAPTER 4

EIGHT MEN OUT AND THE FIXING OF THE 1919 WORLD SERIES (1919)

"Shoeless" Joe Jackson, still playing for the Chicago White Sox in 1920, before being banned permanently from professional Baseball. Photo originally taken by L. Van Oeyen in 1920 and courtesy of the Library of Congress.

As [Shoeless Joe] Jackson departed from the Grand Jury Room, a small boy clutched at his sleeve and tagged along after him.

"Say it ain't so, Joe," he pleaded. "Say it ain't so."
"Yes, kid, I'm afraid it is," Jackson replied.
"Well, I never would've thought it," the boy said.

Chicago *Herald and Examiner*
September 30, 1920

Introduction

Baseball had become America's favorite pastime by the turn of the twentieth century. Gambling on the game was common and widespread, and although there had always been rumors and suspicions that players may have fixed games, it was not until the 1919 World Series that this reality was revealed to baseball fans. Eight members of the Chicago White Sox agreed to orchestrate the loss of the World Series against the Cincinnati Reds. In a conspiracy with several professional gamblers, including Joseph "Sport" Sullivan and former boxer Abe Attell, and backed by New York kingpin Arnold Rothstein's money, first baseman Arnold "Chick" Gandil began working on his teammates to generate enough players to be in on the fix.

Chick eventually recruited starting pitchers Eddie Cicotte and Claude "Lefty" Williams, shortstop Charles "Swede" Risberg, outfielders Oscar "Hap" Felsch and "Shoeless" Joe Jackson, along with third baseman Buck Weaver. Each of these players had, at one time or another, a disagreement and general dislike for Charles "Commie" Comiskey, the team's owner. They agreed, for a price, with the payment of upfront money they would ensure the White Sox lost the World Series to the Cincinnati Reds. Although each participated to various degrees in throwing the series, eight games were played before the White Sox lost.

Several reporters pursued the story, the Baseball Commission was formed, and prosecutors pursued the charges of conspiracy. When the eight players were called before the grand jury, confessions to the corruption were signed. The eight players were indicted and went on trial for conspiracy. When the verdict was read, the players were found not guilty. Despite the acquittal, the following day, the men, now known as the "Black Sox," were banned from playing baseball for life by the new Baseball Commissioner Kennesaw Mountain Landis. The players never played professional baseball again.

In 1963, Eliot Asinof published his book *Eight Men Out: The Black Sox and the 1919 World Series.*[1] Despite the fact the book is now over 50 years old, it still stands as the definitive book on the corruption scandal. In 1988, director John Sayles took on the story for a Hollywood motion picture, writing the screenplay himself, and basing it on Eliot Asinof's book. The film was titled the same as the book, *Eight Men Out.*[2] Although not considered a success at the box office, the film did an admirable job of filming a complicated story that features a large cast of characters.[3] Despite attempts at bringing this historical criminal conspiracy to the silver screen, the film is rife with historical errors and inaccuracies.

Eight Men Out: The History

Although the White Sox of 1919 have often been considered one of the best baseball teams to ever play the game (the best, by some accounts), the team suffered an enormous number of problems and friction between players and with the owner. A number of the White Sox members were college-educated and strait-laced and they did not get along well with the more uneducated blue-collar members of the team.[4] The only thing they all agreed upon was the owner of the Chicago White Sox, Charles "Commie" Comiskey, was a skin flint and treated his players poorly. Comiskey paid his stars, such as outfielder "Shoeless" Joe Jackson and third baseman Buck Weaver, only $6,000; a salary commensurate with the lowest paid members of other baseball teams. The average salary on the White Sox team was around $3,000, half of what the lowest paid players in baseball received. He also cut corners in other places, such as the cleaning of the team's uniforms; hence, most of the White Sox uniforms were soiled, giving them the sobriquet "the Chicago Black Sox."[5]

One example of the greed of Comiskey is found in his relationship with star pitcher Eddie Cicotte. Asinof relays the story in his book that Comiskey had promised Eddie a $10,000 bonus if he won 30 games in the 1917 season.[6] When Eddie reached 28 games, Comiskey had him benched so that he would not have the opportunity to play (or win) the full 30 games. Comiskey also offered a bonus to all of the players on the team if they managed to win the pennant that year. The White Sox did come away with the 1917 pennant, but Comiskey's bonus turned out to be only a case of champagne, and it was flat to boot. While some recent research has called the Cicotte story into question, suffice it to say, Comiskey was abusive toward his players when it came to their salary.[7]

Generally disgruntled with Comiskey, some of the players began entertaining the idea of fixing the 1919 World Series. Asinof makes the claim that the original idea came with first baseman Chick Gandil.[8] Gandil, on the other hand, claimed in a September 17, 1956 article for *Sports Illustrated,* that "Sport" Sullivan came to him in Boston with the idea.[9] Regardless of who came to whom, it is pretty well established that the fix of the World Series began with these two men. Gandil was the ringleader on the players' side and Sullivan would be the ringleader on the gamblers' side.

Sullivan is reputed to have met Gandil in his hotel room where they negotiated how much money was needed up front in order to fix the 1919 World Series, which was three weeks away. Gandil demanded $80,000. The dollar amounts changed several times as more players were brought into the fix or certain players made demands (or were promised) more. When Gandil spoke to Eddie Cicotte, Eddie demanded $10,000 up front, before the first game, with another $10,000 after the series was lost. In his 1920 confession, "Shoeless" Joe was told he would receive a total of $20,000 himself.[10] Once Gandil had the players on board, he notified "Sport" Sullivan that the fix was on.

Suspicions that the World Series was already being fixed (interestingly, even before the real fix took place), had a number of individuals interested in joining the scheme to make money on the throwing of the World Series. "Sleepy"

Bill Burns, a former player and gambler, along with his associate Billy Maharg, approached Eddie Cicotte and offered more money than Sullivan was offering. The original five members in on the fix (Gandil, Cicotte, Williams, Felsch, and Risberg) all agreed to receiving $20,000 in advance. Burns was promising to bankroll the fix through Arnold "Big Bankroll" Rothstein.[11] They did not advise Sullivan that they were double dealing.

Burns and Maharg went to the Jamaica Race Track to meet with Rothstein, but Rothstein noted he was busy and said he would meet them later at a restaurant.[12] Instead of showing in person, Rothstein sent Abe Attell, a former boxer, to listen to the deal. Attell took the information to Rothstein, who refused to get involved. Burns and Maharg then cornered Rothstein in the lobby of the Astor Hotel in Times Square and encouraged him to back the fix. Rothstein again told them no, it was a bad idea and that they should forget about it.

What happened next is somewhat in dispute. Some conjecture that Rothstein changed his mind and bankrolled the $80,000 for the fix on the World Series.[13] Others have argued that he did not bankroll the fix for he knew it was too risky and too many people were involved.[14] Regardless of whether or not he actually bankrolled it, people believed he bankrolled it and, therefore, the fix was on. Playing upon this was, according to Asinof, Abe Attell.[15] Knowing his boss would not support the fix, but sensing an opportunity, he began working his contacts. Attell figured he could use money owed to Rothstein to bankroll the fix himself. Attell's involvement then had the added affect of falsely conveying to the gamblers that Rothstein was in fact involved in the fix through Attell.

What makes the fix and Rothstein all the more interesting (and complicated) is the fact that "Sport" Sullivan also went to Rothstein to bankroll the fix. Rothstein had little to no respect for Burns and Maharg. They were bit players. "Sport" Sullivan, however, was another story. Rothstein respected him, and after he laid out his plan for the fix, Rothstein stated he was on board (although there is the possibility he may already have been on board). While it is possible Rothstein was also double dealing, it is not likely. By refusing Burns and Maharg, Rothstein had plausible deniability. In Sullivan, he knew he had someone who would not turn on him. Rothstein then sent Nat Evans to Chicago, alongside Sullivan, to ensure the players were in on the fix.

The players were still in, but now they wanted $80,000—$10,000 each in advance. Evans returned to Rothstein and confirmed the players were on board, but Rothstein only sent $40,000 back to Sullivan for the players. Sullivan then bet $30,000 of the $40,000, and gave Gandil the other $10,000. Gandil put the $10,000 under Eddie Cicotte's pillow in his hotel room, insurance that he would remain in on the fix.

During the first game of the Series, the Reds won 9–1. Comiskey was suspicious and he asked "Kid" Gleason, the head coach, if he thought there was a fix. Gleason could not confirm it, but he said he thought something was wrong. Cicotte was pulled for Game Two and "Lefty" Williams was sent in to pitch. He too threw the game and that night, Burns delivered $10,000 to "Chick" Gandil. The players played well and in Game Three they won 3–0. They used that as a threat to demand more money. Specifically, Gandil told Sullivan he wanted another $20,000 before Game Four, otherwise they would no longer throw the games. They received $10,000 and lost Game Four. After losing Game Five, again they demanded $20,000 before Game Six. Once again they did not receive the demanded payment, so they won Game Six 5–4 and Game Seven 4–1. If they won Game Eight, the series would be tied. However, they lost Game Eight and the World Series went to the Cincinnati Reds.

Although the White Sox lost it was not entirely clear about the fix. Sports writer Hugh Fullerton and former pitcher Christy Mathewson kept track of the games by scoring them and looking for anything suspicious. They agreed that Games Two and Eight had been thrown. Games One, Three, and Five raised some suspicions, as if attempts were made to throw the game. More specifically, they both suspected Gandil, Williams, Cicotte, and Risberg to be in on the conspiracy. Their play during the games drew the most attention. The other four that they suspected, but could not agree upon, included Jackson, Weaver, Felsch, and McMullin. Fullerton, more than anyone, made the most noise and called for a Baseball Commission to be headed by Federal Judge Kennesaw Mountain Landis.

In the mean time, prosecutors began investigating the possible charges of conspiracy, but Comiskey allowed the players to continue playing in the 1920 season. Things, however, were quickly beginning to unravel. Once the grand jury was seated and began its hearings, confessions from the players provided the evidence necessary to hand down indictments. These came on October 22, 1920, naming the eight players and the four gamblers: Burns, Maharg, Sullivan, and Attell.

Prior to the beginning of the trial, word was received that the confessions and waivers of immunity for Cicotte, Jackson, and Williams had disappeared. Also, it was learned that the eight players now had some of the highest paid lawyers in Chicago representing them, but no one knew who was funding them—clearly not the destitute players. The players were arraigned on February 14, 1921, but none of the gamblers were present—Rothstein had ensured they were well hidden.

The trial began on June 21, 1921, officially titled the case of *State of Illinois v. Eddie Cicotte et al.* Judge Hugo Friend presided. In order to help the prosecution win the case, Billy Maharg was found and with his help they located Bill Burns fishing in Del Rio, Texas, the small town where he was hiding. Given immunity, he returned to Chicago and testified for three days. Maharg also testified, corroborating Burn's story. A month later, the case went to the jury, which deliberated for three hours before returning unanimous "not guilty" verdicts on all of the defendants. That night they celebrated their victory and what they all thought would be their reinstatement to play baseball.

The next day, the Baseball Commissioner, Judge Kennesaw Mountain Landis, issued his famous statement to the newspaper reporters. It succinctly read:

> Regardless of the verdict of juries, no player who throws a ballgame, no player that undertakes or promises to throw a ballgame, no player that sits in conference with a bunch of crooked players and gamblers where the ways and means of throwing a game are discussed and does not promptly tell his club about it, will ever play professional baseball.[16]

The Commissioner was true to his word. None of the eight players ever played professional baseball again.

Eight Men Out: The Film

The film, based on the Eliot Asinof book by the same name, was written and directed for the screen by John Sayles, who also played noted sportswriter (and short story author) Ring Lardner on screen.[17] The film also featured an all-star cast, including John Cusack as George "Buck" Weaver, Charlie Sheen as Oscar "Hap" Felsch, D.B. Sweeney as Joseph "Shoeless Joe" Jackson, and Christopher Lloyd as "Sleepy" Bill Burns. Released on September 2, 1988, the film had an estimated budget of $6 million, but only grossed $5.6 million dollars in the United States.[18] By all accounts, *Eight Men Out* was not a box office success, but is usually included in many top baseball movie lists.[19]

The film opens with time period music and a subtitle states that the film is "based on the book by Asinof."[20] Another subtitle announces it is "Chicago 1919," as the film opens with kids going off to see a White Sox baseball game. The film then moves through a rapid fire change of scenes in order to introduce all of the main characters of the film. Hugh Fullerton and Ring Lardner are shown watching the game. Charles "Commie" "Comiskey walks with reporters to an elegant banquet. "Sleepy" Bill Burns and Billy Maharg are shown in the stands watching the players as they discuss each of them: Collins, Chick, Buck, Eddie, Lefty, Swede, Hap, and Shoeless Joe. Interspersed among the scenes is the mention that Comiskey promised a bonus to the players if they had a successful pennant, which they did. And their bonus was—a case of flat champagne. Then the team photo of 1919 is taken before the film settles into the story.

The scene shifts to a bar with a lady singing and the players hanging out and having a good time. Chick Gandal and Sport Sullivan are in a booth talking about a fix and giving six or seven of the players $10,000 each. Sleepy Bill and Maharg are in a booth nearby and notice the conversation. Everyone talking agrees that Comiskey underpays his players, despite their success, which presents the motivation for them to throw the 1919 World Series. Chick Gandal and Swede become involved in the idea and, while talking about it in the men's bathroom, Freddie overhears and says he wants in on the deal. Swede agrees he is in, but he is told to "keep a lid on it." At this point, the film shows Hugh Fullerton and Ring Lardner arriving at the bar and they talk about the players, and then Sleepy Bill and Maharg are shown talking about a fix, but they acknowledge the need to get Arnold Rothstein on board as they need someone with the funds to be able to back the fix.

The film next begins shifting from scene to scene in order to show how and why various players became involved in the fix. Eddie is shown with his wife, who is rubbing his sore arm and shoulder, and talking about how he does not have much time left with his shoulder. Chick is then shown trying to get Eddie on board, but he refuses. Eddie then goes to Comiskey because he was promised that if he won 30 games he would receive a $10,000 bonus. Eddie had won 29, but Comiskey had Eddie benched to "rest his arm." Eddie argues that had he been allowed to play he would have reached the 30 games, but Comiskey refuses. Eddie meets with Chick, having clearly changed his mind. He tells him he is in as long as he gets "$10,000 grand before the first game. Cash!"

Sleepy Bill and Billy Maharg are next shown in New York at a horse track. They meet the "Little Champ," Abe Attell, who works for Rothstein. Sleepy Bill and Billy Maharg try to convince Abe to convince Rothstein to get in on the fix. Abe hears their plan and says, "No dice." The scene shifts to Lefty telling Swede, "No dice," as well. As Swede wears Lefty down, Lefty says, "If you got Eddie, you got me." Lefty is now in on the fix. The scene then shifts to Abe going to Rothstein with the idea, but not on behalf of Sleepy Bill or Maharg. He is now trying to arrange the fix on his own. Rothstein says, "No." He explains to Abe that there will be no way to keep the players quiet when the fix is in.

Abe decides to try and orchestrate the fix by going to "Sport" Sullivan. Abe then meets with Sleepy Bill and Maharg to tell them Rothstein is in, despite that fact he was not. Sullivan then goes to Rothstein for the money, and Rothstein tells him not to do anything until he hears from him again. Sport is shown receiving a message that Rothstein is in and he is given $40,000 up front. He takes $20,000 of that money, meant for the players, and bets on the Cincinnati

Reds (the other team in the World Series), takes another $10,000 and bets on the Reds winning the whole thing, and then the remaining $10,000 to distribute to the players.

The next scene shows the players on board a train, heading to Cincinnati for the first game. Hugh Fullerton and Ring Lardner are on board and as they pass through the players, they wish them good luck with the Reds and ask how Eddie's shoulder is holding up. Chick is shown trying to get Buck on board, as well as Shoeless Joe. When they arrive in Cincinnati, Hugh explains that the odds are even, but most people are betting on the Reds. Abe is shown telling Chick that most of the money for the players is tied up in bets, but Eddie is seen telling Chick he wants the first $10,000 "before the first game."

Evidence that the players are starting to have doubts about the fix is shown when head Coach "Kid" Gleason tells Buck he does not look so good. To highlight that the fix is in, however, Eddie arrives at his hotel room to find the $10,000 he was promised underneath his pillow. Thus ends the fix and the World Series of 1919 begins.

The scene for Game One begins with Hugh and Ring, believing something suspicious is going on, agreeing to keep separate scorecards based on their observations, and then they will compare them later. The next scene shows Shoeless telling Kid he does not want to play and Kid yelling at him that he will play. Kid then gives the whole team a pep talk. As the game unfolds, it becomes clear that all of the players, except Eddie (the only one to receive money at this point), are unwilling to help throw the game, leaving Eddie by himself. Buck does not go along and Hap makes a difficult catch he could have easily bungled. Eddie is the only one making mistakes until Swede bungles one catch. Kid pulls Eddie, but it is too late: The "Red Legs" win the game 9–1.

The fallout from Game One shows up first in the locker room when Swede accuses Buck of not helping to throw the game. Next, Eddie and Ring Lardner meet. Ring talks about a new ball coming out the next year and that more than likely the spitball will be outlawed. He then asks Eddie straight-up: is the series on the level? Eddie, unconvincingly, states that it is. Finally, Swede comes to Shoeless, places some money on his dresser, and tells him to "ease up on the field."

Game Two of the World Series begins and Lefty is pitching. Buck again makes a big play that he could have avoided for the fix. He is still not going along. Then an airplane is shown flying over the stadium and everyone stops and watches as a dummy falls to the ground. Kid yells out, "Ask it if it can pitch." Once again, Cincinnati wins the game and in the locker room after, the catcher (not in on the fix) goes physically after Lefty. The other players have to physically pull him off. The reporters come charging in and Kid attacks Chick, who is laughing and clearly taking the loss lightly.

The scene shifts to outside Comiskey's hotel, where an effigy of a White Sox player is on fire. Kid Gleason is then shown going to Comiskey's hotel room to talk to him. He tells him he suspects there is a fix. In the same hotel, Sleepy and Maharg visit Abe, saying they need the money for the players. Abe ridicules them and says, what are you "a couple of Boy Scouts?" The scene then shows Comiskey and Sleepy Bill walking the halls of the hotel mad.

Game three begins with Dickie as the pitcher. He talks with Kid about watching him defeat Cy Young and how his grandpa took him to see Kid beat the Indians in a no-hitter. The play on the field begins and they show the players beginning to make mistakes, throwing the game. Hugh and Ring become more suspicious. What is surprising is that out of nowhere, Dickie begins playing extremely well. In the wake of the White Sox win, the scene then shows Buck telling his wife that the fix is in and that Kid knows. He shows remorse.

Games Four and Five are quickly shown with Eddie failing to put a man out on first base and then failing to take a player out as he runs into home. Ring Lardner is shown muttering, "You lied to me Eddie." Game Five shows a new pitcher, but Felsch blows a catch in the outfield and Hap drops a ball. The catcher, frustrated, argues over a slide home and is ejected from the game. After this, Kid and Buck argue over whether or not Buck is in on the fix. Then, on the train, Ring Lardner comes through the team's car with the players singing a song. The song is to the tune of the then popular song "I am forever blowing bubbles," but Ring sings, "I am forever blowing ballgames." No one says or does anything.

Game Six shows Shoeless making an out and Chick at bat. He hits a grounder and Buck runs it in. The White Sox win the game. The scene cuts to a barber shop, where Rothstein is getting a haircut. He is not happy. Swede and Eddie are then shown meeting, trying to figure out how to proceed.

Game Seven begins with Chick threatening the others. Kid and Eddie have an exchange as Eddie is warming up and Kid says he is not playing. Eddie begs and Kid agrees. As Eddie comes out, Ring Lardner asks the question, "How long do you think he will go before he dumps it?" Eddie, however, plays well and the White Sox win the game. In the aftermath Kid is elated, having new confidence in his team. Rothstein, however, calls a man who is shown with a gun. The scene shifts to a bar that evening, where Williams, who is supposed to pitch the next day, is confronted by the gunman, threatening to harm his wife if he does not throw Game Eight.

Game Eight begins with the flag flying and the singing of the National Anthem. The children from the beginning of the movie are in the stands, as are

Comiskey, Abe, and all of the characters of the film. The gunman from the bar sits behind William's wife. Williams begins pitching horribly, but Shoeless hits a home run. Despite that effort, the White Sox lose 10–5 and Cincinnati wins the 1919 World Series.

Ring and Hugh begin investigating the fix. Newspaper articles are written about the fix and headlines are shown on screen. One newspaper headline reads, "Comiskey Offers $10,000." Comiskey is then shown talking to several individuals (other owners is the implication) about creating a baseball commission. They go after Judge Kennesaw Mountain Landis. He agrees as long as he has "absolute power" and a "lifetime contract." The next headline speaks to the grand jury summons.

The scene then moves to the courthouse where various players are waiting to testify before the grand jury. Eddie is called in and admits, "Yeah, we were crooked." Shoeless Joe is asked to sign a waiver of immunity and is seen signing his name with an X. He then departs the courthouse where the young child asks the famous question, "Say it ain't so, Joe." From there the scene shifts to a room that includes the eight accused players being introduced to their lawyers. The lawyers are presented as high class, for in baseball terms, they are the "Cy Young and Babe Ruth" of lawyers. Buck wants to know, if they are the best lawyers in Chicago, then who was paying for them? The players obviously could not afford such lawyers. One of the lawyers advises him not to ask; they are told to simply do and say what they are told. Buck voices his opinion that Comiskey was paying the lawyer's fees.

The scene shifts again to the courtroom, where the people in attendance treat the players as heroes. The courtroom is called to order and the names of the men accused of conspiracy are read. Comiskey takes the stand and testifies that after he learned of the possible fix, he notified Commissioner Johnson. Sleepy Bill testifies that the fix was pitched to him by the players. The confessions made by some of the players are requested as part of the courtroom documents, but the prosecution has to admit that the confessions were stolen. At another point in the trial, Buck demands the opportunity to testify and says he wants a separate trial. He is ignored. Kid Gleason then takes the stand and talks about how he believed there had been corruption in baseball, but he was not in on it or privy to any information. When asked by the lawyer what he thought now, Kid states, "Greatest ball-club I ever seen." The audience gives him a standing ovation.

After a short scene showing Buck with the kids again, the scene shifts back to the courtroom, where the final verdict is read: "Not guilty." There is a huge celebration in the courtroom and an even bigger one in the bar that night. This is interposed with pictures of Commissioner Landis reading his statement to the newspaper reporters that he was banning the eight players from baseball for life.

The scene fades to New Jersey in 1925, where some fans are watching a minor league game. They are talking about one of the players possibly being Shoeless Joe. Buck is there watching and confirms that no, it is not Shoeless Joe (despite the fact it clearly is). The scene fades to black and a final statement conveys that none of the eight players ever played baseball again.

Eight Men Out: Hollywood's Rendering

The film opens with a group of kids who are clearly in love with baseball. At one point, a scene shows them all gathered around the crystal set radio listening to their White Sox playing a game. As the film is largely set in 1919, this would have been impossible. The crystal set radio did not become popular and mainstream until the following year, 1920. Even on the off chance the kids were the first to obtain a crystal radio set, the only thing they would have heard on the radio at the time was static—the first radio station in Chicago, KYW, did not go on the air until 1921.[21]

Early in the film, when the players are being introduced and seen as winning the pennant to enter into the 1919 World Series, they are shown receiving their "bonus" from owner Charles Comiskey. The players had been promised that if they won the pennant, they would be given a bonus. They were shown receiving a case of champagne as their bonus and, to top it off, the champagne was flat. The event did actually happen, but the timing is in error. The players had been promised a bonus if they won the World Series against the New York Giants in 1917. They did win the World Series that year and that was when they were given the "bonus" of flat champagne.

At another point, Comiskey is shown bouncing a game ball, clearly a Rawlings baseball. The problem is, Rawlings did not make game balls until 1976.[22] The official baseball in 1919 for the World Series would have been an A.L. Reach.

An early scene in the film shows everyone in one bar, plotting and scheming to fix the World Series. This is entirely erroneous and none of the major discussions were ever held in such an open forum. Part of the bar scene also shows Fred McMullin accidentally overhearing talk of the fix between Chick Gandil and Swede in the men's bathroom. This too is an error, for they were in the White Sox locker room when McMullin overheard and became part of the conspiracy.

When the sports reporters first identified something amiss in regard to the play of the Chicago White Sox has been somewhat in dispute. It is usually claimed that Hugh S. Fullerton and Christy Mathewson smelled something rotten. Fullerton, however, never said anything negative. The only thing he really pointed out was Chick Gandil's base running in the second inning of Game One. Interestingly, one of the key individuals involved in making later claims that the series was fixed, Christy Mathewson was entirely eliminated from the film. Mathewson had a career with the Giants before spending his last three years with the Reds. Mathewson served in World War I and was exposed to mustard gas, developed tuberculosis, and died in 1925. It was he and Hugh Fullerton who agreed to keep score and compare notes after each game, primarily because rumors that the World Series was being fixed circulated even before the games began. In the film, Mathewson is replaced by Ring Lardner, who serves somewhat as Hugh Fullerton's "sidekick." Still further, Hugh Fullerton was played by Studs Terkel in the film. Terkel was 75 years old at the time. Hugh Fullerton was only 46 at the time of the 1919 World Series.

Just prior to Game One, there is a scene in the dugout where Shoeless Joe is moping in the corner, apparently feeling guilty for agreeing to throw the game. Kid Gleason asks Shoeless Joe what was wrong and he reports that he was sick and he was not going to play. Kid Gleason gets angry and tells Shoeless Joe he will play. There is no recorded evidence to suggest that Shoeless Joe feigned illness or was truly ill prior to Game One of the World Series. Also in the movie, prior to the playing of Game One, there is the singing of the National Anthem, a common event at baseball games today. In 1919, however, it was not common for the National Anthem to be sung prior to sporting events. There is evidence that it had been performed at some baseball games prior to 1919, but the common practice did not begin until World War II.[23] Another mistake that occurs before the start of game one is Buck Weaver is swinging a "powerized" Louisville Slugger. The powerized bat did not come out until 1931, 12 years after the 1919 World Series.[24] And still another error is evident before the first game begins, and that is the field itself. There is a track going around the field, but the first warning track (as they are called) did not appear on a baseball field until 1923, in Old Yankee Stadium. In 1919, there would have been grass all the way up to the walls.

In the play of Game One itself, Cincinnati is the home team, yet they were the first team at bat. In baseball, the visiting team is always at bat first. Later, in the fourth inning, the scoreboard shows a score of 1–0, but by that point the game was tied 1–1. Risberg is also shown making an error in Game One, but only Chick Gandil made a recorded error in the first game of the World Series.

At one point during the 1919 World Series, the film shows Rothstein listening to the game as it is received via the ticker tape. The announcer, reading from the tape, calls the Cincinnati Reds the "Red Legs." In the 1880s, the Cincinnati team became known as the Red stockings for the color of their socks. That was eventually shortened to the Reds by the twentieth century. It was the McCarthy era of the 1950s when the fear of being associated with communism caused the Cincinnati Reds to embrace the nickname "Redlegs."[25] Hence, this is an anachronism in that the Reds were not nicknamed the Redlegs in 1919.

During Game Two of the World Series, a dummy was thrown from an airplane onto the field. This was met first with surprise and then laughter when it was learned that it was an effigy of the White Sox. The pilot was a Reds fan and had dumped the straw-filled body onto the field as a joke against the White Sox. The film makes the dropping of the dummy rather ominous, as if it had more to do with the White Sox throwing the World Series. In fact, in real life it was considered such a humorous spectacle that two police officers walked onto the field, brought it back to the bleachers, and used it as a seat cushion for the remainder of Game Two.

Just prior to Game Three of the World Series, when Cicotte is pulled as the starter and Dickey Kerr is sent in to pitch, the coach, Kid Gleason, has a short conversation with him. Kerr tells Gleason that he saw him pitch a no-hitter against Cy Young. Gleason was impressed that Kerr knew about his history as a pitcher. The problem with the statement is that Gleason did pitch against Cy Young in 1895, but Dickey Kerr was born in 1893, and would have only been two at the time. Kid Gleason also never pitched a no-hitter.[26] In addition, the film makes it appear that Gleason was a pitcher. In reality, he had been primarily a second baseman and sometime pitcher. Further, Kerr is shown in the film as a right-handed pitcher, while in real life he was left-handed.

In one scene where Abe Attel is talking with some of the players, he mockingly says, "What are you, a couple of Boy Scouts?" In 1919, the Boys Scouts of America were less than a decade old. During World War I, they had gained notoriety for assisting on the home front, and in some cases, preparing future World War I soldiers for service. The Scouts were held in high esteem and their name was not used in the pejorative for most of the twentieth century. The pejorative use of the group entered the lexicon in the later twentieth century and is used to denote someone, usually negatively, who plays by the rules.

The film depicts an encounter between one of Rothstein's henchmen with pitcher Lefty Williams. In this scene, after Game Seven and the night before Game Eight, Rothstein's strong man enters the bar and confronts Lefty Williams. He tells him that if he does not throw Game Eight his wife, who is across the bar, will be physically harmed. On the day of Game Eight, Lefty looks into the stand and sees Rothstein's man sitting behind his wife in the bleachers. We are led to believe that Lefty threw Game Eight to save his wife. The reference to this scene is taken directly from Eliot Asinof's book *Eight Men Out,* so one would assume it had to be correct. Unfortunately, it was not. According to Doug Linder, "Asinof admitted in 2003 that the story was made up ... but it made for a good story and added drama to the 1988 movie."[27] Linder does note that some people claimed there were threats made against the players, but none of them have ever been substantiated.

The film attempts to use newspaper headlines to convey the advancement of time and events. In several cases, however, the dates and information prove to be wrong. The first Baseball Commissioner, Kennesaw Mountain Landis, was appointed to the position on November 12, 1920. The paper in the film carries the proper headline, but the date on the newspaper reads January 14, 1920. Later, there is a newspaper headline discussing the trial and it is dated February 2, 1920; however, the trial of the eight players did not open until June 27, 1921. One of the headlines also mentions that after the Series, Comiskey was offering $10,000 for anyone who had evidence the Series had been fixed. In reality, Comiskey offered $20,000. The mistake may have been intentional, in order to tie the same figure that the players had ultimately requested to fix the game. As if these newspaper headline mistakes were not enough, even the use of the newspaper font featured on those newspapers has been called into historical question.[28] The font is Helvetica typeface, which was not developed until 1957.

In one scene, Comiskey makes the announcement that the players are suspended until the outcome of the trial. In real life, nearly all of the players continued to play through the 1920 season. The only one who sat out that season was Chick Gandil, as he was having an individual contract dispute with Comiskey.

When the eight players are indicted and are charged with conspiracy, they end up in a meeting with their new high-paid lawyers. They are told that the lawyers who will be representing them are like the Ty Cobb and Babe Ruth of lawyers. In 1920, Babe Ruth was making a name for himself, being sold from the Boston Red Sox to the New York Yankees. However, he was not yet the legend he is considered today, and therefore referring to the lawyer as the "Babe Ruth of Lawyers" would be an anachronism.

The trial scene opens with everyone in suits, ties, and overcoats coming into the courtroom. The film seems to suggest that the trial took place in February of 1921, or at least during the winter months. In fact, the trial opened in July of 1921 and concluded in August, and at some points the temperatures were in the high 90s. No one was wearing an overcoat and few were wearing jackets. During photo ops they often wore their suit jackets, but most photos of the trial participants show them without their suit jackets on.

During the trial scene itself, White Sox owner Comiskey is called to the stand. When asked what his reaction was when he first learned that the World Series was possibly fixed, he responded that he had informed Commissioner Ben Johnson. This is clearly a mistake, for they show in the film Kennesaw Mountain Landis being named the first baseball commissioner. Therefore, Comiskey would never had referred to another commissioner. Also, it is unknown who the writer/director had in mind when this name was used; although there was a U.S. House Representative by the name of Ben Johnson serving in 1921, he had nothing to do with baseball.

At another point in the trial scene, Buck Weaver becomes angry with the proceedings and demands a separate trial. He makes the claim that he did not throw the World Series because he had a batting average of .327. In the actual trial transcript, Buck had stated that he had a batting average of .324.[29]

Conclusion

Assessing the overall historical accuracy of the film *Eight Men Out* is a little unique in comparison with the previous three films. In this particular example, the film was based on one book by the same name. The film may do an exemplary job of bringing the book to film, but the historical accuracy then may solely be based on the historical accuracy of that one book. Interestingly, it has been reported that in some cases, Eliot Asinof did take some liberties with the truth in his seminal book. For instance, the threat against Lefty William's wife, which created more tension in the final game played, was later discovered to have been entirely a fictional account by Asinof.[30] Hence, when that scene made it into the film, the historical inaccuracy lies with the author, not the director. Yet, there are many instances where the director did take liberties or made mistakes in moving the contents of the book to the screen.

John Sayles, the director of *Eight Men Out*, when asked in an interview about the sort of things he would do to recreate the history, answered, "You do the things that you think are going to strike people. For instance, I got hold of the rules of baseball from that era and the records of the World Series. We knew what happened on every play of every game because they kept those kind of line scores then. If somebody hit a ground ball to the shortstop in the third inning of the fourth game, that was the way it was shown on the screen."[31] Unfortunately, that was not entirely true, for there were many instances where the way the World Series progressed on screen were not in keeping with the way it unfolded in real life. One example: in Game One during the fourth inning the score was shown as 1–0 on screen, but was tied 1–1 by that point in the true 1919 World Series.

Despite these various mistakes, there were a number of things that the director shows in the film that were entirely correct. The White Sox never came on field with clean uniforms—even during the World Series—because Comiskey was too cheap to have the uniforms sent out to be laundered. Or when the players came in from the outfield, they were always seen tossing their mitts into the air and leaving them behind on the field. This was entirely accurate for the time period, for sharing gloves was a cost saving measure for all the baseball teams during that time period. Thus, the numerous examples of minor historical inaccuracies, when combined with this attention to detail, seem to balance each other out. Thus, in the end, while many of the techniques Hollywood often uses in portraying historical crime stories are present in *Eight Men Out* (e.g., time compression, character elimination, etc.), overall the film does an adequate job of conveying the true historical events surrounding the conspiracy to fix the 1919 World Series.

Further Reading

Asinof, Eliot. (1991). *1919: America's Loss of Innocence.* New York: Plume.

Asinof, Eliot. (1963). *Eight Men Out: The Black Sox and the 1919 World Series.* New York: Henry Holt and Company.

Axelson, Gustaf W. (1919). *"Commy": The Life Story of Charles A. Comiskey.* Chicago: Reilly & Lee Company.

Burns, Ken. (1994). "The Faith of Fifty Million People." *Baseball: Inning 3.* BMG Video.

Carney, Gene. (2006). *Burying the Black Sox: How Baseball's Cover-Up of the 1919 World Series Fix Almost Succeeded.* Dulles, VA: Potomac Books.

Cook, William A. (2001). *The 1919 World Series: What Really Happened?* Jefferson, NC: McFarland.

Fleitz, David L. (2001). *Shoeless: The Life and Times of Joe Jackson.* Jefferson, NC: McFarland & Company.

Linder, Douglas. (2010). *The Black Sox Trial: An Account.* Retrieved online at http://law2.umkc.edu/faculty/projects/ftrials/blacksox/blacksox.html.

Nathan, Daniel. (2003). *Saying It's So: A Cultural History of the Black Sox Scandal.* Champaign, IL: University of Illinois Press.

Pietrusza, David. (2011). *Rothstein: The Life, Times, and Murder of the Criminal Genius Who Fixed the 1919 World Series.* New York: Basic Books.

Yardley, Jonathan. (2001). *Ring: A Biography of Ring Lardner.* New York: Rowman & Littlefield.

Endnotes

1. Asinof, Eliot. (1963). *Eight Men Out: The Black Sox and the 1919 World Series.* New York: Henry Holt and Company.

2. *Eight Men Out* (Orion Pictures, 1988) (John Sayles, Director).

3. See Internet Movie Database. (2011). Retrieved online at http://www.imdb.com/title/tt0095082/.

4. The 1919 Black Sox. (2010). Retrieved from www.1919blacksox.com.

5. Linder, Doug. (2010). The Black Sox Trial: An Account. Retrieved online at http://law2.umkc.edu/faculty/projects/ftrials/blacksox/blacksoxaccount.html.

6. Asinof, Eliot. (1963). *Eight Men Out: The Black Sox and the 1919 World Series.* New York: Henry Holt and Company.

7. Carney, Gene. (2006). *Burying the Black Sox: How Baseball's Cover-Up of the 1919 World Series Fix Almost Succeeded.* Dulles, VA: Potomac Books.

8. Asinof, Eliot. (1963). *Eight Men Out: The Black Sox and the 1919 World Series.* New York: Henry Holt and Company.

9. Gandil, "Chick" Arnold. (1956). "This is My Story of the Black Sox Series." *Sports Illustrated,* September 17.

10. Asinof, Eliot. (1963). *Eight Men Out: The Black Sox and the 1919 World Series.* New York: Henry Holt and Company; Linder, Doug. (2010). The Black Sox Trial: An Account. Retrieved online at http://law2.umkc.edu/faculty/projects/ftrials/blacksox/blacksoxaccount.html.

11. Pietrusza, David. (2011). *Rothstein: The Life, Times, and Murder of the Criminal Genius Who Fixed the 1919 World Series.* New York: Basic Books.

12. Asinof, Eliot. (1963). *Eight Men Out: The Black Sox and the 1919 World Series.* New York: Henry Holt and Company; Linder, Doug. (2010). The Black Sox Trial: An Account. Retrieved online at http://law2.umkc.edu/faculty/projects/ftrials/blacksox/blacksoxaccount.html.

13. Seymour, Harold. (1989). *Baseball: The Early Years.* New York: Oxford University Press.

14. Katcher, Leo. (1994). *The Big Bankroll: The Life and Times of Arnold Rothstein.* New York: De Capo Press.

15. Asinof, Eliot. (1963). *Eight Men Out: The Black Sox and the 1919 World Series.* New York: Henry Holt and Company.

16. Asinof, Eliot. (1963). *Eight Men Out: The Black Sox and the 1919 World Series.* New York: Henry Holt and Company, p. 273.

17. Asinof, Eliot. (1963). *Eight Men Out: The Black Sox and the 1919 World Series.* New York: Henry Holt and Company; *Eight Men Out* (Orion Pictures, 1988) (John Sayles, Director).

18. See Internet Movie Database. (2011). Retrieved online at http://www.imdb.com/title/tt0095082/.

19. See for instance Baseball Almanac. (2011). Top Ten Baseball Movies. Retrieved online at http://www.baseball-almanac.com/moviebat.shtml; Brown, Phillip. (2011). Best Baseball Movies. Retrieved online at http://www.askmen.com/top_10/celebrity/best-baseball-movies_5.html; Movie Mavericks. (2011). Top 10 Baseball Movies. Retrieved online at http://moviemavericks.com/2010/04/top-10-baseball-movies/.

20. This section is based on the film *Eight Men Out* (Orion Pictures, 1988) (John Sayles, Director).

21. Samuels, Rich. (2011). It All Began with an Oath and an Opera: Behind the Scenes at Chicago's First Broadcast. Retrieved online at http://www.richsamuels.com/nbcmm/kyw.html.

22. Lynch, William. (2011). History of the Rawlings Baseball. Retrieved online at http://www.livestrong.com/article/270577-history-of-the-rawlings-baseball/.

23. Sports Illustrated. (2011). Musical Traditions in Sports. Retrieved online at http://sportsillustrated.cnn.com/multimedia/photo_gallery/0711/music.traditions.sports/content.3.html.

24. Louisville Slugger. (2011). Our History. Retrieved online at http://www.slugger-museum.org/sluggerhistory.aspx.

25. Cincinnati Reds. (2011). Reds History. Retrieved online at http://cincinnati.reds.mlb.com/cin/history/index.jsp.

26. See Wikipedia. (2011). Dickey Kerr. Retrieved online at http://en.wikipedia.org/wiki/Dickie_Kerr.

27. Linder, Doug. (2010). The Black Sox Trial: An Account. Retrieved online at http://law2.umkc.edu/faculty/projects/ftrials/blacksox/blacksoxaccount.html.

28. Simonson, Mark. (2011). Typecasting: The Use (and Misuse) of Period Typography in Movies. Retrieved online at http://www.ms-studio.com/typecasting.html.

29. Linder, Doug. (2010). The Black Sox Trial: An Account. Retrieved online at http://law2.umkc.edu/faculty/projects/ftrials/blacksox/blacksoxaccount.html.

30. Linder, Doug. (2010). The Black Sox Trial: An Account. Retrieved online at http://law2.umkc.edu/faculty/projects/ftrials/blacksox/blacksoxaccount.html

31. Carnes, Mark C. (1995). *Past Imperfect: History According to the Movies.* New York: An Owl Book, Henry Holt & Company, p. 15.

CHAPTER 5

St. Valentine's Day Massacre and the American Gangster Al Capone (1929)

Mug shot of the famous Al Capone after being arrested for tax evasion and before being sentenced to Alcatraz. Capone was never held accountable for the St. Valentine's Day Massacre. Photo courtesy of the United States Department of Justice (Bureau of Prohibition).

You can get further with a smile, a kind word, and a gun than you can with a smile and a kind word.

—Al Capone

Introduction

The 1920s was the time of Prohibition across the nation. Alcohol was illegal and providing it became a multi-million dollar business for gangsters. Chicago had hundreds of speakeasies, brothels, and gambling establishments operated by organized crime groups like the North Side Gang and the South Side Gang and by their leaders, George "Bugs" Moran and Alphonse Capone. Moran, a safecracker and petty thief, ran the North Side Gang. He was aggressive, tough, and hated Capone. He controlled the area from the Chicago River to Evanston and along Lakeshore Drive. Moran was popular there because he provided the German, Polish, and Irish immigrants who had settled in that area with the beer and whiskey they wanted.

Capone operated the bootlegging operations on the South Side of Chicago. Capone was born in Brooklyn, New York, on January 17, 1899 to immigrant parents from Sicily. As a youth, he held legitimate jobs such as a clerk in a candy store, a pin boy in a bowling alley, and an employee at an aluminum factory. At the age of 17, he obtained a job in a saloon and joined the Five Points Gang, where he learned how to fight with a knife and how to use a revolver. In 1919, to escape a murder charge, he was sent to Chicago to work for crime-figure Johnny Torrio, starting as a body guard. He rose quickly in the underworld and moved into Torrio's business, which expanded when Prohibition became law on January 17, 1920. People on the South Side of Chicago liked Capone. He was generous, even opening a soup kitchen during the depression that fed 3,000 people a day. It was estimate that by 1929, Capone was worth $60 million a year from his businesses.

Both the North Side and the South Side Gangs wanted to control the alcohol commerce in Chicago. In the early years of Prohibition, the heads of the North Side Gang, Torrio and Capone, sought peace with the South Side Gang.[1] They understood that there was plenty of business for everybody. When a disagreement flared, the two groups would have their dispute mediated peacefully by the Unione Siciliane, led by Mike Merlo.[2] The Unione Siciliane was an organization that ruled over all gangs in Chicago, but especially the Italian mobs. Merlo was considered to be a person who would solve disputes fairly. But when he died in 1924, the gangland peace was shattered and the Great Beer Wars between the North Side Gang and South Side Gang began. The war was made more deadly by the development and popularity of a new weapon, the Tommy gun. Originally invented for use in World War I, the gun became the weapon of choice for gangsters in Chicago. It was small and easy to carry, with incredible firepower. It was much more violent (and effective) than mere pistols.

Both Moran and Capone fought fiercely and violently for control of the city. Chicago became a killing field that resulted in the deaths of over 1,000 people. The culmination of the Beer War was the St. Valentine's Day Massacre in which seven men from the Moran gang were brutally executed by the Capone organization. It was the most violent event in mob history and the single most shocking event of that period. The massacre made Capone the king of the Chicago underworld, but only briefly. The public was outraged by the viciousness and violence that was a product of Prohibition and demanded that it be stopped. Law enforcement responded and sent Capone to federal prison for tax evasion, effectively bringing down the Capone organization for good.

The St. Valentine's Day Massacre and the life story of Al Capone have long been fodder for journalist and authors alike, from the days he took over the North Side Gang, to his conviction for tax evasion, to his days confined to *The Rock*—Alcatraz. It is no wonder that Hollywood also became endeared with the story and has featured Al Capone in nearly a dozen films. Perhaps the most noted film, Roger Corman's 1967 *The St. Valentine's Day Massacre*, featuring actor Jason Robards as Al Capone, attempts to convey the historical events leading up to the massacre.[3] While in many ways based on historical events, the film takes numerous liberties with history in order to appeal to the cinematic patronage.

St. Valentine's Day Massacre: The History

In the span of a few years, the North Side Gang saw their leaders killed one by one, presumably by gunmen from the South Side. One early boss of the North Side Gang was Dion O'Banion, the owner of the Schofield Flower Company, located in a posh area on the North Side of Chicago across from Holy Name Cathedral. O'Banion himself was a murderer and it was estimated that he killed over 60 people in his career. Like many others, he was greedy and sought to enhance his beer distribution in the city. To do this, he first had to take out the head of the South Side Gang, Johnny Torrio.

O'Banion attempted to do that in 1924. At that time, O'Banion oversaw a large beer operation and decided to use that to trap Torrio. On May 19, he told Torrio that he wanted to sell one of his extra breweries. The two agreed to meet at the brewery to discuss the sale of the property. In the midst of the meeting, the police raided the building, arresting everyone present. O'Banion, because he had no previous prohibition violations, was not sent to jail. However, since Torrio had been arrested previously for violating prohibition laws, he was sent to jail for a year. To make matters worse, O'Banion refused to return the money Torrio had given him.[4]

When Torrio was released from prison, he arranged to have O'Banion killed. He called Frankie Yale from New York to do the job. On November 10, 1924, O'Banion was preparing flowers in his shop for the funeral of a fellow mobster. He shook hands with some customers who were in the store to buy flowers, but they did not let go. Instead, they shot him point blank, killing him instantly. The second in command of the North Side Gang, Hymie Weiss, then became the leader of the North Side Gang, along with George "Bugs" Moran.[5]

It was now Weiss's turn to go after Torrio. On January 24, 1925, Weiss and Moran waited for Torrio to return to his home so they could kill him in front of his apartment building. When Torrio arrived, Moran put a gun to his head and pulled the trigger, but the chamber was empty. After the ambush, Torrio decided to get out of the beer business and handed the position of boss of the North Side Gang to Capone.[6]

Three months later, Angelo Genna from the Capone gang was killed by the Moran gang while in his car.[7] Eighteen days after Genna's death, his brother attacked Moran and Weiss. Moran and Weiss escaped, but they planned their revenge on Capone.

At the time, Capone's headquarters was located in a suburb of Chicago called Cicero. Capone operated out of the Hawthorne Hotel and Smoke Shop. In late September, Moran arranged for a ten-car caravan to pass by the hotel while Capone was eating lunch. Seven cars drove down Main Street, past the building, with Tommy guns blazing but shooting blanks. Everyone in the restaurant fell to the floor, unaware that they were not real bullets. When the shooting stopped, Capone leaped up and started to run, but his bodyguard pulled him back down. The Moran gang quickly returned, shooting again, this time with real bullets. One car stopped directly in front of the restaurant, and a man jumped out. He knelt in the doorway of the hotel, shooting from close range. The gunmen shot over 1000 bullets into the building, ruining the store, but killing no one. After the attack, Capone again vowed vengeance against the North Side Gang.[8]

Capone had his men rent a room in front of the Holy Name Cathedral. As Weiss and other members of the North Side Gang were walking across the steps of the church, machine guns started firing. Weiss was killed, making Moran the leader of the North Side Gang. This time, Capone knew he would have to get rid of Moran to have complete control of Chicago.

Capone also knew that Moran operated his gang out of the SMC Garage (SMC Cartage Company) at 2122 North Clark Street. When Capone found out that Moran's gang was hijacking his whiskey, he was furious. He made up his mind to kill Moran.[9] At the end of December, Capone went to his vacation home in Florida to mastermind the St. Valentine's Day Massacre. It was complicated but a well thought-out crime, one that took a great deal of planning to pull off successfully.

The massacre began with Capone's men renting rooms in a boarding house across the street from the SMC Cartage Company. The men told the landlady they were cab drivers who worked at night. For about three weeks they watched the comings and goings of the Moran gang members, taking notes about their behavior. They also arranged for four men to come to Chicago from elsewhere to help them carry out the crime, as these men would not be recognized by the victims. They decided to carry out their plan on February 14, 1929.

The day before the massacre, a man placed a phone call to Moran and offered him a good price on a truckload of high-quality illegal booze (Old Log Cabin) that belonged to Capone. Moran agreed to buy the liquor and to be at the garage to accept the delivery at 10:30 AM.

On the morning of the massacre, Valentine's Day, it was snowing and only 18 degrees. The Capone men in the apartment across the street watched as seven men entered SMC Cartage Company to wait for the shipment of illegal booze. The men were John May (a mechanic), Adam Hire (Moran's business manager), James Clark (Moran's gunman), Dr. Schwimmer (an optometrist), Al Weinschank (a speakeasy owner), and Frank and Pete Gusenberg.[10] The last man to enter the garage appeared to be Moran, but was not. Moran was running late that day and as he neared the garage he saw a police car outside of the building. Assuming it was a raid, Moran ducked into a nearby drug store for a cup of coffee.

Meanwhile, the Capone men, assuming Moran and his entire gang were in the garage, set their plan into motion. They signaled to four other men who were waiting in a nearby garage. Two of the men were dressed in civilian clothes and the other two were dressed as Chicago cops. All four got into a car that was the same model used by Chicago police. The Capone men drove their *police car* to the SMC garage. The fake police car pulled up in front of Cartage Company and the four men went inside, appearing to be raiding the business.

The men inside the garage also thought it was a raid, but were not concerned. Most gangsters in Chicago at the time did not fear the police ,who, more often than not, were typically paid off by the gangsters to "look the other way."[11] The seven men went along peaceably with the orders given by the police, turning over their guns and lining up to face a brick wall, their hands above their heads. Suddenly, the two men in civilian dress pulled out machine guns and began shooting the Moran men. Some of the shooters aimed at the victims' heads, some at their middles, some at the knees, waving their guns back and forth. When they were done, the gunmen walked over the bodies to make sure no one was still alive. May let out a groan, so the Capone men shot him again at close range.[12]

When the shooting was over, the men in civilian clothes left the garage holding their hands in the air. They were followed by the men dressed as police, who were holding guns to the backs of the civilians. All four got into the police car and drove away. To witnesses outside the garage, it appeared to be a simple arrest. Inside the garage, May's dog howled. A neighbor went in to investigate, then fled the scene to call the police.

The police found a gruesome scene inside the garage. There were seven crumpled bodies on the garage floor, some cut almost in half by the bullets, and some even had bullets lodged in their toes. There was blood streaming out of the bodies and pooling on the ground. One member of the Moran gang, Frank Gusenburg, was still alive. He was found crawling toward the front door with 22 bullet wounds in his body. He was taken to the hospital, where police tried to question him.[13] He refused to answer any questions, claiming that nobody shot him. His last words were "I ain't no copper."[14] He died three hours later.

While all of this was happening, Capone was in Florida on a private beach on Palm Island, near Miami, where he had purchased a 14 room mansion to escape Chicago's brutal winters. At the time of the massacre, he was meeting with the Dade County solicitor who was questioning Capone's finances.[15] He also took a swim in his swimming pool, wearing an all-black bathing suit. This all gave him a good alibi when the Moran gangsters were killed. He read about the massacre in the newspaper and reportedly said, "The only man who kills like that is Bugs Moran."[16]

The extreme brutality of the murders shocked and sickened Chicagoans. Before this, the gangsters largely killed each other so it was easy to look the other way. But now the people of Chicago demanded that the violence be stopped. Even the President of the U.S., Herbert Hoover, showed concern over the increasing severity of the crimes carried out as a result of Prohibition. He immediately ordered the attorney general to "get Capone." [17]

There was little evidence by which the police could identify the killers. A week after the massacre, officials found a burning car. It turned out to be the car used by the murderers during the massacre. Besides this, little is known about the real killers. One may have been "Machine Gun" Jack McGurn, a member of Capone's gang, but the Moran gang knew him and probably would not have let him inside the garage. McGurn claimed to have been with his girlfriend at the time of the massacre. Other men, including Fred "Killer" Burke, were questioned about their role in the crime, but witnesses at the scene were unable to identify them. Some have theorized that one gunman was Anthony Accardo (Joe Batters). After the massacre his career took off and he became boss of a Chicago organization, never spending a night in jail.

Capone was called to appear in court to give testimony about his role in the massacre, but he claimed to be too sick to appear. After being charged with contempt of court, he showed up eight days later, but the grand jury questioned him only briefly.

Moran survived the assassination attempt on his life, but the massacre essentially destroyed his gang. He attempted to rebuild his organization, but he was unable to do so. He returned to being a petty criminal and was arrested for forging money and travelers checks. In 1946, Moran was arrested for robbing a tavern in Dayton, Ohio, and was sentenced to ten years in the Ohio State Prison. Bugs died in 1957 of lung cancer. He was buried without fanfare in a prison casket.[18]

Capone became the undisputed leader of organized crime in Chicago for a while, but on June 5, 1931, he was indicted on 22 counts of tax evasion. The

IRS declared that his income was taxable despite being illegal. He was sentenced to 11 years in federal prison.[19] Capone first went to the federal penitentiary in Atlanta, then to Alcatraz. He had syphilis and was released in 1939 because of health reasons. He was taken to Florida and died in 1947 of heart failure and was buried in Mt. Carmel Cemetery, next to his rivals from the North Side Gang.[20]

The St. Valentine's Day Massacre: The Film

The movie *The St. Valentine's Day Massacre* was originally released in July 1967 and starred Jason Robards as Al Capone, George Segal as Peter Gusenberg, and Ralph Meeker as George "Bugs" Moran.[21] Because it was produced prior to movie ratings, the film is unrated but involves mild violence. To ensure the credibility of the events depicted in the movie, the director, Roger Corman, had the actors portraying the seven murdered men study photographs of the massacre scene. When the scene was shot, each man collapsed in the same position as the victims in the photos.

The movie is set in a snowy Chicago. The subtitle tells viewers it is February 14, 1929, and Herbert Hoover is president. It is 10:25 AM and only 18 degrees above zero. From the SMC Cartage Company, a woman hears gunshots and leaves her apartment to see a police car drive away. The woman approaches the Cartage Company and looks through a window. A dog is howling. She sees seven bodies on the ground and screams.

A narrator tells viewers that in the years following the Prohibition Act of 1920, the nation's underworld rises to power and battles amongst itself. There are periods of warfare between competing gangs, followed by peace treaties. There are attempts at consolidation; but each is shattered and new warfare erupts. It is estimated that in 1929, the gangs of Chicago operated 21,207 speakeasies, and their gross income reached $357 million. As a result of the wars, 618 members of the underworld were murdered within a nine-year span.

A man named Peter Gusenberg, a member of Moran's gang, enters a saloon where a few men are drinking beer. The men in the saloon immediately go quiet and Gusenberg threatens the owner. The barkeep admits to serving beer supplied by Slauson, who gets his beer from Capone. The gangster forces the bar owner to purchase Moran's beer from then on. The narrator tells viewers that Gusenberg was born in Chicago on September 27, 1898. He came home at the age of 13 to find his mother dead and proceeded to pawn her wedding ring. He was an ex-con, mail robber, burglar, hijacker, and professional killer, and a member of Moran's North Side Gang. His younger brother, Frank

Gusenberg, was also born in Chicago, on October 11, 1902. Also a member of Moran's gang, he was a burglar, car thief, extortionist, and professional gunman. He was reportedly married to two women at the same time but lived with neither one.

The film switches its focus on Capone's gang. One member, "Machine Gun" Jack McGurn, as the narrator tells viewers, was born in Brooklyn on July 7, 1903. When he was nine, his father was murdered. By the age of 20 he had killed every man connected to his dad's death. He eventually became a top trigger man for Capone.

The film reports that Capone, born in Italy on January 6, 1899, had no criminal record. He was raised in a Brooklyn slum and went to Chicago, where he climbed from saloon bouncer to be the unchallenged leader of the under-world organization. In his headquarters in the Hawthorne Hotel, Capone, also known as "Scarface," is shown at a meeting with the members of his gang. The men are discussing *donating* about a half a million dollars into "Big Bill" Thompson's campaign fund to put Anton Cermak into office. That way, the mob could control what happened in the city. At the meeting is Charles "The Fixer." Born in Italy, he was a second cousin to Capone. He served as the chairman at executive committee meetings. He was known for being able to bribe many state and city leaders. Also at the meeting is Jake Guzik, who was in charge of bootlegging sales and distribution for Capone.

Capone sits at the head of table. He tells the others that they are making money on the South Side and the West Side, but he asks, "what about the North Side?" They were not making money in that part of the city. He told his men that there were 28,000 joints there, and Moran had pushed Capone beer out of 28 joints.

Capone becomes angry over the Moran gang's attempt to shoot at Jack McGurn and the execution of Tony Lombardo. He reports being concerned about staying alive. He believes Moran wants him dead, as do other gang leaders: Dion O'Banion and Hymie Weiss.

The film switches to a scene with Capone eating lunch at the Hawthorne Hotel, his headquarters. Moran gang members slowly drive by the restaurant, shooting at it the entire time. Everyone in the place falls to the floor and waits for the cars to go by and the shooting to end. When it does finally end, everyone begins to rise, but some notice that there is little damage. A bodyguard pushes Capone back down to the ground. Immediately, Moran's men drive by again, this time shooting real bullets. One man leaves the car and continues to shoot into the restaurant from the sidewalk. It was Peter Gusenberg.

Back in the meeting, Capone yells that Weiss was responsible for the Hawthorne Restaurant shooting. He believes Moran is getting set to pull something just as crazy. But Capone tells his gang that "We're gonna get him before he gets me. I want that Irish son of a bitch hit." He considers two men for the job. The first is Frank Nitti. Born in Italy, Nitti eventually became the head of the Chicago underworld after Capone's death. Capone ultimately gave the task of getting Moran to "Machine Gun" Jack McGurn.

The narrator gives more information about Moran. Born in Minnesota, he is an ex-con, burglar, hijacker, and horse thief. He sometimes uses the alias "George Miller." There is no question that he hates Capone. Moran is at war with the Capone organization for control of Chicago's bootlegging and gambling profits. During the previous five years, every leader of the North Side Gang has been killed by Capone's South Side Gang. Moran is shown saying, "It's time to put Capone and his bums out of business for good." A member of the Moran organization is shown telling Moran that his chance of beating Capone is slim because every Italian in town is working for him. But Moran knows one man who is not: Joe Iello. He proposes working with Joe Iello to get Capone.

The movie flashes to Dion O'Banion in his flower shop. He greets customers and shakes their hands. The visitors reach out and grab his hand and hold onto it, shooting O'Banion at close range. The movie then shows Hymie Weiss being shot outside of the Holy Cathedral Church from a window across the street.

Moran complains that Capone promised to stay out of the North Side but has not. He tells others that Capone's protection comes from the Mafia, and that Capone cannot make a move without permission from their leader. But Capone cannot be the head himself because he is not Sicilian. Instead, Patsy Lolardo runs the outfit. Joey Iello was a friend of Lolardo's. If they could convince Iello to help Moran's gang kill Lolardo, then Iello could take over the mafia. Moran puts James Clark in charge of getting rid of Lolardo. Clark, a German, was an ex con, burglar, car thief, and was married to Morans' sister. He was the *number two man* in Moran's gang.

Another man helping Moran was John May. Born in Chicago, he was married with seven children. He had been in trouble in the past for safe blowing and burglary. He worked for Moran's gang in the past as an auto mechanic. He promised his wife he would stay out of trouble, but he was behind in the rent and needed money. The Moran gang asks him to drive the car for them, for which he would be paid $100.

The movie switches to show Nick Cirelli, an Italian immigrant who was born in Sicily in 1872, and brought to the U.S. with his parents. He has five children and 11 grandchildren. According to the narrator, Cirelli had a difficult time learning the ways of the new world. He went to see McGurn, and when asked, told McGurn he owned a truck and had a moving business. McGurn offers him a job for which he would give Cirelli $500. He tells Cirelli that there will be a car left in front of his house. The car will be stolen, so McGurn tells Cirelli to get rid of it as soon as he can. He tells Cirelli to be on 33rd street at 9:00 AM on the nose, and that he will need a gun. McGurn gives him one from his personal armory. Cirelli agrees to the job, telling McGurn that it will be an honor to serve him.

Cirelli holds up the truck as scheduled, then calls Moran. He tells Moran he has 80 cases of Old Log Cabin Whiskey (Capone's brand) and wants to sell it to Moran. Moran agrees and gives Cirelli $56 a case. After, Moran has his men check Cirelli out. To Moran, it appears that Cerilli has hijacked Capone's whiskey and is selling it to Moran.

In attempting to kill Capone, Moran's gang begins watching him to get his schedule. They know that Capone regularly goes to see Lolardo at a specific time. In one of those meetings, Capone tells Lolardo that Moran has been stepping out of line. He has his men ready to "fix his wagon." Lolardo tells Capone to try and talk things over with Moran. Capone states that he has tried to talk to the previous leaders, O'Banion and Weiss, but they would not talk. They just tried to kill him. Capone tells Lolardo that he is getting rid of Moran and that McGurn is going to do it. McGurn wants two mafia boys on the killing: Scalise and Alsamni. They would give them the same money they paid him for killing Hymie Weiss.

Capone tells Lolardo that he has heard that Iello is going to take over the Mafia in Chicago and they have Lolardo's name on a bullet. Lolardo says he has nothing to fear from Iello and that the rumors are not true.

Meanwhile, Cirelli brings the hijacked liquor to Moran's headquarters. Moran's men test the liquor and find it is good quality. Cirelli tells the men he talked to Moran himself and was promised $56 cash for each case, or $4,592 for the entire truckload. Nonetheless, the Moran gang keeps $500 for "handling charges." Later, Cirelli gives the money to Jack McGurn, who then tells Cirelli he has another job to do. This time, all it will be is a phone call.

The narrator tells viewers that Dr. Reinhart Schwimmer was a man who was fascinated with gangsters. He had no criminal record, but in the last few months had became acquainted with the Moran gang and started to hang out with them. He even abandoned his practice and was being supported by his widowed mother.

Viewers also learn about another Moran gang member, Adam Hire. He had one conviction for operating a con game, and served as an accountant for the Moran organization. He often paid off politicians and police. His wife is ill and does not know what he does.

Peter Gusenberg is living with a lady as husband and wife, but they are not married. The movie shows them in a long, somewhat violent fight over a fur coat she purchased with his money. He wants her to return it, but she refuses to do so.

The Moran gang chose January 7 as the day to kill Mafia Chieftain Lolardo. Pete and Frank Gusenberg plan to use Iellos's friendship with Lolardo as a means to enter his apartment. Their next step is to kill the bodyguards, then for Frank and Pete Gusenberg to kill Lolardo.

The next scene is a party at Capone's mansion, where he is talking to a judge. Their conversation is interrupted by a phone call in which Capone is told that Lolardo was killed in his own house by two of Moran's gang and with the help of Iello. Capone declared that Moran will go, as will Iello.

The narrator tells viewers about Al Weinshank. He was born in Chicago and has no criminal record. He has been associated with North Side Gang for three years and is now in charge of "cleaning and dryer" operation controlled by Moran.

Cirelli calls Moran again and offers him more hijacked liquor. Moran agrees to buy liquor from Cirelli again. They agree to meet Thursday morning at 10:30, and Moran agrees to be present this time to guarantee Cirelli will get the promised price for the liquor. The phone call is really for Capone and McGurn. Meanwhile, Capone gang members are shown buying a used car, for which they paid cash.

On February 11, the second cousin to Iello buys a train ticket. Iello knows that Capone is aware of his role in Lolardo's death and he is trying to escape Chicago and Capone by train. But Capone gets a phone call from Frank, who tells him that Iello is boarding the train. Capone rushes to the train and is able to board as well. He kills Iello on the train.

Capone's men are seen renting a room in a boarding house that faces Clark Street. To do so, they pretended to be members of an orchestra with the last names of White and Johnson. The instruments in their cases were really guns. They ask for a room facing the front to overlook the Cartage Company. They place a call to Vic at Omeara's, a local garage.

The men posing as White and Johnson meet other Capone men in a bar to plan the massacre. McGurn leads the meeting. He explains that two men, Albert Alsamo and John Scalise, are coming from New York to help with the massacre so they won't be recognized. The visitors have participated in 31 murders, including the murders of O'Banion and Weiss. McGurn gives two men police hats and tells them to act like cops. He then tells the men that Moran wears a brown suit, overcoat, hat, and shoes.

Capone is shown in Miami, swimming in pool. He receives a phone call from McGurn who tells him the murder will happen Thursday in the morning around 10:30.

At 6:45, May takes a bus to work. He plans on replacing the gang's car transmission. May, Clark, Gusenberg, Schwimmer, Frank Gusenberg, Hire, and Weinshank enter the Cartage Company. The Capone men are in their rented room across the street, watching the men enter the building. A final man enters the Carthage Company. He appears to be Moran but isn't. Moran is late because of a phone call.

The Capone men call Vick at Omeara's. Vick rides his scooter to the garage, where the men are waiting. One man is shown putting garlic on bullets. He tells others, if the bullets don't kill you then you will die of blood poisoning. Two of the men are dressed like policemen and two are dressed in plain clothes. The car appears to be a police car. The men drive out of the garage and toward the Carthage Company in the police car. They arrive at the Company and enter it. Moran is outside, watching, and decides to get coffee instead of entering the Cartage Company. He believes the police are raiding the place because Cirelli will soon be there with the stolen, bootleg liquor.

The "police" line up the men along the wall. They put their hands on the wall, thinking they are being arrested. The men are searched and their guns taken. Then the men in plain clothes shoot them all, and keep shooting, even after the seven men are dead. The men dressed as police lead those dressed as civilians to the car, pretending to arrest them. They all get in the police car and drive away.

Moran, having coffee, hears sirens and thinks there is an accident. But a man comes into the coffee shop and yells that a cop has just killed a bunch of hoods and one of them is Bugs Moran.

One of the seven Moran men from the shooting, Frank Gusenberg, survives the massacre. In the hospital, real police asked who shot him, but he will not say.

Reporters then find Moran, who pretends to be sick and out of town when the shooting happened. When asked by reporters if he thought it was possible that the police killed the men, Moran responded, "only Capone kills like that."

The day of the massacre, Capone was shown hosting a party, giving him an alibi. He claimed to be in a meeting with the district attorney that morning. When asked if he was behind the shooting, he says that the media always blames him for everything. He then says that they don't call that guy "Bugs" for nothing.

The narrator tells viewers that the public outrage brought an end to open gang warfare. But the gangs rebuilt so that in the 1960s their power was higher than what it was in the 1920s. Once more, the police will not prosecute gangs until the public demands that they be brought to justice, as they did in 1929.

No one was ever brought to trial for the slaughter of the seven men killed in the massacre. Within the following 19 months, the four involved were all killed through some act of violence. On May 7 1929, John Scalise and Albert Alsamo were invited to a banquet at one of Capone's mansions. Capone had discovered their plot to kill him and take over his empire. At the dinner, Capone repeatedly hits them with a baseball bat. One of the men who pretended to be a police officer in the massacre was shot to death while attempting to rob a jewelry store. The body of the other "policeman" was found in a pond in Missouri.

Machine Gun Jack McGurn was killed in a Chicago bowling alley almost seven years after massacre. George Moran disappeared from Chicago soon after the massacre. He served a ten year sentence for burglary in Leavenworth and died of lung cancer on February 25, 1957. Capone was never tried for St. Valentine's Day Massacre although his role as the man behind it is unquestioned. Three months after the massacre, Capone was imprisoned and more than half of the remaining 18 years of his life was spent in federal penitentiaries. He died in his sleep on January 25, 1947. His mind was gone, his body ravaged by syphilis. His body was interred in family plot in Chicago cemetery.

St. Valentine's Day Massacre: Hollywood's Rendering

Even though the producer of the *St. Valentine's Day Massacre* attempted to make it realistic, the movie has many inaccuracies, many of which have to do with Al Capone himself. These may be because at the time the movie was produced, few people understood the true nature of organized crime and the people involved in it. For example, the narrator tells viewers that Capone was born in Italy and raised in a slum in Brooklyn, New York. However, in reality, Capone was born in Brooklyn on January 17, 1899.[22] His parents, Gabriele and Teresina, were originally from Italy and immigrated to the U.S. Additionally, the movie made it seem as if Capone was not married in the years leading up to the massacre because his wife and child are never mentioned. In fact, he was married and had one son.[23]

In the movie, the narrator states that Capone has no criminal record, but he had been arrested a few times prior to arriving in Chicago for disorderly conduct. He was also charged with the murder of two men in New York. The only reason he did not end up in prison was that the witnesses suddenly forget anything they heard or saw, so Capone was never tried for the crimes.[24]

The number and viciousness of the crimes Capone ordered as boss of the Chicago crime family were not shown in the movie. He also had many illegal gambling and vice operations, as well as numerous speakeasies, which were not shown in the film. Capone more or less ran Chicago during Prohibition and operated hundreds of illegal enterprises, and the movie only showed a few examples of this. The movie also never mentions how Capone bribed most of the city's law enforcement, paying them to ignore his activities. The police would not arrest him, and when it did happen, all of the charges would be quickly dropped.

The actor chosen to play Capone was tall and thin, and made him appear as a madman who was feared throughout the city. In reality, Capone was 5'1" and weighed around 250 pounds. Most people in Chicago trusted and liked Capone. He was generous, successful and prominent, and people looked up to him. Part of the reason for the mistake in casting this role was that the original actor chosen by the director to play Capone was Orson Welles, but he was unable to play the role and was replaced by Robards.[25] However, this meant that Capone was portrayed by a 47-year-old actor in the film when Capone was actually only turning 30. The inaccurate casting of the Capone character gave the impression that Chicago's underworld was being run by an older man. In reality most of the Capone gang were in their twenties and early thirties.

The movie depicts Capone's home as a palatial mansion. In fact, Capone's real home was quite different. Capone and his family members lived at 7244 South Prairie Ave in Chicago, in a working class Southside neighborhood. He purchased the home just after moving to Chicago in 1923. It was a modest, two-story brick duplex home and by no means flashy or a mansion.[26] Similarly, the car that Capone used in the movie was shown as an ordinary stock car, but in reality his car had bullet proof glass and weighed 9,000 pounds, with flashing red police lights and siren, and a police band receiver.[27]

The movie also inaccurately portrayed Capone's power. In the movie, Moran declares that Capone had to seek the approval from the Mafia and could not make decisions on his own. However, he did not seek the Mafia's protection, nor did he need it.[28] Capone was not incapable of making decisions for his gang, nor was he a foot soldier for Lolardo.

The *mafia* to which Moran is referring was the Unione Siciliana, an organization originally established to sell insurance to Sicilian immigrants upon their arrival in the U.S. During the years of Prohibition, one of its leaders, Mike Merlo, was able to keep the peace between O'Banion and Torrio. When Merlo died of cancer, the organization split into many factions. One of those factions was headed by Pasqualino "Patsy" Lolardo. Some allege that he was able to hold office because of Capone's support. Another organized crime figure, Joe Aiello, had also sought to be the head of the Unione Siciliana. Aiello had Moran's support. Moran believed that if Aiello became the organization's leader, Capone would be less powerful. So Moran arranged for Lolardo's execution. On January 8, 1929, unidentified gunmen entered Lolardo's home and proceeded to shoot him.[29]

Aiello also wanted to kill Capone. One time, Aiello sent one of his men to Capone's favorite cigar shop with a submachine gun and told him to shoot Capone. Before he could do that, he was spotted and had to flee. In another attempt, Aiello tried to bribe the chef at Capone's favorite restaurant with $35,000 to put acid in Capone's soup. Instead, the chef told Capone.

Thus, the film's portrayal of the role Aiello played in Lolardo's death was largely accurate. Aiello had become allies with Moran and conspired in the murder of Lolardo and the conspiracy to kill Lolardo. The film, however, shows that Aiello and Gusenberg killed Lolardo. But since the gunmen remain unidentified to this day, that scene may be inaccurate. There are some who believe that the Genna gang carried out the actual murder. In the past, O'Banion and the Gennas had worked together and had caused friction with the Capone organization. Capone had actually only sanctioned the killing, but the Genna gang actually carried out the murder.[30] Nonetheless, the Aiello clan was very powerful and was quite capable of killing without any help from the Moran gang.[31]

In the movie, Lolardo's murderers kill him in his living room in front of his wife, and then they laid his head on the pillow. In the actual event the killers ran out of the house after the shooting.[32]

In the film, Capone avenged Lolardo's death by killing Aiello on a train in 1929. This was not true. Aiello was not slain by Capone, nor was he slain on a train. Aiello did, in fact, after learning of his imminent death have a train ticket purchased for him by his cousin so he could leave town to avoid death. Capone, however, did not kill him, nor did Aiello die in the massacre. Aiello was actually killed well over a year after the massacre, in October 1930, by machine gun fire while he was leaving to catch a train. He had allegedly made plans to permanently leave Chicago and move to Mexico. Aiello was waiting for a cab inside a building. When the cab arrived, he walked out of the building. A gunman across the street in the second-floor window fired on him with a submachine gun. He ran around the corner to the side of the building to escape the gunfire, but there were more shooters in another building. He was shot 59 times.[33]

More inaccuracies revolved around Capone's gang members. One of his men was Jake "Greasy Thumbs" Guzik, as shown in the film. He was an overweight, round-shaped man who lacked in personal hygiene.[34] In the movie he was portrayed as a tall, well-dressed confident man. Moreover, Guzik did not control the liquor sales and distribution as indicated in the movie. In reality, Capone's brother Ralph did that. But Ralph was not mentioned or shown in the film. The film also shows conflict between Guzik and Capone, but this probably never happened. In fact, Capone once killed a man who humiliated Guzik as a show of support for him.

Other men in the Capone organization were also not accurately portrayed. One of those, "Machine Gun" Jack McGurn, was shown to be a young, up-and-coming gangster, eager to please Capone. But in reality, McGurn was already a top lieutenant in the Capone organization at the time of the massacre.[35]

The entire Capone gang appeared to be unfamiliar with George Moran in the movie. In fact, he had been the right-hand man for both O'Banion and Weiss for many years, and the Capone organization had known him for at least that long.[36]

In this same scene, Capone is shown discussing the threat Moran posed and ordered a hit on him. He put Jack McGurn in charge of the operation. In reality, McGurn and other members of the Capone organization visited Capone in Miami over the winter months leading up to the massacre, and during those meetings, McGurn discussed his feelings about the threats Moran posed to the Capone gang. He told Capone about the assassination attempt from Moran not long before that. McGurn wanted Moran dead as much as Capone. After that meeting, Capone agreed and put McGurn in charge of the plan. Capone ultimately gave the task of getting Moran to "Machine Gun" Jack McGurn.

The movie included multiple errors regarding the massacre itself, which detracts from the historical accuracy of the production. Prior to the massacre, the movie shows one of the victims to be Dr. Reinhart Schwimmer, one of the men killed in the SMC Cartage Company, an optician who had let his practice go and instead chose to gamble in horse racing and associate with the Moran gang. Though Schwimmer called himself an *optometrist* he was actually an optician (an eyeglass fitter) without any medical training.[37]

In the film, the Capone men rented an apartment with a window overlooking the garage operated by the North Side Gang. It appears that they only watched the Moran gang for a couple of days before the massacre occurred. In reality, the men watched the garage for three weeks.

In the actual massacre, the Capone gang realized that Moran had not entered the garage but decided to go through with the plan nonetheless.[38] The film indicates that the men watching the garage truly believed that the intended victim, Moran, had entered the garage to wait for the shipment of bootleg liquor.

The movie accurately indicated that Frank Gusenberg, a Moran gang member, survived the massacre, but died shortly afterwards in a hospital. Before he died the police tried to question him and find out who committed the massacre. In the movie Gusenberg's last words were, "I didn't see nothing." In reality, it was documented that his last words were "I ain't no copper."[39]

The true identity of the phony police officers has never been revealed even to this day and no one knows who they were. The movie indicates to viewers that the two policemen in the massacre were Boris Chapman and Adolph

Muller, and that two men named Scalise and Alsamo did the killing. As shown in the movie, Capone had brought them to Chicago from New York so they would not be recognized by the Capone men. But that may not have been true.

On January 8, 1935, agents from the FBI arrested Byron Bolton, a member of the Barker-Karpis gang. Upon questioning, Bolton told the agents that he played a key role in the St. Valentine's Day Massacre. According to Bolton, the massacre was planned in October or November of 1928 at a resort in Couderay, Wisconsin. The men involved in the planning stage were Capone, his second-in-command Frank Nitti, and many other trusted Capone men. Bolton told the FBI that he, along with a man named Jimmy Moran, was responsible for watching the Cartage Company and then giving the signal that the Moran gang was in the garage. The killers were waiting at the Circus Café when they were informed that Moran had entered the garage. Bolton continued to describe the massacre, indicating that all four Capone men shot the Moran gang. Afterwards, according to Bolton, Capone was furious that the lookout men had misidentified Moran. Others have identified one of the killers as Tony Accardo, a driver for McGurn.[40]

The movie quickly indicates the fate of some of those who participated in the massacre, which were not accurate. The narrator in the movie tells viewers that three months after the massacre, Capone was indicted for income tax evasion. Capone was actually not indicted for tax evasion until 1931, two years after the massacre.[41]

In the wake of the massacre, Aiello tried to partner with two of Capone's men, Anselmi and Scalise, to kill Capone. He told them they would all be more powerful with Capone gone. Aiello would then take over the North Side (as Moran had left the city), and Anselmi and Scalise could have the South Side. But Capone heard of the plot, and in April 1929, Capone invited Anselmi and Scalise to dinner and beat them to death (or had them killed). The movie shows Capone killing the men with a baseball bat, but some reports suggest others carried out the beatings.[42]

Conclusion

The St. Valentine's Day Massacre was a pivotal event in the Chicago Beer Wars. Not only did it decimate the Moran organization and raise Capone to the position of the sole bootlegger in the city of Chicago, it was a turning point in the way gang violence was viewed by those who lived in the city. Before the massacre, the carnage carried out by the gangs was viewed by many as an annoyance and generally accepted throughout the city. Mostly the gang members killed each other and rarely were innocent people harmed or murdered.

After the massacre, the public simply got tired of the violence associated with Prohibition and started to make demands of politicians to do something and put an end to the bloodshed. Politicians responded to the public concerns. In the end, the massacre led to the downfall of Capone and his organization. The facts surrounding the St. Valentine's Day Massacre still fascinate viewers, explaining the success of the movie, despite its many inaccuracies.

Further Reading

Allsop, Kenneth . (1961). *The Bootleggers: The Story of Chicago's Prohibition Era.* New Rochelle, NY: Arlington House.

Balsamo, William and George P. Carpozi, Jr. (1999). *Crime Incorporated: The Inside Story of the Mafia's First 100 Years.* Far Hills, NJ: New Horizon Press.

Bergreen, Laurence. (1994). *Capone: The Man and the Era.* New York: Simon & Schuster.

Eig, Jonathan. (2010). *Get Capone: The Secret Plot that Captured America's Most Wanted* Gangster. New York: Simon & Schuster.

Enright, Richard T. (1987). *Capone's Chicago.* Lakeville, MN: Northstar Maschek Books.

Iorizzo, Luciano. (2003). *Al Capone: A Biography.* Westport, CT: Greenwood Press.

Kobler, John. (1971). *Capone: The Life and World of Al Capone.* New York: G.P. Putnam's Sons.

Kohn, Aaron. (1974). *The Kohn Report: Crime and Politics in Chicago.* New York: Arno Press.

Lyle, John L. (1960). *The Dry and Lawless Years.* Englewood Cliffs, NJ: Prentice Hall.

Ness, Eliot. (1987). *The Untouchables.* New York: Pocket Books.

Ovid, Demaris. (1969). *Captive City.* New York: L. Stuart.

Russo, Gus. (2001). *The Outfit: The Role of Chicago's Underworld in the Shaping of Modern* America. New York: Bloomsbury.

Schoenberg, Robert J. (1992). *Mr. Capone.* New York: Morrow.

Shmelter, Richard. (2008). *Chicago Assassin: The Life and Legend of Machine Gun Jack McGurn and the Chicago Beer Wars of the Roaring Twenties.* Nashville, Tennessee: Cumberland House.

Endnotes

1. Balsamo, William and George P. Carpozi, Jr. (1999). *Crime Incorporated: The Inside Story of the Mafia's First 100 Years.* Far Hills, NJ: New Horizon Press.

2. Allsop, Kenneth. (1961). *The Bootleggers: The Story of Chicago's Prohibition Era.* New Rochelle, NY: Arlington House.

3. *St. Valentine's Day Massacre* (Los Altos Productions, 1967). (Roger Corman, Director).

4. Russo, Gus. (2001). *The Outfit: The Role of Chicago's Underworld in the Shaping of Modern America.* New York: Bloomsbury; Allsop, Kenneth. (1961). *The Bootleggers: The Story of Chicago's Prohibition Era.* New Rochelle, NY: Arlington House; Kobler, John. (1971). *Capone: The Life and World of Al Capone.* New York: G.P. Putnam's Sons.

5. Russo, Gus. (2001). *The Outfit: The Role of Chicago's Underworld in the Shaping of Modern America.* New York: Bloomsbury.

6. Lyle, John H. (1960). *The Dry and Lawless Years.* Englewood Cliffs, NJ: Prentice Hall; Russo, Gus. (2001). *The Outfit: The Role of Chicago's Underworld in the Shaping of Modern America.* New York: Bloomsbury.

7. Allsop, Kenneth. (1961). *The Bootleggers: The Story of Chicago's Prohibition Era.* New Rochelle, NY: Arlington House.

8. Russo, Gus. (2001). *The Outfit: The Role of Chicago's Underworld in the Shaping of Modern America.* New York: Bloomsbury.

9. Allsop, Kenneth. (1961). *The Bootleggers: The Story of Chicago's Prohibition Era.* New Rochelle, NY: Arlington House.

10. Lyle, John H. (1960). *The Dry and Lawless Years.* Englewood Cliffs, NJ: Prentice Hall.

11. Kobler, John. (1971). *Capone: The Life and World of Al Capone.* New York: G.P. Putnam's Sons.

12. Kobler, John. (1971). *Capone: The Life and World of Al Capone.* New York: G.P. Putnam's Sons.

13. Lyle, John H. (1960). *The Dry and Lawless Years.* Englewood Cliffs, NJ: Prentice Hall.

14. Russo, Gus. (2001). *The Outfit: The Role of Chicago's Underworld in the Shaping of Modern America.* New York: Bloomsbury, p. 40.

15. Russo, Gus. (2001). *The Outfit: The Role of Chicago's Underworld in the Shaping of Modern America.* New York: Bloomsbury.

16. Russo, Gus. (2001). *The Outfit: The Role of Chicago's Underworld in the Shaping of Modern America.* New York: Bloomsbury, p. 40; Balsamo, William and George P. Carpozi, Jr. (1999). *Crime Incorporated: The Inside Story of the Mafia's First 100 Years.* Far Hills, NJ: New Horizon Press; Lyle, John H. (1960). *The Dry and Lawless Years.* Englewood Cliffs, NJ: Prentice Hall.

17. Marion, Nancy E. (2008). *Government Versus Organized Crime.* Upper Saddle River, NJ: Pearson/Prentice Hall.

18. Balsamo, William and George P. Carpozi, Jr. (1999). *Crime Incorporated: The Inside Story of the Mafia's First 100 Years.* Far Hills, NJ: New Horizon Press.

19. Marion, Nancy E. (2008). *Government Versus Organized Crime.* Upper Saddle River, NJ: Pearson/Prentice Hall.

20. Allsop, Kenneth. (1961). *The Bootleggers: The Story of Chicago's Prohibition Era.* New Rochelle, NY: Arlington House.

21. *St. Valentine's Day Massacre* (Los Altos Productions, 1967). (Roger Corman, Director).

22. Internet Movie Database. (2011). *St. Valentine's Day Massacre.* Retrieved online at http:www.imdb.com/title/tt0062301; Balsamo, William and George P. Carpozi, Jr. (1999). *Crime Incorporated: The Inside Story of the Mafia's First 100 Years.* Far Hills, NJ: New Horizon Press.

23. Kobler, John. (1971). *Capone: The Life and World of Al Capone.* New York: G.P. Putnam's Sons.

24. History on Film. (2011). *St. Valentine's Day Massacre*. Retrieved online at http://www.historyonfilm.com/reviews/st-valentines-day-massacre.htm.

25. Turner Classic Movies. (2011). *St. Valentine's Day Massacre*. Retrieved online at http://www.tcm.com/tcmdb/title/88919/The-St-Valentine-s-Day-Massacre/trivia.html.

26. DOMU: Chicago Apartments. (2001). *Al Capone Family*. Retrieved online at http://www.domu.com/chicago/history-map/al-capone-family-residence.

27. Allsop, Kenneth. (1961). *The Bootleggers: The Story of Chicago's Prohibition Era*. New Rochelle, NY: Arlington House.

28. History on Film. (2011). *St. Valentine's Day Massacre*. Retrieved online at http://www.historyonfilm.com/reviews/st-valentines-day-massacre.htm.

29. Allsop, Kenneth. (1961). *The Bootleggers: The Story of Chicago's Prohibition Era*. New Rochelle, NY: Arlington House.

30. History on Film. (2011). *St. Valentine's Day Massacre*. Retrieved online at http://www.historyonfilm.com/reviews/st-valentines-day-massacre.htm.

31. History on Film. (2011). *St. Valentine's Day Massacre*. Retrieved online at http://www.historyonfilm.com/reviews/st-valentines-day-massacre.htm.

32. La Costra Nostra Database. (2001). *American Mafia*. Retrieved online at http://www.lacndb.com.

33. Lyle, John H. (1960). *The Dry and Lawless Years*. Englewood Cliffs, NJ: Prentice Hall; Internet Movie Database. (2011). *St. Valentine's Day Massacre*. Retrieved online at http:www.imdb.com/title/tt0062301;

Allsop, Kenneth. (2001). *The Bootleggers: The Story of Chicago's Prohibition Era*. New Rochelle, NY: Arlington House.

34. Allsop, Kenneth. (2011). *The Bootleggers: The Story of Chicago's Prohibition Era*. New Rochelle, NY: Arlington House.

35. History on Film. (2011). *St. Valentine's Day Massacre*. Retrieved online at http://www.historyonfilm.com/reviews/st-valentines-day-massacre.htm.

36. History on Film. (2011). *St. Valentine's Day Massacre*. Retrieved online at http://www.historyonfilm.com/reviews/st-valentines-day-massacre.htm.

37. History on Film. (2011). *St. Valentine's Day Massacre*. Retrieved online at http://www.historyonfilm.com/reviews/st-valentines-day-massacre.htm.

38. History on Film. (2011). *St. Valentine's Day Massacre*. Retrieved online at http://www.historyonfilm.com/reviews/st-valentines-day-massacre.htm.

39. Ward, David with Gene Kassenbaum. (2009). *Alcatraz: The Gangster Years*. Berkeley, CA: University of California Press, p. 16.

40. History on Film. (2011). *St. Valentine's Day Massacre*. Retrieved online at http://www.historyonfilm.com/reviews/st-valentines-day-massacre.htm.

41. Kobler, John. (1971). *Capone: The Life and World of Al Capone*. New York: G.P. Putnam's Sons; Internet Movie Database. (2011). *St. Valentine's Day Massacre*. Retrieved online at http://www.imdb.com/title/tt0062301/.

42. Allsop, Kenneth. (1961). *The Bootleggers: The Story of Chicago's Prohibition Era*. New Rochelle, NY: Arlington House; Kobler, John. (1971). *Capone: The Life and World of Al Capone*. New York: G.P. Putnam's Sons.

CHAPTER 6

PUBLIC ENEMIES AND THE HUNT FOR JOHN DILLINGER (1934)

Public Enemy Number One of the Federal Bureau of Investigation—John Dillinger. After an extensive search to bring down Dillinger, he was finally given away by the "Lady in Red" and was gunned down in front of the Biograph Theater. Photo courtesy of the Federal Bureau of Investigation.

Stranger, stop and wish me well
Just say a prayer for my soul in hell
I was a good fellow, most people said
Betrayed by a woman all dressed in red.

> —A poem scribbled on the wall in the alley
> near the Biograph Theater after Dillinger was shot

Introduction

It was the mid-1930s and the middle of the Great Depression in America. John Dillinger, Public Enemy Number One, was one of the country's most notorious gangsters and bank robbers. He stole more than $500,000 from banks in the Mid-West, a fortune for the time. Dillinger's crimes allowed him the luxuries of expensive clothes, exotic women, and high-priced social outings. Despite his crimes, Dillinger was popular with the public. Most people knew that he was not a violent man. He did not seek to hurt people. He was also not involved with Prohibition or the violence associated with running alcohol.

117

Instead, the public viewed him as an all-American outlaw, out to seek revenge on the banking industry that had been ruining families by wiping out people's savings accounts and foreclosing on their homes. He quickly became known to the public as the *Gentleman Bandit.*

For about a year, law enforcement in four states aggressively pursued the flamboyant Dillinger. The head of the FBI, J. Edgar Hoover, knew that capturing the famous criminal would be a publicity coup for both him and his agency. Hoover made Dillinger the most wanted man in America and assigned special agents the task of finding and arresting the outlaw. But Dillinger knew how to evade the police, often hiding in plain view. On the rare occasions when he was captured, Dillinger found ways to escape, boasting that no jail could hold him. He outgunned local police and escaped their pursuits in state-of-the-art luxury cars that could easily outrun police vehicles at the time. Law enforcement looked inept as their attempts to arrest Dillinger failed. In the end, the FBI, led by special agent Melvin Purvis, finally succeeded. With the help of the so-called *Lady in Red*, Anna Sage, Dillinger was killed outside the Biograph Theater on a crowded Chicago street. His body was displayed to the public in the Cook County morgue, where thousands came to see the famous criminal's remains.

Many films have told the story of John Dillinger, beginning with a 1945 portrayal of the outlaw's career in which Lawrence Tierney played the lead role. The most recent version of the Dillinger story, by director Michael Mann, was entitled *Public Enemies.*[1] Released in 2009, the film was based on Bryan Burrough's book *Public Enemies: America's Greatest Crime Wave and the Birth of the FBI, 1933–43.*[2] Actor Johnny Depp starred in the role of Dillinger, Christian Bale portrayed FBI agent Purvis, and Marion Cotillard played the role of Evelyn "Billie" Frechette. The movie provided an entertaining description of the events surrounding Dillinger, but also had some historical inaccuracies, as discussed in this chapter.

Public Enemies: The History

John Herbert Dillinger was born on June 22, 1903. His father, John Wilson Dillinger, was a local grocery store owner. John's mother, Mary Ellen "Mollie" Dillinger, passed away from a stroke when he was three. After her death, John's 17-year-old sister, Audrey, acted as his mother and showered him with love and affection. In school, John's math skills were weak but he loved to read. When he was nine, John's dad married Elizabeth Fields, whom John admired. His father was strict, with some reports claiming violent, toward his son.[3]

Like many others at the time, Dillinger quit school at age 16 and held various jobs, including in a wood mill, the Indianapolis Board of Trade, a machine shop, and the Indianapolis Power and Light Company. When his father bought a farm, Dillinger worked on it for a short time. During this period, he spent a lot of time hunting and playing baseball. He played shortstop for a semi-pro team called the Mooresville Athletics. At age 18, Dillinger fell in love with a local woman named Francis Thornton. He courted her and sought to marry her, but her stepfather refused to allow the marriage.[4]

After a brief run-in with police, John joined the navy. Five months later he deserted the service and returned home, where he met 16-year-old Beryl Ethel Hovious. They were married in April 1924, but it was not a good marriage. He spent most of his free time with friends instead of earning a living for his family.

On the evening of September 6, 1924, Dillinger conceived a plan to rob a grocery store with a man named William Edgar "Eddie" Singleton, Dillinger's cousin, an ex-con who sometimes umpired John's baseball games. Singleton was in a get-away car while Dillinger robbed the store owner, Frank Morgan. During the robbery, Dillinger hit the grocer over the head and pulled out a revolver. Morgan knocked the gun out of John's hand and the gun went off. No one was shot, but Singleton was frightened and left without Dillinger, who was forced to flee on foot. Both men were later arrested for the crime.

Dillinger's father did not hire a lawyer for his son because he believed John should confess his sins. Although John was only 21 and this was his first offense, the judge sentenced Dillinger to a term of 10–20 years in prison. His accomplice, Singleton, appeared in front of a different judge and only received a sentence of two years in prison.[5] The discrepancy between the sentences angered Dillinger. On the way to the prison, Dillinger attempted to escape but was recaptured before he could get away.[6]

Dillinger was sent to the Pendleton Reformatory in Indianapolis, where he attempted, but failed, to escape. His wife filed for divorce in 1929, shortly before Dillinger went up for parole. Prison officials denied his parole and instead transferred him to prison in Michigan City, Indiana's *Big House*. There, Dillinger found himself living with professional bank robbers including "Handsome Harry" Pierpont, John "Red" Hamilton, Charles Makley, and Russell Clark. These men taught Dillinger many new techniques for becoming a successful criminal.

In May 1933, Dillinger was finally allowed to leave prison after almost nine years in the institution. He was anxious to leave because his stepmother had suffered a stroke and was near death. By the time Dillinger got home she had been dead only about 20 minutes.[7]

When Dillinger left prison, almost immediately, he began to use the new skills he learned in the institution. After a series of small robberies, Dillinger and two other ex-cons went to Daleville, Indiana, and robbed the bank there. The robbers took $3,500 without any resistance from law enforcement. Then, on July 19, he and an accomplice robbed the Rockville National Bank but nabbed only $120. Not long after, on August 4, Dillinger robbed the First National Bank in Montpelier, Indiana. He stayed in the bank only ten minutes and left with over ten thousand dollars. Later that month, he robbed the Citizen's National Bank in Bluffton, Ohio, for another $6,000 dollars. Dillinger and his crew took $24,000 from the Massachusetts Avenue State Bank in Indianapolis on September 6.[8]

The police always found themselves one step behind the outlaw. Dillinger had the fastest cars of the day, even faster than those owned by the police. But what made it more difficult for law enforcement to pursue Dillinger was that they were unable to chase him across state lines. Police were required to stop at the state border because they did not have the legal authority to enter into another state's jurisdiction. There was also limited communication between police agencies in different states.

When some of Dillinger's friends were sent to the Michigan City prison, Dillinger devised a scheme to get them out. He snuck some automatic guns into a box of thread that was to be delivered into the prison's shirt factory. With Dillinger's help, ten men were able to walk out of the state penitentiary. It was the biggest prison break in Indiana history. After the escape, the men remained together to commit a series of bank robberies.[9]

During this time, Dillinger had been courting Mary Longnaker, and moved to Ohio to be close to her. In September, 1933, law enforcement agents learned about his new love interest, raided her apartment and found him there. Dillinger was arrested and sent to prison in Lima, Ohio.[10]

Two weeks later, on Columbus Day, his friends from the Michigan City escape plot returned Dillinger's earlier favor and helped him escape from the Lima prison. The men pretended to be police officers from Indiana who wanted to meet with Dillinger. When the sheriff, Jess Sarber, asked to see their credentials, Pierpont killed him. Dillinger grabbed his coat and hat and walked out of the jail, getting into a car with the men and driving away. It was later reported that Dillinger was angry over the sheriff's death.[11]

Now that they were all back together, the men needed more guns so they could rob more banks. The gang raided two police stations in Indiana and stole weapons, including Tommy guns, pistols, rifles, ammunition, and bullet proof vests. They were now prepared to commit more bank robberies. On October 23, the gang, including Dillinger, Pierpont and two others, robbed the Central National Bank in Greencastle, Indiana. Pierpont went to the main vault while Dillinger cleared the cages of cash. Throughout, the gang was polite to the employees and customers. After about ten minutes, the robbers got into their cars and drove away with about $75,000.[12]

The men then went to Chicago, where it was easier to hide from police. On November 20, the gang drove to Racine, Wisconsin, where they robbed the American Bank and Trust. An employee hit the alarm so police were outside, ready to shoot the robbers as they left the bank. Dillinger grabbed some hostages to protect him. The gang took $28,000 and drove to rural Wisconsin to drop the hostages off.

The gang returned to Chicago. After spending a short time there, the men decided to rob the American Bank and Trust Company in Wisconsin. In the middle of the robbery, the police arrived, and there was a shootout between the robbers and police.

In January of 1934, the Dillinger gang robbed the First National Bank of East Chicago in Indiana. Despite alarms going off and attracting attention of law enforcement, the robbers finished collecting money before leaving the bank. Dillinger, wearing a bullet proof vest and carrying a Thompson submachine gun, led the way out. Detective Sergeant Patrick O'Malley was one officer who was waiting outside for the men. He shot Dillinger four times in the chest, but the bullets bounced off of the vest he was wearing. Dillinger returned fire at O'Malley, aiming for his knees. O'Malley dropped to the ground and one bullet went through his heart, killing him instantly. This was the first and only time Dillinger shot and killed a man. Afterwards, he appeared to be genuinely upset about killing the officer.

After the robbery, Dillinger and his gang then went to Tucson, Arizona, for a short vacation. Not long after they got there, the men got to know some firemen who recognized the robbers and called the police.[13] The gang members were arrested and sent back to Lima for killing the sheriff, and John was returned to Indiana for killing O'Malley. As they arrived at the jail in Crown Point, Indiana, reporters asked Sheriff Lillian Holley and prosecutor Robert Estill to pose with Dillinger. Dillinger smiled for the cameras and seemed to be enjoying the attention.

While Dillinger was being held in the Crown Point jail, over 100 armed guards surrounded the building to ensure that it was escape-proof. Dillinger was a model prisoner who remained calm and friendly throughout his stay. But Dillinger had other plans. He carved a gun out of wood and used it to escape. He locked the guards in a cell, then stole real weapons from the jail and calmly walked out through the kitchen. He drove away in the sheriff's personal car.

Nobody was hurt in the escape, but FBI Director J. Edgar Hoover was furious that Dillinger was allowed to break out and evade authorities again. Robbing banks was not yet a federal crime, but when Dillinger stole the sheriff's car to escape he drove a stolen car across state lines, which was a federal offense. As a result, Hoover announced an FBI campaign to catch Dillinger. Hoover knew the outlaw's capture would not only bring media attention to the FBI but would also help him convince Congress of the need for a federal agency that could pursue criminals across state lines. Hoover assigned FBI special agent Melvin Purvis the task of arresting Dillinger.

On March 6, 1934, just three days after the escape from the Crown Point Jail, Dillinger and his crew, which now included Baby Face Nelson and Homer Van Meter, robbed the Security National Bank and Trust Company in Sioux Falls.[14] Nelson had a reputation for being violent and often killing innocent people. Within the next week, the gang pulled off a robbery at the First National Bank in Mason City, Iowa. The bank was equipped with a guard tower with tear-gas ports that filled the bank with noxious fumes. Although the gang got $52,000 dollars, a shootout ensued and Dillinger was shot in the shoulder.[15]

After he recovered from the injury, Dillinger headed north to St. Paul, Minnesota, where he and his girlfriend Billie rented a room in the Lincoln Court Apartments. The landlady of the building became suspicious when the pair rarely left the apartment. She called the FBI, who sent agents to investigate. When they knocked on the door, Billie answered, telling the agents she was not dressed and they would have to wait. This gave Dillinger time to grab a gun and shoot their way out. When Hoover was told of the events, he ordered more agents onto the case.

Despite the FBI search, Dillinger continued to evade the FBI without much trouble. At one point, he went to his family's home for a family reunion. The FBI was watching the area but did not respond to all of the cars and activity at the farm.[16]

Dillinger and Billie returned to Chicago once again. Billie arranged to meet some men in a pub who were arranging for a place for her and Dillinger to stay. The FBI had been tipped off about the meeting, and Purvis arrested Billie as she walked in. Billie was interrogated for hours, deprived of food and sleep. She was put on trial and sentenced to two years in prison for harboring a fugitive.

Dillinger and other outlaws headed to a retreat called the Little Bohemian in Wisconsin, where they could make plans for the future. The couple who owned the inn, Emil and Nan Wanatka, recognized them and contacted the FBI Purvis and other FBI agents arrived and surrounded the hotel. They shot at a car leaving the hotel. The gang members heard the gunfire and began to flee.

Dillinger escaped through a second story window in the back of the hotel, and the others followed. FBI agents threw tear gas into the building the entire night. The next morning, the agents went in and found only the girlfriends, who were left behind.[17]

In the end, the raid was a disaster. The robbers escaped, but in the chase Baby Face Nelson killed a federal agent. There were public calls for Hoover to be fired. In an effort to restore the agency's reputation, Hoover increased the reward for Dillinger to $15,000.[18]

On May 3, Dillinger and his men robbed a bank in Fostoria, Ohio. They took about $11,000 in cash and an undisclosed amount of bonds. On May 21, they robbed a small bank in Galion, Ohio, netting $5,400. But Dillinger was becoming increasingly paranoid about being recognized in public. He had plastic surgery to alter the look of his face and had an acid treatment on his fingers to obliterate his fingerprints.

Back in Chicago, John had a new girlfriend named Polly Hamilton, whom he met through Anna Sage, and took up residence with the women. Sage, a Romanian, was to be deported for running a brothel and for other criminal activities. She contacted Purvis and tried to make a deal with the FBI. She told them she would give them Dillinger if the FBI would stop her deportation and give her the reward money.

On Sunday July 22, 1934, Anna called the FBI and informed them that Dillinger was taking Anna and Polly to the movie that evening at the Biograph Theater. Before the movie, federal agents surrounded the theater. Purvis was to signal the other agents by lighting a cigar when Dillinger left the theater. When the movie ended, Dillinger walked out with Polly on one arm and Anna on the other. Agents rushed in on Dillinger. As he ran from them, Dillinger pulled out a gun from his pocket. Agents Winstead and Hurt fired at Dillinger at close range. He was shot first in his chest. A second bullet entered the base of his neck, went through the brain stem and came out beneath his right eye. He stumbled to his knees and agents shot him again. Women ripped their slips and men ripped their straw hats to dip them in Dillinger's blood as souvenirs.

As Dillinger's body was taken to morgue, thousands followed. The coroner put the corpse on public display. Word of his death spread quickly and 15,000 people came to see his body. Skeptics wondered if it was really Dillinger, claiming that the eye color was wrong and his body was heavier. Even though his fingerprints were scarred, what remained closely matched his original prints.

Dillinger was buried in the family plot in Indianapolis. Later, the family went on a tour in an effort to make money. The theme of their tour was to prove that crime never pays.

Public Enemies: The Film

The movie takes place in 1933, the fourth year of the Great Depression. When the movie begins, Dillinger had been paroled just eight weeks earlier after serving nine years in the penitentiary. The first scene is in the Indiana State Penitentiary in Michigan City, Indiana. The prisoners are in lockstep, wearing striped uniforms. A car pulls up and a man with a badge gets out, pulling Dillinger from the back seat. He appears to be taking a new inmate into the prison. They walk across the yard and into the prison. The inmates are involved in a work program. A package is unloaded. Inside the package is thread for the sewing machines. Buried beneath the spools of thread are weapons. The prisoners use the guns to overpower the guards. In the commotion, a guard is shot, another beaten, and an inmate is shot. The alarm sounds. Amid gunfire, Dillinger and four other inmates leave the prison and run to the car. The injured inmate is Walter Dietrich. A friend of Dillinger, he soon dies.

The men drive to a nearby farm. They thank a man named Red for getting them out and welcome back a man named Pete (Pierpont). They decide to go to Chicago and make some money.

The scene switches to an apple orchard, where Pretty Boy Floyd is running through the woods being pursued by FBI agent Purvis. Purvis shoots Floyd with precision as he is running away. Purvis kicks a gun out of Floyd's hand as he lays on the ground, wounded. They talk for a few seconds and Floyd dies.

The scene again switches back to a brothel/safe-house where they are preparing weapons for a bank robbery. A man named Harry Berman has rebuilt some cars so they are fast. Anna Cumpanas, or Anna Sage, tells the men she has opened up some new houses (brothels) and invites them to come by and see the girls. Dillinger is seen paying off a cop, who tells Dillinger that he has safe haven as long as he is in Chicago.

In the next scene, the gang is robbing a bank. One robber takes the bank president to the safe and forces him to open it, while another robber steals the cash from the teller's windows. An alarm is going off. The lookout man outside the bank spots the police and indicates to those inside that the police are there. A getaway car pulls up for the robbers and a shootout begins. Dillinger allows a bank customer to keep his money, saying he only wants the bank's money. As they leave the bank, the robbers take hostages. Dillinger gives the female hostage his coat because she is cold. They take the hostages to a rural area, tie them to a tree, and leave.

The scene shifts to show an appropriations committee meeting on Capitol Hill in Washington, D.C. A congressman asks Hoover why there is a need to pass a law to create a federal police agency that can chase suspects across state borders. Hoover explains that criminals flee in fast automobiles across state lines and get away because state agents cannot stop them. A federal police force could stop them. The Congressman asks Hoover how many bank robbers he has apprehended, Hoover claims that the agency had captured 213 felons. When asked how many *he himself* had arrested, Hoover tells the panel that he administers the agency and has not personally arrested any criminals. The Congressman tells Hoover that because he has no field experience, he is shockingly unqualified to run the FBI. He then denies Hoover's appropriations increase request.[19]

Later, Hoover announces the promotion of FBI Agent Purvis to be the special agent in charge of the Chicago Field Office. Hoover also congratulates the agent on killing Pretty Boy Floyd. In a press conference, Hoover announces the first war on crime by introducing Purvis to the media. Hoover describes Purvis's new task as being the apprehension of Public Enemy Number One: John Dillinger.

The scene switches to the bank thieves, who are in a posh nightclub. Dillinger meets with Alvin Karpis, who tells Dillinger about a plan to kidnap a St. Paul banker, but they need a few more people to help out. Dillinger tells Karpis he does not like kidnapping because the public does not like kidnappers. He explains that since he hides out among the public, he has to care what they think. Karpis then tells Dillinger that they are also planning a heist of a Federal Reserve train shipment and need two or three guys to help stick it up. They believe they can get about $1,700,000 from the train heist. Dillinger tells Karpis he has no plans for the future, but Karpis tells him he ought to think about it because what they are doing isn't going to last forever. Karpis gives Dillinger the name of Louis Piquett, a syndicate lawyer who can help him if needed.

Anna Sage is also at the nightclub and introduces the men to some of her ladies. But Dillinger is more interested in meeting a woman he saw earlier. John introduces himself to her, telling her his name is Jack. The woman's name is Evelyn "Billie" Freschette. They dance to the song "Bye, Bye Blackbird" and she tells him she is a coat-check girl at the Steuben Club. They leave the nightclub and go to a restaurant where he tells her he is really John Dillinger and he robs banks.

On their way out of the restaurant, Dillinger runs into someone he knows, and asks Billie to wait for him outside. The man works for Frank Nitti, the boss of Chicago's organized crime family. A man named Phil D'Andrea introduces himself to Dillinger.[20] When Dillinger goes outside, Billie is gone. Later, Dillinger goes to Steuben Club to find Billie. The two trade stories about their childhoods.

The Dillinger gang robs another bank and gets $74,000. Purvis asked Hoover for agents with special qualifications to augment the staff in Chicago because his current agents cannot get the job done. He tells Hoover that there are some former Texas and Oklahoma lawmen currently with the Bureau in Dallas that could help. Hoover just hangs up the phone. Soon, some lawmen get off a train and are met by Purvis. They include Special Agent Charles Winstead and Special Agent Clarence Hurt.

In another scene, Dillinger is at a race track in Miami. Nitti is there with D'Andrea, who waves at Dillinger. Dillinger and other bank robbers agree to meet in Tucson. While at the Hotel Congress in Arizona, agents storm into the hotel room and arrest Dillinger. There was a fire in the hotel and the firemen found the outlaws' guns and called the cops.

Purvis comes to see Dillinger in the jail and tells him he is being sent back to Indiana to face charges there. In Indiana, a crowd of people are waiting to see Dillinger, and people are lined up on the road, cheering and waving, as Dillinger is driven to the Indiana jail. At the jail, officials take pictures with him, including the female sheriff, Lillian Holley.

Dillinger's attorney in his arraignment is Piquett, the lawyer Karpis had recommended. At the arraignment, the prosecution argues that Dillinger is a dangerous man who should be sent to the Indiana State Penitentiary in Michigan City, because it is the only prison that can hold him. When Dillinger's attorney teases him that that the Indiana jail is not strong enough to hold Dillinger, Holley takes offense and tells the judge they have a strong jail that can hold the outlaw and she was not afraid of him escaping. The judge ordered that Dillinger remain in the jail and set the trial for one month from then.

While in jail awaiting trial, Dillinger overpowers a guard using what appeared to be a gun. He forces his way into the gun room and steals real guns. Dressing in the guard's street clothes, Dillinger takes Sheriff Holley's personal car as an escape vehicle because it was the fastest. He drives right past all the guards outside the jail and escapes without harming anyone.

After the escape, John drives to a safe house and is told he cannot stay there anymore. To find out why, Dillinger goes to a cigar shop that housed an illegal wire service owned by the Chicago syndicate. There, D'Andrea tells him the operation makes a large amount of money because they know who wins the third race before anyone else. He continues by telling Dillinger that he attracts attention from police, which is bad for business. The Syndicate's new policy is that they can no longer associate with Dillinger, Karpis, or Baby Face Nelson. They will no longer launder their money nor provide safe houses for the bank robbers.

In the next scene, Dillinger is in a movie theater where he and other men discuss robbing another bank, but Dillinger says he does not like working with Baby Face Nelson. Other men tell him that Nelson knows of a bank in Sioux

Falls with $800,000 and a place to stay until the heat is off. Dillinger says after the robbery they have to bust out Pierpont and Makley from prison. As they were talking, a news clip shows Dillinger as Public Enemy Number One. He looks around the theater but no one recognizes him.

The gang pulls off the bank robbery at the First National Bank in Sioux Falls. They took hostages again and there is a shootout with police. Dillinger is shot in the arm. Nelson shoots randomly and many people are hurt. To recover, the robbers go to the Little Bohemia Lodge in Wisconsin. There they count the money and discover they only got $26,000, or $8,000 a man.

FBI agents are shown in a hospital, questioning an injured robber from the bank heist. According to the doctors, he has a bullet in his head and needs a shot for the pain. Agents will not allow the shot until the man answers their questions. They even apply pressure to the wound to make it hurt more. Agents keep asking the man where the rest of the gang is hiding. The man claims to not know. He finally tells Purvis the gang is at the Little Bohemia Lodge.

The agents immediately go to the lodge. An agent tells Purvis they do not have enough men to block an escape because there too many ways to get out. He recommends they wait until some more local agents arrive. But Purvis does not want to risk the robber's escape and orders an attack.

A car starts to drive away from the lodge and the agents order the driver to stop, but they keep driving so the agents shoot at it, killing one man. The shots wake up Dillinger, who had fallen asleep in one of the rooms. There is another shootout and Dillinger escapes out of a second story window in the back of the lodge and runs through the woods. Red and Nelson are both shot, as is an FBI agent, but Dillinger gets away. All of Dillinger's friends are now dead.

On the radio, it is announced that Dillinger helped law enforcement in one way. Now Congress was considering the first national crime bill that would make criminal enterprise across state lines a federal crime. This angered Chicago boss Frank Nitti and other men in organized crime, who knew law enforcement could use the new laws against them.

Dillinger is able to meet Billie and tells her that there is one more big job to carry out, then they can leave the country and go anywhere they want. Billie goes in to see a bartender because he has the keys to an apartment they are going to rent. As Billie goes in, she is ambushed by FBI agents. Dillinger is waiting in the car and sees Billie being arrested. At the station, the agents interrogate Billie. They slap her and do not allow her to sleep or use the bathroom. She tells agents that she and Dillinger were to meet at an apartment at that moment. The agents go there and find the place empty. They return to Billie and cuff her to the chair. The secretary tells Purvis that they cannot treat a woman this way. Purvis will not let the agents beat her any more and gives her permission to use the restroom. Because she cannot stand, Purvis carries her to the bathroom.

Nitti is shown getting angry at the bank robbers. He has one of his men talk to Anna, who tells him she is being deported back to Romania. The man convinces Anna to help them get rid of Dillinger. The mob convinces her that the FBI will block her deportation if she gives up Dillinger. Sage meets with Purvis and tells him she wants a guarantee that she will not be deported if she helps get Dillinger. Purvis tells her he will do anything he can do to influence immigration, but Purvis will not give her a guarantee. He then threatens her by saying, if she does not help get Dillinger then she will be on a boat to Romania in 48 hours.

Back in Chicago, Dillinger starts dating a new woman, Polly Hamilton, one of Anna's girls. He also meets with Karpis and some other men to begin planning for the big train heist. They expected to get between $1,500,000 to $1,700,000, which would average out to about $300,000 each. Dillinger tells him if they pull this on Tuesday then he would be gone by Wednesday.

That night, Dillinger made plans to go to a movie with Anna and Polly. Before that, Polly needs to go to get her waitressing license so Dillinger offers to take her. While they are gone, Anna calls Purvis and tells him that they are going to a movie that night. She will be with Dillinger, wearing a white blouse over an orange skirt. They will be attending either the Marlboro or Biograph Theater. But the agents discover that the movie at the Marlboro is a Shirley Temple movie and the movie showing at the Biograph was a gangster movie with Clark Gable. From that they know Dillinger will be at the Biograph. Just to be sure, Purvis sends two agents from the East Chicago Police Department as well as Agent Winstead and Purvis to the Biograph. Other police are sent to the Marlboro.

While in the city with Polly, Dillinger walks into the Chicago Police Department unrecognized. He enters the room marked "Dillinger Squad" and looks around. He sees pictures of himself, Billie, and his gang. He even asked men the score of a baseball game.

Later that night, Dillinger and the two women go to the theater. Purvis and the other agents are also at the theater. The three go in to and watch *Manhattan Melodrama* starring Clark Gable. Purvis tells the other agents posted around the theater that he will light his cigar when Dillinger comes out. When Dillinger exits the theater, Purvis indicates when the outlaw appears. Dillinger is walking between Anna and Polly. The agents follow him with their guns drawn, pointed at Dillinger from behind. He turns around and starts to pull out a gun. Agent Winstead shoots him in the back of the head and in his back, three times in all. He leans down to hear Dillinger's last words but claims he couldn't hear them. People swarmed around Dillinger's body, taking pictures.

Later, Agent Winstead visits Billie in prison. He tells her that he and other agents shot Dillinger. He also told her that Dillinger's last words were, "Tell Billie for me, bye, bye blackbird."

Public Enemies: Hollywood's Rendering

Despite many accurate descriptions of events throughout the film, there are multiple historical inaccuracies in *Public Enemies* that takes away from its effectiveness. One set of inaccuracies occurs in the first scene of the movie. The film begins with Dillinger breaking his friends out of Indiana State penitentiary on a sunny day in 1933. There are many things wrong with this scene. To begin with, it was a cold and rainy September day. More importantly, Dillinger was not present for the escape because he was in jail in Lima, Ohio.

Many years before this famous escape, Dillinger and the other bank robbers (including Pierpont) had made a deal whereby Dillinger, upon being granted parole first, would help the remaining imprisoned men escape. In exchange, Dillinger would become a member of Pierpont's gang. When he was released from the prison, Dillinger made good on his deal. He first robbed a few banks to get enough money to purchase guns, then had them sent into the jail inside a shipment of thread going to a shirt factory. Thus, Dillinger's role was only to figure out a way to smuggle the guns into the prison, but he left the others to finish the job. He only orchestrated the breakout but did not participate in it, as shown in the movie.

Additionally, the movie shows a full-fledged shootout between the inmates and the guards as part of the escape, but in reality, few shots were fired.[21] Only one man, a clerk, was wounded.[22] That scene also shows that inmate Walter Dietrich was killed during the breakout from the jail. But Dietrich was actually captured on January 6, 1934, and returned to Indiana State Prison at Michigan City. Further, Dietrich died after Dillinger.[23]

The demise of other bank robbers and associates of Dillinger's were not portrayed accurately in the movie. In the film, Dillinger's friends were all killed prior to him. But in reality, Dillinger actually died before everyone else.[24] When Dillinger was shot, Pierpont, Makley and Clark were in the Ohio state prison. About a month after Dillinger's death, Pierpont and Makely tried to escape using fake guns made from soap, wire, jigsaw-puzzle pieces, cardboard tubes and tin foil from cigarette packages. In the attempt, Makley was shot and killed instantly and Pierpont was wounded and later executed.[25] Chase was later captured and sent to Alcatraz. Homer Van Meter was gunned down in an alley in St. Paul a month after Dillinger was killed.

Baby Face Nelson's death was also not accurate in the movie. In the film, Nelson was killed in a shootout with police in Wisconsin after they robbed the Security National Bank of Sioux Falls, South Dakota. In fact, he was injured in a shootout with FBI agents in a northwest suburb of Chicago on November 27, 1934.[26] Baby Face Nelson and John Paul Chase were followed to Lake Geneva in Wisconsin after Chase's girlfriend ratted on them. Nelson killed two agents with a .351 automatic, then stole their car. During the shootout, Nelson was shot multiple times. His nude body was found the following day, covered by a blanket.[27] Nelson had been named Public Enemy Number One upon Dillinger's death.[28] Baby Face Nelson was also inaccurately portrayed during a scene in the movie where there is a shootout in an apartment building between the FBI agents and Nelson. This did not happen. There was a shootout at the Lincoln Court Apartments in St. Paul, Minnesota, where Dillinger and Frechette were staying under the alias of Mr. and Mrs. Carl Hellman.

Another bank robber, Pretty Boy Floyd, was killed on October 22, 1934 (four months after Dillinger) by agents from the Department of Investigation on a farm in East Liverpool, Ohio, not as shown in the movie. The raid was led by Purvis, but he was just one of several agents who shot at Floyd, and there are no accounts that Purvis shot him. The movie shows Purvis chasing Pretty Boy Floyd through a field and shooting him. Floyd was killed in an open field beside a barn, not in an apple orchard.[29]

It can be argued that Purvis' role in capturing Dillinger was overplayed in the movie. He was not the lead agent on the FBI's case against Dillinger. In fact, Purvis was not in charge of anything except overseeing the Chicago office of the FBI. This meant that in the public's eye, Purvis was the man overseeing the search for Dillinger. In reality, it was FBI agent Samuel Cowley who took Dillinger down.

The movie exaggerates Purvis's role in capturing Dillinger in other ways as well. There is a scene in the movie in which Purvis calls Hoover and asks him to bring in more experienced lawmen from Texas and Oklahoma, because the men in Chicago were not qualified to track down Dillinger. This is probably not accurate. Most agents were fearful of Hoover and would not have questioned his decisions. Instead, it is likely that Hoover did that on his own because he thought Purvis was not qualified for the job.[30]

The relationship between Purvis and Dillinger was exaggerated throughout the movie. In the film, the characters have a conversation in which the FBI agent tells Dillinger he is being extradited to Indiana, to which Dillinger replies, "Why? I have absolutely nothing I want to do in Indiana." But in reality, Purvis and Dillinger never met, so this conversation could not have taken place.[31]

Purvis was also inaccurately portrayed during the scene where Billie Frechette was being interrogated. She testified during her trial that she was struck by

FBI agents and deprived of food and water for two days of interrogation, as depicted in the movie. However, the film shows Purvis stepping in to stop agents from abusing her, and shows him then carrying Billie to the bathroom. It is not true that Purvis helped Billie during her interrogation.[32]

Not only was Purvis portrayed inaccurately, there were many other inaccuracies concerning other FBI agents as well. The movie includes a scene in which FBI agents torture a suspect in his hospital room by applying pressure to a wound as a way to get information on Dillinger. This never happened.[33] There was an FBI agent in the movie who had to be restrained by others for using extreme tactics such as slapping Frechette during her interrogation. There was no such agent. The use of this character by the director shows the frustration many agents felt when Dillinger was able to escape so often.

The agents were also frustrated because of the support that Dillinger had from the general public. This was not shown in the movie. Many average citizens liked Dillinger and supported what he was doing. They saw him as an average man who had the courage to stand up against the banks during the economic hardships of the day. Banks had been foreclosing on people's properties and many families lost their entire savings. When public announcements were shown in theaters warning the public about Dillinger, people often cheered for him and booed the federal agents who were looking for him.[34]

It could be argued that the movie portrays too much violence and killing than what actually occurred as a result of Dillinger's gang. Although it is true that Dillinger and his men were responsible for the deaths of many people, the film portrays many more deaths than actually occurred. Dillinger himself was not a violent man and made an effort not to harm others. It is thought that he probably only killed one man, Sgt. O'Malley, and that was accidental.[35] Further, the movie shows that Homer Van Meter and Baby Face Nelson are shot to death by Purvis after a car chase outside of the Little Bohemia Lodge. In reality, no one was killed during that shoot-out. Both men were actually killed by law enforcement officers in separate incidents after Dillinger died. The movie did not show the agents filling the lodge with tear gas.

The movie had some other minor inaccuracies. For example, in the Crown Point jailbreak scene in the movie, Dillinger is seen entering the gun safe and taking a .45, a Thompson submachine gun, and a B.A.R. (Browning Automatic Rifle). Dillinger actually left the jail with a .45 and two Thompsons, one for him and one for Herbert Youngblood.[36] In another scene in the movie, Dillinger is shown receiving a wound during the holdup of the Security National Bank of Sioux Falls, South Dakota. In reality, he received a shoulder wound a week later during the First National Bank of Mason City heist.[37] Finally, he and Billy did not meet in a nightclub, as depicted in the film. Instead, they were introduced to each other by her roommate, Pat, in the summer of 1933.[38]

The movie included many inaccuracies about the events surrounding Dillinger's death. One of those has to do with how Dillinger died. In real life, when Dillinger realized he was being chased, he ran toward an alley to escape his pursuers and pulled out a gun. Before he could shoot, law enforcement agents fired five shots at Dillinger, two of which hit the outlaw. Even today, there is debate as to whether or not Dillinger pulled his gun on the agents before he was shot. Although some say he was unarmed, others reported that Dillinger was carrying a Colt .380 in his pants when he died.[39] Nonetheless, the movie shows that Dillinger is shot once in the head from behind as he was walking down the street away from the theater.[40] He was not shown running into an alley and reaching for a gun.

After he is shot, the movie shows Dillinger saying, "Bye Bye Black Bird" as he died, but no one can verify if he really said anything at all. Because of the type of injuries he suffered as a result of being shot, it would have been difficult for him to speak. His jaw was shattered because of where the bullet exited. Some reported that Dillinger said "You got me" after he was shot. But he did not say "Bye Bye, blackbird."[41]

In one of the last scenes in the film, FBI agent Charles Winstead tells Billie he was the agent who shot Dillinger. In reality, three agents were recognized for killing Dillinger. They were Winstead, Clarence Hunt, and Herman Hollis, not Winstead alone.[42]

The movie did not show that two women passersby were injured during the shooting at the Biograph theater. One received a slight flesh wound to the hip and the other a bullet wound between the knee and thigh. Neither had any permanent damage.[43]

The movie implies that there was at least some kind of relationship between Dillinger and the organized crime family in Chicago. This is shown a few times throughout the film. First, Dillinger pays off a police officer standing in Anna Sage's kitchen, to which the officer responds, "you will always have safe haven as long as you are in Chicago." In a more obvious scene, after Dillinger and Billie's conversation in a restaurant, they run into some members of organized crime and have a quick conversation. In a third instance, Dillinger, Billie and some of the other bank robbers are shown at a race track in Miami and they wave to Frank Nitti, head of the Syndicate in Chicago. Fourth, Nitti is shown on the telephone complaining about new laws that are being considered in Congress concerning criminals who cross state lines to commit crimes that were proposed because of Dillinger. Fifth, Dillinger is shown barging in on the Syndicate's bookmaking operation and is told that Nitti no longer wants to be associated with the likes of Dillinger. The film also implies that organized crime wanted to get rid of Dillinger because of the attention he was bringing to the criminals by law enforcement. The movie shows organized crime urging Anna Sage to go to the FBI and turn in Dillinger. This all implies that the Syndicate had something to do with Dillinger's death. This relationship is not known to be true. There is little evidence that organized crime and bank robbers associated with each other. Organized crime families, such as the one in Chicago, had chosen members with whom they associated and rarely dealt with people outside of the organization.[44]

Anna Sage, however, did supposedly have some kind of relationship with Martin Zarkovich, a policeman from Lake County, Indiana, who took bribes from speakeasy owners during Prohibition. These were the same people who allegedly sheltered Dillinger.[45] If there was a connection between Dillinger and organized crime, it was through Anna Sage as opposed to Frank Nitti.

Conclusion

Even today, the public remains fascinated by the Dillinger story and the crimes he committed. Many of the true facts surrounding John Dillinger may never truly be known. He was blamed for bank robberies he did not commit, and was not named in robberies in which he did participate. But many changes resulted from Dillinger's crimes. Local police agencies equipped their officers with better weapons, faster cars, and better equipment. The FBI was given the authority to arm their agents and given them the power to arrest offenders. New federal laws were passed that outlawed robbing a federally insured bank and taking stolen cars across state lines. There were also prison reforms that lead to more secure prisons, and banking reforms to prevent more robberies.[46] The interest that Dillinger's crimes still evokes is demonstrated in the success of the film *Public Enemies*, despite its sometimes inaccurate representation of the true events.

Further Reading

Clement, Henry. (1973). *Dillinger.* New York: Curtis Books.

Cromie, Robert. (1962). *Dillinger: A Short and Violent Life.* New York: McGraw Hill.

Girardin, G. Russell. (1994). *Dillinger: The Untold Story.* Bloomington: Indiana University Press.

Gorn, Elliott J. (2009). *Dillinger's Wild Ride.* New York: Oxford University Press.

Higgins, Jack. (2010). *Dillinger.* New York: Open Road Integrated Media.

King, Jeffrey S. (2005). *The Rise and Fall of the Dillinger Gang.* Nashville, TN: Cumberland House Publishing.

Matera, Dary. (2004). *John Dillinger: The Life and Death of America's First Celebrity Criminal.* Cambridge, MA: Da Capo Press.

Nash, Jay Robert. (1972). *Citizen Hoover: A Critical Study of the Life and Times of J. Edgar* Hoover and His FBI Chicago: Nelson-Hall.

Nash, Jay Robert. (1983). *The Dillinger Dossier.* Highland Park, Ill: December Press.

Powers, Richard G. (1983*). G-Men, Hoover's FBI in American Popular Culture.* Carbondale: Southern Illinois University Press.

Purvis, Alston. (2005). *The Vendetta: Special Agent Melvin Purvis, John Dillinger, and* Hoover's FBI in the Age of Gangsters. New York: Public Affairs.

Streissguth, Thomas. (2002). *J. Edgar Hoover: Powerful FBI Director.* Berkeley Heights, NJ: Enslow Publishers.

Theoharis, Athan G. (1988). *The Boss: J. Edgar Hoover and the Great American Inquisition* . Philadelphia: Temple University Press.

Toland, John. (1995). *The Dillinger Days.* New York: Da Capo Press.

Endnotes

1. *Public Enemies* (Universal Pictures, 2009)(Michael Mann, Director).

2. Burroughs, Bryan. (2004). *Public Enemies: America's Greatest Crime Wave and the Birth of the F.B.I., 1933–34.* New York: Penguin Books.

3. Matera, Dary. (2004). *John Dillinger: The Life and Death of America's First Celebrity Criminal.* Cambridge, MA: Da Capo Press; Gorn, Elliott J. (2009). *Dillinger's Wild Ride.* New York: Oxford University Press, 2009.

4. Gorn,Elliott J. (2009). *Dillinger's Wild Ride.* New York: Oxford University Press.

5. Gorn, Elliott J. (2009). *Dillinger's Wild Ride.* New York: Oxford University Press.

6. Matera, Dary. (2004). *John Dillinger: The Life and Death of America's First Celebrity Criminal.* Cambridge, MA: Da Capo Press.

7. Gorn, Elliott J. (2009). *Dillinger's Wild Ride.* New York: Oxford University Press.

8. Matera, Dary. (2004). *John Dillinger: The Life and Death of America's First Celebrity Criminal.* Cambridge, MA: Da Capo Press.

9. Matera, Dary. (2004). *John Dillinger: The Life and Death of America's First Celebrity Criminal.* Cambridge, MA: Da Capo Press.

10. Gorn, Elliott J. (2009). *Dillinger's Wild Ride.* New York: Oxford University Press.

11. Gorn, Elliott J. (2009). *Dillinger's Wild Ride.* New York: Oxford University Press.

12. Matera, Dary. (2004). *John Dillinger: The Life and Death of America's First Celebrity Criminal.* Cambridge, MA: Da Capo Press.

13. Burroughs, Bryan. (2004). *Public Enemies: America's Greatest Crime Wave and the Birth of the F.B.I., 1933–34*. New York: Penguin Books; Matera, Dary. (2004). *John Dillinger: The Life and Death of America's First Celebrity Criminal*. Cambridge, MA: Da Capo Press.

14. Burroughs, Bryan. (2004). *Public Enemies: America's Greatest Crime Wave and the Birth of the F.B.I., 1933–34*. New York: Penguin Books; Matera, Dary. (2004). *John Dillinger: The Life and Death of America's First Celebrity Criminal*. Cambridge, MA: Da Capo Press.

15. Matera, Dary (2004). *John Dillinger: The Life and Death of America's First Celebrity Criminal*. Cambridge, MA: Da Capo Press.

16. Burroughs, Bryan. (2004). *Public Enemies: America's Greatest Crime Wave and the Birth of the F.B.I., 1933–34*. New York: Penguin Books.

17. Gorn, Elliott J. (2009). *Dillinger's Wild Ride*. New York: Oxford University Press.

18. Matera, Dary (2004). *John Dillinger: The Life and Death of America's First Celebrity Criminal*. Cambridge, MA: Da Capo Press.

19. McKellar (R: TN) was a U.S. Representative from 1911–1917 and then U.S. Senator from 1917–1953. He was the Chair of the Appropriations Committee

20. D'Andrea was a bodyguard to Al Capone.

21. Gorn, Elliott (2009) "Is Michael Mann's Public Enemies Historically Accurate?" *Slate*. Retrieved online at http://www.slate.com/id/2222070/.

22. Internet Movie Database. (2001). "Public Enemies-Goofs." *The Internet Movie Database*. Retrieved online at http://www.imdb.com/title/tt1152836/goofs.

23. Jones, J.R. (2011). "History vs. Hollywood: Public Enemies." *Chicago Reader*. Retrieved online at http://www.chicagoreader.com/chicago/history-vs-hollywood/Content?oid=1138125; Internet Movie Database. (2001). "Public Enemies-Goofs." *The Internet Movie Database*. Retrieved online at http://www.imdb.com/title/tt1152836/goofs.

24. Gorn, Elliott (2009) "Is Michael Mann's Public Enemies Historically accurate?" *Slate*. Retrieved online at http://www.slate.com/id/2222070/.

25. Dary Matera, *John Dillinger: The Life and Death of America's First Celebrity Criminal* (Cambridge, MA: Da Capo Press, 2004).

26. Internet Movie Database. (2001). "Public Enemies-Goofs." *The Internet Movie Database*. Retrieved online at http://www.imdb.com/title/tt1152836/goofs.

27. Matera, Dary. (2004). *John Dillinger: The Life and Death of America's First Celebrity Criminal*. Cambridge, MA: Da Capo Press.

28. Internet Movie Database. (2001). "Public Enemies-Goofs." *The Internet Movie Database*. Retrieved online at http://www.imdb.com/title/tt1152836/goofs.

29. Chasing the Frog. (2011). "Chasing After the Truth Behind Movies Based on True Stories—Public Enemies." *Chasing the Frog*. Retrieved online at http://www.chasingthefrog.com/reelfaces/publicenemies.php.

30. Gorn, Elliott (2009) "Is Michael Mann's Public Enemies Historically accurate?" *Slate*. Retrieved online at http://www.slate.com/id/2222070/.

31. Gorn, Elliott (2009) "Is Michael Mann's Public Enemies Historically accurate?" *Slate*. Retrieved online at http://www.slate.com/id/2222070/.

32. Chasing the Frog. (2011). "Chasing After the Truth Behind Movies Based on True Stories—Public Enemies." *Chasing the Frog*. Retrieved online at PERLINK"http://www.chasingthefrog.com/reelfaces/publicenemies.php"http://www.chasingthefrog.com/reelfaces/public enemies.php.

33. Jones, J.R. (2011). "History vs. Hollywood: Public Enemies." *Chicago Reader*. Retrieved online at http://www.chicagoreader.com/chicago/history-vs-hollywood/Content?oid=1138125.

34. Chasing the Frog. (2011). "Chasing After the Truth Behind Movies Based on True Stories—Public Enemies." *Chasing the Frog.* Retrieved online at http://www.chasingthefrog.com/reel faces/publicenemies.php.

35. Gorn, Elliott (2009) "Is Michael Mann's Public Enemies Historically Accurate?" *Slate.* Retrieved online at http://www.slate.com/id/2222070/.

36. Internet Movie Database. (2001). "Public Enemies-Goofs." *The Internet Movie Database.* Retrieved online at http://www.imdb.com/title/tt1152836/goofs.

37. Internet Movie Database. (2001). "Public Enemies-Goofs." *The Internet Movie Database.* Retrieved online at http://www.imdb.com/title/tt1152836/goofs.

38. Matera, Dary. (2004). *John Dillinger: The Life and Death of America's First Celebrity Criminal.* Cambridge, MA: Da Capo Press.

39. Chasing the Frog. (2011). "Chasing After the Truth Behind Movies Based on True Stories—Public Enemies." *Chasing the Frog.* Retrieved online at http://www.chasingthefrog.com/reel faces/publicenemies.php.

40. Internet Movie Database. (2001). "Public Enemies-Goofs." *The Internet Movie Database.* Retrieved online at http://www.imdb.com/title/tt1152836/goofs.

41. Chasing the Frog. (2011). "Chasing After the Truth Behind Movies Based on True Stories—Public Enemies." *Chasing the Frog.* Retrieved online at http://www.chasingthefrog.com/reel faces/publicenemies.php.

42. Chasing the Frog. (2011). "Chasing After the Truth Behind Movies Based on True Stories—Public Enemies." *Chasing the Frog.* Retrieved online at http://www.chasingthefrog.com/reel faces/publicenemies.php.

43. Chasing the Frog. (2011). "Chasing After the Truth Behind Movies Based on True Stories—Public Enemies." *Chasing the Frog.* Retrieved online at http://www.chasingthefrog.com/reel faces/publicenemies.php.

44. Marion, Nancy E. (2008). *Government Versus Organized Crime.* Upper Saddle River, New Jersey: Pearson/Prentice Hall.

45. Matera, Dary. (2004). *John Dillinger: The Life and Death of America's First Celebrity Criminal.* Cambridge, MA: Da Capo Press.

46. Matera, Dary. (2004). *John Dillinger: The Life and Death of America's First Celebrity Criminal.* Cambridge, MA: Da Capo Press.

CHAPTER 7

IN COLD BLOOD AND THE CLUTTER FAMILY MURDERS (1959)

Mug shots of Richard Eugene Hickock (bottom) and Perry Edward Smith (top) after their arrest for the Clutter family murders. Photo courtesy of the Garden City Police Department, Garden City, Kansas.

No one will ever know what 'In Cold Blood' took out of me. It scraped me right down to the marrow of my bones. It nearly killed me. I think, in a way, it did kill me.

—Truman Capote

Introduction

In 1959, in a small Kansas town, a respected father, mother, and two of their teenage children were brutally murdered in their home by two ex-convicts. The killers broke into the home after being told there was a safe in the office that held a large amount of money. Upon entering the house, the offenders discovered there was neither a safe nor any money. Because they had agreed that they would leave no witnesses and commit the "perfect crime," all of the family members in the home at the time were tied up, gagged, and shot at close range with a 22-gauge shotgun. The father's throat had been slit, leaving a large pool of his blood on the basement floor. The murderers left the home with only a radio, binoculars, and $50, leaving very little evidence for law enforcement.

After fleeing to Mexico to evade police, the fugitives quickly ran out of money and returned to the United States. They bounced checks for cash, stole cars, and travelled throughout the country before being captured in Las Vegas. They were returned to Kansas and a trial was held in the community where the killings took place. The pair were found guilty of murder and sentenced to death by hanging. After many appeals, the men were executed, one right after the other.

The gruesome story was first made popular by a reporter, Truman Capote, who wrote a book about the events entitled *In Cold Blood*. He considered it to be a new style of writing, the non-fiction novel. In researching the case, Capote traveled to Kansas to interview not only the townspeople who knew the crime victims, but also spent many hours with the offenders while they were awaiting trial and then execution. The book became a best-selling novel, and a movie followed in 1967 based on Capote's book. In 1996, a version of the story was made into a television miniseries. Both depicted the crime and the outcome.

In Cold Blood: The History

In mid-November, 1959, Herb Clutter was a 48-year-old farmer and owner of the River Valley Farm. The farm encompassed over 800 acres of land, with sheep and cattle.[1] Although Mr. Clutter was not the wealthiest man in town, he was one of the community's most widely known residents.[2] He chose not to smoke or drink,[3] and even tried to avoid socializing with those who did. Everyone in town knew that although Mr. Clutter had plenty of money, he chose to pay for everything by check[4] because it served as a way to keep track of his purchases.

His wife, Bonnie, suffered from "nervous spells" and had been an occasional psychiatric patient for many years,[5] possibly suffering from post-partum depression.[6] His youngest child, Kenyon, 15, was a respected young person within the community, even though he occasionally smoked cigarettes. His daughter, Nancy, was 16 and a straight-A student who often taught other girls in town how to cook and sew, and helped with their music lessons. She was the president of her class, a leader in the 4-H program and the Young Methodists League. She was a skilled horse rider and played clarinet and piano.[7] Nancy and her father sometimes fought over her boyfriend, Bobby Rupp.[8] Although Mr. Clutter liked Bobby, he was opposed to the relationship because Rupp's family was Roman Catholic and the Clutters were Methodist. Mr. Clutter would sometimes find the two kissing and would remind his daughter that they could not remain together.[9]

The Clutter family farm became the target for two ex-cons, Dick Hickock and Perry Smith, who had met in the Kansas State Penitentiary.[10] Of the two, Hickock was released first from prison on the condition he live with his parents on their farm near Olathe, Kansas. He found a job in an auto-repair garage, earning about $60 a week. He was 28, had been married and divorced twice, and had three young sons. Hickock was very intelligent, having an IQ of 130.[11]

The second convict, Smith, was involved in a motorcycle accident years earlier and spent six months in a hospital recovering. He remained in severe pain, becoming an aspirin addict.[12] Upon his release from prison, Smith found a temporary job as a truck driver. He received a letter from Hickock in which he described the "perfect score": a robbery of the Clutter farm in Kansas. Smith decided to return to Kansas to meet up with Hickock so he packed his collection of maps and books, and bought a ticket for a Greyhound bus.[13] He met Hickock at the bus station, carrying a cardboard suitcase, an old Gibson guitar, and two big boxes of books and maps that weighed about a quarter of a ton.[14]

The pair went to Hickock's parents' farm, where they planned their crime. The men told Mr. Hickock they were going to see Smith's sister in Fort Scott and pick up some money she owed him.[15] When they left the house, they took a 12-gauge shotgun with them. The men stopped at the garage where Hickock worked to change the oil, adjust the clutch, recharge the battery, and put new tires on the rear wheels of the car.[16] The two drove west 400 miles to the Clutter farm, bringing the shotgun, a fishing knife, and enough rope to tie up a dozen people. They drank alcohol along the way.[17]

The morning of the murders, Nancy helped a friend bake a cherry pie, then helped another friend learn a trumpet solo. Kenyon worked on a hope chest for his sister Beverly.[18] Their mother was in bed resting. Mr. Clutter had been at a 4-H meeting[19] and had purchased a new $40,000 insurance policy that, in the event of death by accidental means, would pay double indemnity.[20]

During the trip from Olathe to Holcomb, Hickock and Smith stopped in Emporia, Kansas, and bought some supplies they needed for the crime, including a pair of gloves for Smith (Hickock brought his own from home) and nylon cord,[21] later used to tie up Mr. Clutter and Kenyon. The men considered purchasing black stockings to wear as masks, but Hickock reminded Smith it was unnecessary because there would be no witnesses left after the crime was committed. The men stopped for dinner, then made another stop for adhesive tape. The men made one last stop for gas as they got closer to the Clutter house[22] where Hickock bought candy. During the trip, Smith told Hickock that he had killed a man with a chain simply for the hell of it.[23] The story made Hickock believe that Smith would go through with the crime.[24]

It was dark when the men turned onto the road that led up to the Clutter farm. They waited until the last light went out in the home, vowing one last time to leave no witnesses. The men walked into the house through an unlocked door. Hickock believed the safe was in the office, on the first floor. They searched the office and when they did not find the safe, the men woke Mr. Clutter. They told him once they got the money they would leave quietly without harming him or his family. Clutter told the intruders that he did not have a safe, only money in his wallet, which was around $50 dollars. The men did not believe Mr. Clutter. They took the father upstairs and woke the rest of the family. They again demanded that the family show them the safe, giving them a choice: come up with the money or die.

The invaders realized their perfect score seemed to be a failure. The convicts separated the family members. Smith took the men to the basement while Hickock stayed upstairs with the women. Mrs. Clutter pleaded with them not to hurt her family, and the convicts told her not to worry. Hickock had an urge to "bust" Nancy, but Smith stopped him. After killing the family, the men fled with Kenyon's radio, binoculars, and about $50.

In the morning, Nancy's friend came to pick her up for church. When she knocked at the front door, there was no response. Concerned, the young girl went to another door and knocked, again with no response. The friend knocked at the door to Mr. Clutter's office, then the back door, with no answer. The girl ran to a nearby apartment building and called the Clutter house. No one answered the phone.

Concerned, two of Nancy's friends entered the house and went to her bedroom. There they found her dead in her bed, lying on her side facing the wall, with covers up to her shoulders. She appeared to have turned away as intruders shot her in the back of the head. She was wearing pajamas, socks and slippers, and her ankles were tied together.[25]

The sheriff came immediately to the home and discovered Mrs. Clutter's body in her bedroom, gagged and tied with a rope, her hands in front of her. The rope went down to her ankles, which were bound together, tying her to the footboard of the bed. She was wearing a robe, white nightgown and white socks, and was still wearing two rings.[26] Mrs. Clutter had been shot in the side of her head while looking straight up, and her eyes were still open.

Kenyon's body was found in the basement, in the playroom. He was lying on a couch, gagged with tape. His hands and feet were tied together and to the bed in a similar manner as Mrs. Clutter. He was wearing a t-shirt and jeans, but no shoes. He had been shot in the face.[27]

Mr. Clutter's body was found in the furnace room, on a mattress box in front of the furnace. He was wearing striped pajamas. His mouth was taped and he also had tape wound around his head. His ankles were tied together but his hands were free. He had been shot in his face and his throat had been cut twice.[28]

The violent murders of the Clutter family members shook the town's residents. The Clutters were a popular family. Most community members attended the funeral of the four family members.[29] After the initial shock wore off, the residents' shock turned to fear. For the first time, they locked their doors at night, trusting no one else in the small town.

The Kansas Bureau of Investigation (KBI) was called in to help solve the crime. Agent Alvin Adams Dewey, the former county sheriff and FBI agent, was responsible for the investigation. He and the 18 men assigned to the case[30] had few clues as to who killed the Clutters. At first they believed that robbery was the motive, because they found Nancy's gold watch in her shoe[31] and thought that Nancy had hid it there from burglars. They had also found a woman's purse on the floor in the kitchen, opened. But there was little else missing. The only item missing item the maid could identify was Kenyon's radio.[32]

Investigators were also stumped because no one heard any gunshots. A family friend who lived about a hundred yards from the Clutter home had heard nothing. Mr. Clutter's ranch hand also heard little. He reported hearing a car drive away from the home around 10:30 or quarter to 11 that night, but thought it was Bob Rupp. Rupp was the primary suspect at first,[33] but after being questioned at length and passing a polygraph, was ruled out.[34] The only clue investigators had were two photos taken at the crime scene that showed a bloody bootprint of a Cat's Paw half sole and a bootprint with a diamond-patterned sole.[35] A local newspaper, The Hutchinson News, offered $1,000 for information leading to the solution of the crime.[36]

After they committed the murders, Dick and Perry went to Olathe, where Smith stayed at a hotel and Hickock went to his parents' house, where he ate dinner and fell asleep.[37] The pair had plans to flee to Mexico, but needed money to get there. They went to a clothing store and purchased some expensive suits, successfully conning the clerk into cashing a check for $80 more than the cost of the clothes.[38] They then bought jewelry, a video camera, and a television with forged checks and pawned them.[39] They left for Mexico,[40] spending the first night in a brothel.[41] They then drove to Acapulco, where they fished every day. It wasn't long before Hickock and Smith ran out of money. They decided to drive to Mexico City so Hickock could find a job.[42] There they sold Kenyon's radio and the binoculars to a policeman,[43] and then sold the car. Smith had to ship his books, some clothes, and his boots to himself in Las Vegas.[44]

While the outlaws were in Mexico, investigators continued to search for clues. A big break came when Hickock's former prison cellmate, Floyd Wells, heard an appeal for information about the Clutter murders[45] and about the reward on the radio. Wells approached the warden and told him about conversations he had with Hickock in which he told Hickock that he had worked for Clutter as a farmhand, and that Mr. Clutter had a safe in which he kept $10,000. Even though the story was a fabrication, Hickock believed Wells and asked for more details. Wells gave Hickock directions to the farm and a layout of the house. Hickock began to talk about killing Clutter, robbing the family and killing all the witnesses.[46] He reportedly also mentioned including another inmate on the crime, Perry Smith. It would be the perfect score, according to Hickock.

The warden immediately called the KBI, and investigators travelled to interview Hickock's parents at the Hickock farm. Mr. Hickock told them that his son had met up with Smith just days before the murders, saying that he came to Kansas to claim $1,500 from his sister, who lived in Fort Scott, Kansas. They left on the night of the murders and returned the next day around noon. Upon returning, Hickock and Smith told Mr. Hickock that they were unable to find Smith's sister. In the week that followed, Hickock maintained his normal routine but disappeared a few days later.[47] At the Hickock farm, investigators found the shotgun and the knife with blood on it that matched Mr. Clutter's blood type. They also found a shoe with a sole that matched the bloody foot print.

In Mexico, Hickock was unable to find a job, so the two fugitives hitchhiked back to the United States. A salesman traveling to Omaha picked up the men. The fugitives had planned to kill the driver with a belt, rob him, and take the car.[48] But just as they were about to strangle the driver, he stopped to pick up a third hitchhiker, a soldier home on leave from the military.[49]

Hickock and Smith hitchhiked through the West, ending up in Iowa. There, they ran into a barn to seek shelter from a rain storm.[50] In the barn was a 1956 Chevrolet with a key in the ignition.[51] Dick switched the plates on the car[52] and the men drove the stolen car to Kansas City. There, Hickock began to bounce checks for money, using his own name. Police from Kansas City notified Agent Dewey that Hickock was in town, writing bad checks. A store clerk smartly wrote down the license plate number of Hickock's car as he drove away after writing a check in the store. The men were driving a 1956 black and white, two-door Chevy with Kansas license plates.[53] But the killers escaped law enforcement.

Over Christmas of 1959, the fugitives drove to Miami.[54] Because they couldn't find jobs in Miami, the killers didn't stay long and decided to head west again.[55] On the trip back, Smith and Hickock picked up a young boy and his grandfather. As they were driving through Texas, the group picked up empty Coke bottles for money and got $12.60.[56]

Investigators were following other leads, one of which took them to a hotel in Las Vegas where a clerk reported that Smith had stayed a few times.[57] She showed them a box that Smith had shipped from Mexico. Knowing that Smith might return to pick up his belongings, they notified the Las Vegas Police and told them to be watching for the men, reminding them that the men were probably armed and dangerous. Las Vegas police put out an APB on Smith and Hickock and on December 30, police spotted their license plates. As the fugitives stopped at the hotel to pick up Perry's boxes, investigators arrested them. They soon discovered that a pair of boots in the box matched the footprints from the Clutter house.[58]

During the first eight hours of interrogation, Hickock and Smith were not asked about the murders. Instead, the investigators asked about check cashing schemes and parole violations. Eventually agents asked Hickock about the murders, and he immediately denied pulling the trigger, saying that he and Perry were in Fort Scott at the time. But when the agents pulled out the boots that matched the footprints at the crime scene, Hickock confessed about being part of the robbery, but revealed that Smith committed all the killings.

Hickock told investigators that at first, Smith locked all the Clutters in the bathroom,[59] but later went back upstairs and took Mr. Clutter downstairs, and tied him up.[60] Smith then took the boy out of the bathroom and down to the basement and tied him up. Smith returned to the bathroom to tie up Mrs. Clutter and Nancy, after which he went to the basement. The soon-to-be murderers had agreed that they would slit the throats of the victims because it would be quieter than shooting them. But when Smith cut Mr. Clutter's throat, he did not cut very deep and Mr. Clutter gurgled and made a lot of noise, but did not die. The sound bothered Smith so much he shot Mr. Clutter. Smith then shot Kenyon, after which he went upstairs, took Nancy out of the bathroom, put her in her bed, and shot her in the back of the head. Hickock picked up the shotgun shells and ran out of the house to start the car. From there he heard another shot and knew that Smith had killed Mrs. Clutter.

Since investigators wanted to file murder charges in Kansas, Smith and Hickock had to be returned there. Smith did not admit to anything until they were back in Kansas, when he gave his version of the night's events. At first, Smith claimed that Hickock killed the women, but the next day he changed his story, admitting that he killed all of the Clutters. Smith said he lied because he did not want Hickock's mom to think her son killed the women.

Smith told investigators that after they left the Clutter house, he and Hickock drove onto a country road and they buried the shells, extra rope, and tape. Later they stopped at a rest stop to burn the gloves and Smith's shirt. Then Hickock dropped Smith at the hotel and he went to his parents' house.[61] He told them about Mexico and how they sold the binoculars and radio.

The murder trial was scheduled to start on March 12, 1960.[62] If the men pleaded guilty, their sentence would be handed down by the judge. Knowing that the presiding judge would probably sentence them to death, the defendants did not want to take a chance with him. Their only possible way out of being sentenced to death was a jury trial. They entered a plea of not guilty and were appointed lawyers to represent them.

The jury was chosen in four hours. It consisted of 14 men and two alternates. The trial itself lasted only one week. Throughout the trial, Smith and Hickock seemed uninterested.[63] After the evidence was presented, the jurors deliberated only 40 minutes, finding the defendants guilty and handing down a sentence of death by hanging.[64]

The men were sent to Kansas State Penitentiary in Leavenworth County, Kansas.[65] Their execution was scheduled for Friday, May 13, but the Kansas Supreme Court granted the men a stay of execution pending the outcome of an appeal.[66] Hickock began writing letters protesting his conviction. One letter was sent to Everett Steerman, Chairman of the Legal Aid Committee of the Kansas State Bar Association. In it, Hickock reported that there was a "hostile atmosphere" that made it impossible to have an unbiased jury and a change of venue should have been granted. He claimed that the attorneys were incompetent and no real defense had been presented.

The Bar Association appointed a young attorney, Russell Shultz, to investigate the charges.[67] Based on his work, the Kansas Supreme Court commissioned a retired justice, Walter G. Thiele, to conduct a hearing. The case was retried,[68] but Judge Thiele ruled that the inmates had received a fair trial and denied a petition to abolish the verdict. He then set a new execution date of October 25, 1962.[69]

Two other lawyers then replaced Shultz on the case. They filed numerous appeals as a way to avoid three execution dates. The case went to the Supreme Court three times and on each occasion the justices refused to grant a writ of certiorari.[70] The Kansas Supreme Court set another execution date for April 14, 1965. A clemency appeal was filed with the newly elected Governor of Kansas at the time, William Avery, but Avery refused to intervene[71] and the men were hanged that day.

Hickock was executed first and died at 12:41, at the age of 33. Before being executed, Hickock said: "I just want to say I hold no hard feelings. You people are sending me to a better world than this ever was." He shook hands with the warden and the men who had investigated the case, all of whom had requested permission to attend the executions.[72] The prison chaplain administered last rites. The trap door fell. Hickock hung for 22 minutes before being declared dead.

Smith died at 1:19, at the age of thirty-six.[73] He had some Doublemint chewing gum in his mouth just prior to his execution. He said "I think it's a helluva thing to take a life in this manner. I don't believe in capital punishment, morally or legally. Maybe I had something to contribute, something . . . I would be meaningless to apologize for what I did . . . Even inappropriate . . . But I do . . . I apologize." [74] He spit his gum into the chaplain's hand before being hanged. The warden read the warrant of execution to Smith, who pleaded for a second chance. He would not walk up the steps and had to be carried to the top of the gallows. Once that was accomplished, Smith was dead 17 minutes later.

In Cold Blood: The Film

The movie opens with a scene showing Smith strumming a guitar on a Greyhound bus. His feet are propped on the seat in front of him, clearly showing his boot tread that has the impression of a cat. The scene quickly shifts to the family home of the second criminal, Hickock. He is in the shed with a shotgun and he tells his dad that he's got a big day ahead of him. He has promised to help a friend, Perry Smith, and places the gun into the back seat of a car.

The scene again shifts to Smith as he climbs off the bus carrying a large box, a guitar, and a suitcase. He purchases some aspirin and a root beer, and pulls out a letter from Hickock in which he describes the "perfect score." Meanwhile, Hickock tells a gas station attendant that the guns that are clearly visible in the back seat are for pheasant hunting. He has broken the terms of his parole by quitting his job.

The movie shifts to the Clutter family in Kansas. They are going about their typical day on their farm. The son, Kenyon, is shown sneaking a cigarette in the basement. His older sister, Nancy, is making breakfast. Their father is drinking a glass of milk. Kenyon brings a glass of milk to his mom, who is not feeling well. Nancy promises to help a friend make a cherry pie and to help another friend with a trumpet solo. Because she is so busy, their dad says he will do her mom's errands.

Smith is shown in the bathroom of the bus station, gazing at himself in the mirror. He sees himself as a singer in a Las Vegas club. Hickock wakes him from his daydream, and they begin their drive to Kansas. Along the way, Dick tells Perry about a safe in the Clutter's home with $10,000 that his former cellmate, Floyd Wells, described to him. This means that they will each get $5,000 for about an hour of work. The men stop at a hardware store and buy rope, gloves, and tape. Smith is upset that they were not able to buy black stockings, but Hickock reminds him, they do not need any because they will leave no witnesses. Hickock tells Smith that he was chosen because Smith killed a man before, for no reason.

At the Clutter farm, Nancy asked a friend to pick her up for church in the morning. Mr. Clutter purchased new insurance. In the case of his death, his family will receive $40,000 dollars, but in the case of accidental death, they will be paid double. Nancy's boyfriend, Bobby, comes to watch television. After a short time, Bobby leaves and Mr. Clutter finishes watching the news and weather report. Nancy picks out her clothes for church the next day and says a prayer on her knees beside the bed. They all say goodnight and head off to bed.

Smith and Hickock pull up to the farm with the headlights off. Smith appears nervous. Hickock says, "Look at that spread. Don't tell me this guy ain't loaded." Smith is beginning to have second thoughts. He tells Dick to pull out of here "now before it's too late."

In the next scene, the doorbell rings at the Clutter house. There is no answer. The church bells are ringing. Ladies enter the house, thinking the Clutters are still asleep. They go up the stairs and the viewer hears screams. The police come to the scene and see Nancy's purse on the ground. They find Nancy's body in her bed, and her mother's body in her bed. The bodies of Mr. Clutter and his son are found in the basement. Mr. Clutter had been placed on a mattress and his throat had been cut. A pillow had been placed under Kenyon's head. All of the bodies were tied with the same rope and the same square knot. Their mouths had been taped. One officer takes photos of some footprints found in Mr. Clutter's blood. There are no shell casings, no fingerprints, and no murder weapon. The women had not been molested.

In thinking the motive for the crime was robbery, the housekeeper was called in to look for missing property. The only thing she noticed missing is the boy's radio.

The police note that Mr. Clutter paid for everything with checks so there was no money in the house. Agent Dewey tells reporters that there is little evidence. They report that no one heard gun shots. When asked how the offenders entered the house, police responded that they probably just walked in. They describe that the victims were killed with a 12-gauge shotgun. Two bloody boot prints were found near Mr. Clutter. Because of that, the police knew there were at least two people involved in the crime.

Hickock is shown at his family's house where he ate dinner and watches a news report on television about the Clutter crime. Smith is at a local hotel. He is shown listening to Kenyon's radio, which is broadcasting a report of the Clutter crime.

Because there were so few clues, the police make an appeal to public. To back it up, the offers a reward of $1,000 for any information. A prisoner in the Kansas State Penitentiary, Floyd Wells, hears about the reward and calls the police. He once shared a cell with Hickock, and told him that he once worked for Clutter. Wells told Hickock about Clutter's safe and how much money he had. Hickock told Wells he was going to rob the Clutter's home for the safe and then kill all the witnesses. Based on the information provided by Wells, the police put out a warrant for Hickock and Smith.

The criminals need money to leave the country, so they pass some bad checks. They first buy suits for Smith, some jewelry, video cameras, and a television. They then pawn them and flee to Mexico City. There, Smith dreams about deep sea diving and finding the Cortez jackpot in the Yucatan. It is not long before the two run out of money and have to leave Mexico. Perry mails his belongings back to Las Vegas before they hitchhike back to the US. A man picks them up. Smith is planning to strangle the driver, but he stops to pick up a soldier who also needed a ride.

The police continue to look for clues. They go to interview Smith's father who reported that he has not seen his son in years. They also go to see Hickock's father. At the Hickock farm they find a shotgun and a knife.

Once back in the United States, Hickock and Smith find a car in Iowa. Smith agrees to go to Kansas City with Hickock as long as they go to Las Vegas first to pick up his belongings. They write some bad checks in Kansas, and a salesman writes down the license plate number of the car they are driving. The police look for the stolen car, but the fugitives get away.

As they are driving to Las Vegas, Dick and Perry pick up two hitchhikers, a young boy with his grandfather. They do not have gas money, but have bottles that could be traded in for a deposit. The young boy and Smith picked up bottles along the side of the road and trade them in for $12.60.

The men arrive in Las Vegas to pick up Smith's belongings. They are arrested for driving a stolen car and interrogated separately by the police. Hickock admits to driving a stolen car and breaking parole. Both men explain that they went to see Smith's sister in Fort Scott, but police knew he did not have a sister there. Over time, the police find other discrepancies in their answers. When asked about the Clutter murders, both deny taking part.

The police tell Hickock that the men made three mistakes. First, they left a living witness who could testify against them. Second, the post office in Fort Scott is closed on Saturday so that their alibi does not hold up, and third, the footprint. They showed Hickock the footprints found in Mr. Clutter's blood. One print was Smith's and the other was Hickock's. At that point, Dick blames Perry for everything, saying that Perry pulled the trigger on all of the victims. Then Hickock passed out.

The police drive Hickock and Smith to Kansas. On the way, detectives inform Smith that Hickock blamed all the murders on Smith. At that point,

Smith gives police his version of the crime. He tells them that he tried to back out before committing the crime, but Hickock talked him into it. They parked the car, loaded the weapons, and entered the house through unlocked doors.

Smith continued to explain that they first found Mr. Clutter and took him to the office and asked him about the safe. He denied having one. Smith ripped out the phone lines and took the money from Mr. Clutter's wallet. They went upstairs and into Mrs. Clutter's room. The criminals asked her about the safe but she denied having one. Hickock and Smith made her go into the bathroom, and tied up Mr. Clutter's hands behind his back. They got the son and tied his hands behind his back. At that point, Nancy came out of her room, asking what was going on. The intruders put her in the bathroom with her mother.

They took Mr. Clutter and his son downstairs to the basement, where they tied Mr. Clutter to an overhead pipe. They then tied Kenyon to a couch. Dick went back upstairs to continue to look for the safe. Smith, who was still in the basement, untied Mr. Clutter because he seemed to be cold. He put Mr. Clutter on a mattress on the floor, hogtied him, and taped his mouth shut. Hickock continued to ransack the office looking for the safe or anything of value. He went to the second floor and tied up the daughter. He put her on the bed, returning to tie up Mrs. Clutter, who pleaded for the safety of the children. Hickock started to sexually abuse the girl, but Smith stopped him. They grabbed the son's radio. Smith looked around the girl's room and talked with her about music, art, and horses. He told Nancy that his mother was in the rodeo.

When they could not find a safe, Smith started to panic. He told Hickock that what they were doing was ridiculous. He ran downstairs and had a flashback to when his dad threatened to kill him. Afterwards, he slit Mr. Clutter's throat, leaving a boot print in the blood. Mr. Clutter did not die right away so Smith shot him. He then shot Kenyon, went upstairs and shot Mrs. Clutter, and then shot Nancy.

In their trial, Hickock and Smith plead for mercy and asked for a sentence of life in prison, instead of death. The prosecutor reminds the jury that the crime was planned for the money, and that the family was slaughtered like hogs. The criminals brought weapons with them to commit the crime, including a shotgun, a dagger, and rope. It was obviously not a crime of passion. The offenders got $40 — 10 dollars a life. They reminded the jurors of the passage from the Bible: "This is the sign of the covenant which I am making between me and you and every living creature that is with you, for all successive generations" (Genesis 9:12).

The defense took one and a half hours to present their case. An expert in forensic medicine claimed that neither man would have done it alone, but together they made a third personality and that is the one that did it.

It took the jury only 40 minutes to find the defendants guilty. The offenders were taken to death row and an execution was planned for Friday, May 13. As a matter of routine, the convicts appealed their sentences and were granted a stay of execution, also routine. In Kansas at that time, the legal machinery typically ran a year or more for sentences of death. The case went to the US Supreme Court three times. After five years, the execution date was set. They were to be executed on April 14, 1965.

Hickock was executed first. Prison officials read him the court order mandating his hanging. He said he had no hard feelings, and that they were sending him to a better world than this ever was. After the execution took place, officials put Hickock's body in a hearse and drove it away. Smith was then brought in. He wanted to apologize, but asked, whom to? Officials place a hood over his head, he spit out his chewing gum, and was hanged.

In Cold Blood: Hollywood's Rendering

The movie *In Cold Blood* was released in 1967 and was based on a book of the same name by Truman Capote. The movie was directed by Richard Brooks and starred Robert Blake as Perry Smith, Scott Wilson as Dick Hickock, and John Forsythe as Alvin Dewey. The film was nominated for four Academy Awards. In 1996, there was a television remake of the movie and book. To portray the events realistically, parts of the movie were filmed at the actual locations. For example, the bus station in Kansas City where Smith met up with Hickock, the gas station where Hickock stopped on the way to meeting Smith, sites in Las Vegas, the actual store where the men bought the tape that was used to bind the Clutters, and the Clutter home itself were all filming sites. Many of same spectators and reporters were in the crowd when the men were brought back to Kansas. Seven jurors appearing in the film were actual jurors who served on the trial.

Despite the use of actual settings and people, there were multiple historical inaccuracies in the movie. To begin with, members and details of the Clutter family are omitted from the story. There are four children in the actual family, but the two older daughters are not mentioned in the film. In fact, there are only two children in the framed family pictures on Mr. Clutter's desk. At the time of the murders, the oldest daughter, Eveanna, lived in Northern Illinois with her husband and 10-month-old son. The next oldest child was Beverly, who was studying to be a nurse in Kansas City, Kansas, and was engaged to a biology student. Additionally, Clutter's wife, Bonnie, had a long history of mental illness. This was alluded to but not made explicit in the film.

There were some inaccuracies about the events surrounding the murders and the events that followed. In the movie, Smith is shown slicing Mr. Clutter's throat but then it quickly turns to the next scene. In actuality, that event was much more gruesome. Smith didn't cut deep enough and Mr. Clutter was left gasping for air and struggling to stay alive. This went on for some time before he was shot.

The film made it clear that there was little evidence left by the murderers, which is what really happened. However, some of the evidence had been buried by the offenders, which was not portrayed in the film. In reality, Smith and Hickock buried some of the evidence of their crime upon leaving the Clutter home. They buried the knife, the extra rope and the shotgun shells that remained after shooting the evidence. This was not shown in the movie. Still further, neither Smith nor Hickock were seen picking up the shotgun shells or disposing of the evidence after leaving the home in the film.

More inaccuracies appear in the events after the murders take place. In the movie, the Clutters' murdered bodies were found by ladies on their way to church who stop by the Clutters home. But in reality, Nancy's friend entered the home first and found Nancy's body in her bedroom. After that, the sheriff was called to the home. He later found the remains of the other family members.

Some inaccuracies revolve around the investigation of the murders. Although the film shows that a footprint was found at the scene, the footprint in the movie was much more detailed than the footprint found at the scene of the crime. At the true murder scene, only a print of Perry's heel was found. Furthermore, the movie does not show that the investigator's first suspect was a man named Bobby Rupp, Nancy Clutter's boyfriend, who was not in favor with Mr. Clutter. Investigators gave him a lie detector test, which he passed. This was omitted from the film.

After the crimes were committed, the offenders traveled extensively to escape law enforcement. Although this was partly shown in the film, there was no mention of Hickock and Smith travelling to Miami over Christmas. In the movie the killers are shown travelling to Mexico, California, and Las Vegas, but the producers neglect to mention they spent time in Miami, Florida, as well.

After they were caught, Hickock talked to the police immediately and pointed to Smith as the murderer. In the movie, Smith never actually blamed Hickock for murdering the family members. However, in real life Smith first admitted only to killing the two men, and claimed that Hickock was the one responsible for killing the two women. It was not until a while later that he eventually admitted that he did in fact kill all the family members and confessed that Dick had told the truth originally. He wanted Dick's mother to know that her son did not kill them.[75]

In the movie, the detectives are having a conversation with Perry while in transport back to Kansas. During this conversation they reveal to Perry that Dick has told them that it was he alone who pulled the trigger on the entire family. It is at this point that Perry admits to the murders and recounts the entire night's events. This is inaccurate for a couple reasons. First of all, Perry did not make a statement regarding the murders until he was back in custody in Kansas. The second problem with this is that Perry originally blamed Dick for murdering the women although he later told detectives that it was he alone who pulled the trigger on all of them. In the movie he admits to all four killings the first time.

This fact, as well as those mentioned earlier, may have been omitted to keep the film at a reasonable length. The movie as produced was over two hours. Other details were omitted from the film, more than likely due to time constraints. One of those is a hunger strike by Smith. In the period after his trial but before he was executed, Smith did not eat for a period of time as a sign of protest. He started eating again only after receiving a letter from his father. This was not shown in the movie.

In the criminal trial for Hickock and Smith, the quote used from the Bible is actually Genesis 9:6, not Genesis 9:12. In the movie's version of the court proceedings, the prosecutor cited, "This is the sign of the covenant which I am making between me and you and every living creature that is with you, for all successive generations." In real life court the actual quote was from Genesis 9, verse 6, which states, "Whoever sheds man's blood, by man, shall his blood be shed."[76]

In the movie, Hickock's last words were "goodbye, I'm going to a better place" and then he smiled and walked up the stairs. In reality he said goodbye to some of the people attending the execution, and said, "I just want to say I hold no hard feelings. You people are sending me to a much better place than this has been." On his way to the gallows he saw Dewey and stopped to shake his hand. He said, "Nice to see you." Then climbed the steps.[77]

Smith's final words were also inaccurate. The film had Smith say "I guess I'd like to apologize for this and I'm sorry for what happened to the Clutter family." In actuality, Smith said, "I am surprised this is my sentence," and "I really have a lot to offer the world." He would not walk up the stairs to the noose and employees were forced to carry him. This also did not appear in the movie.

Truman Capote, who was largely responsible for the public's knowledge and interest in the killings, was never mentioned in the film. After reading a short article about the killings, Capote decided to write a series of articles for the *New Yorker*. Eventually, the articles were turned into a novel. Capote worked on his novel for years, and often visited the men while they were in prison and spent time getting to know them. He analyzed their personalities and the decisions they made. Capote watched Hickock's execution, but could not stay for Smith's. In his will, Smith left his belongings to Capote. The movie did not show this.

Some allege that Smith and Capote had a sexual relationship, or that Smith and Hickock had a relationship. This would explain why Smith reacted when Hickock was about to rape Nancy Clutter. It is also alleged that Hickock was attracted to young girls, which disgusted Perry, which also would explain why he stopped Hickock from raping Nancy.[78]

The movie includes a character of a reporter, but that was a fictional character used to show the media was involved in the case and to help provide some information to the viewers. The reporter was shown talking with police much of the time, attempting to gather information and clues from them so he could publish them. He is seen throughout the film, from the beginning, when he interviews the police after the murders, until the courthouse when Smith and Hickock are on trial. He was also shown at the execution.

Finally, the movie doesn't expand on the appeals to the Kansas State Supreme Court. There were multiple automatic appeals because it was a death penalty case, and the appeals went on for quite some time. If one were to simply watch the movie, they would have the impression that the killers were executed soon after the trial, which did not happen.

Conclusion

The movie *In Cold Blood* was based on an event made popular by the book by Truman Capote. The movie was one of the first that detailed the gruesome murders of an entire family for no real reason from start to finish: from before the crime occurred to the execution of the offenders and all the events in between. The film was entertaining yet at the same time factual, despite small inconsistencies throughout that distort the reality of what happened the night of the Clutter murders. It is an example of a successful motion picture that adequately depicts the true events fairly accurately, possibly because it is based on one specific book.

Further Reading

Algeo, Ann M. (1996). *The Courtroom as a Forum.* New York: P. Lang.
Capote, Truman. (1965). *In Cold Blood.* New York: Random House.
Clarke, Gerald. (1989). *Capote: A Biography.* New York: Ballantine.

Creeger, George R. (1967). *Animals in Exile: Imagery and Theme in Capote's* In Cold Blood. Middletown, Connecticut: Center for Advanced Studies.

Davis, Deborah. (2006). *Party of the Century.* Hoboken, N.J.: John Wiley.

Goad, Craig M. (1967). *Daylight and Darkness, Dream and Delusion: The Works of Truman Capote.* Emporia, Kansas: Kansas State Teacher's College.

Guest, David. (1997). *Sentenced to Death: The American Novel and Capital Punishment.* Jackson: University Press of Mississippi.

Malin, Irving. (1968). *Truman Capote's* In Cold Blood: *A Critical Handbook.* Belmont, CA: Wadsworth.

Nance, William L. (1973). *The Worlds of Truman Capote.* New York: Stein and Day.

Windham, Donald. (1989). *Footnote to a Friendship: A Memoir of Truman Capote and Others.* New York: Paragon House.

Endnotes

1. As the film was based upon the book by Truman Capote, and for the fact Capote's book is the primary source for this particular case, the majority of citations for this chapter will come from Capote's research. In addition, for closer scrutiny and verification, even when paraphrasing, page numbers will be included in the citations. Capote, Truman. (1965). *In Cold Blood.* New York: Random House, p. 12.
2. Capote, Truman. (1965). *In Cold Blood.* New York: Random House, p. 6.
3. Capote, Truman. (1965). *In Cold Blood.* New York: Random House, p. 5.
4. Capote, Truman. (1965). *In Cold Blood.* New York: Random House, p. 46.
5. Capote, Truman. (1965). *In Cold Blood.* New York: Random House, p. 7.
6. Capote, Truman. (1965). *In Cold Blood.* New York: Random House, p. 27.
7. Capote, Truman. (1965). *In Cold Blood.* New York: Random House, p. 18.
8. Capote, Truman. (1965). *In Cold Blood.* New York: Random House, p. 20.
9. Capote, Truman. (1965). *In Cold Blood.* New York: Random House, p. 8.
10. Capote, Truman. (1965). *In Cold Blood.* New York: Random House, p. 22.
11. Capote, Truman. (1965). *In Cold Blood.* New York: Random House, pp. 30–31.
12. Capote, Truman. (1965). *In Cold Blood.* New York: Random House, p.31.
13. Capote, Truman. (1965). *In Cold Blood.* New York: Random House, p. 45.
14. Capote, Truman. (1965). *In Cold Blood.* New York: Random House, p. 14.
15. Capote, Truman. (1965). *In Cold Blood.* New York: Random House, p. 23.
16. Capote, Truman. (1965). *In Cold Blood.* New York: Random House, p. 23.
17. Capote, Truman. (1965). *In Cold Blood.* New York: Random House, p. 48.
18. Capote, Truman. (1965). *In Cold Blood.* New York: Random House, p. 38.
19. Capote, Truman. (1965). *In Cold Blood.* New York: Random House, p. 35.
20. Capote, Truman. (1965). *In Cold Blood.* New York: Random House, pp. 40, 46, 48.
21. Capote, Truman. (1965). *In Cold Blood.* New York: Random House, p. 37.
22. Capote, Truman. (1965). *In Cold Blood.* New York: Random House, p. 53.
23. Capote, Truman. (1965). *In Cold Blood.* New York: Random House, p. 54.
24. Capote, Truman. (1965). *In Cold Blood.* New York: Random House, p. 55.

25. Capote, Truman. (1965). *In Cold Blood*. New York: Random House, p. 62.
26. Capote, Truman. (1965). *In Cold Blood*. New York: Random House, p. 63.
27. Capote, Truman. (1965). *In Cold Blood*. New York: Random House, p. 64.
28. Capote, Truman. (1965). *In Cold Blood*. New York: Random House, p. 65.
29. Capote, Truman. (1965). *In Cold Blood*. New York: Random House, p. 96.
30. Capote, Truman. (1965). *In Cold Blood*. New York: Random House, p. 80.
31. Capote, Truman. (1965). *In Cold Blood*. New York: Random House, p. 102.
32. Capote, Truman. (1965). *In Cold Blood*. New York: Random House, p. 102.
33. Capote, Truman. (1965). *In Cold Blood*. New York: Random House, pp. 72, 84.
34. Capote, Truman. (1965). *In Cold Blood*. New York: Random House, p. 102.
35. Capote, Truman. (1965). *In Cold Blood*. New York: Random House, p. 83.
36. Capote, Truman. (1965). *In Cold Blood*. New York: Random House, p. 102.
37. Capote, Truman. (1965). *In Cold Blood*. New York: Random House, pp. 73–74.
38. Capote, Truman. (1965). *In Cold Blood*. New York: Random House, p. 97.
39. Capote, Truman. (1965). *In Cold Blood*. New York: Random House, pp. 98–99.
40. Capote, Truman. (1965). *In Cold Blood*. New York: Random House, p. 106.
41. Capote, Truman. (1965). *In Cold Blood*. New York: Random House, p. 108.
42. Capote, Truman. (1965). *In Cold Blood*. New York: Random House, p. 119.
43. Capote, Truman. (1965). *In Cold Blood*. New York: Random House, p. 118.
44. Capote, Truman. (1965). *In Cold Blood*. New York: Random House, p. 125.
45. Capote, Truman. (1965). *In Cold Blood*. New York: Random House, p. 159.
46. Capote, Truman. (1965). *In Cold Blood*. New York: Random House, pp. 161–162.
47. Capote, Truman. (1965). *In Cold Blood*. New York: Random House, p. 171.
48. Capote, Truman. (1965). *In Cold Blood*. New York: Random House, p. 172.
49. Capote, Truman. (1965). *In Cold Blood*. New York: Random House, p. 174.
50. Capote, Truman. (1965). *In Cold Blood*. New York: Random House, p. 187.
51. Capote, Truman. (1965). *In Cold Blood*. New York: Random House, p. 189.
52. Capote, Truman. (1965). *In Cold Blood*. New York: Random House, p. 195.
53. Capote, Truman. (1965). *In Cold Blood*. New York: Random House, p. 198.
54. Capote, Truman. (1965). *In Cold Blood*. New York: Random House, p. 200.
55. Capote, Truman. (1965). *In Cold Blood*. New York: Random House, p. 202.
56. Capote, Truman. (1965). *In Cold Blood*. New York: Random House, p. 211.
57. Capote, Truman. (1965). *In Cold Blood*. New York: Random House, p. 175.
58. Capote, Truman. (1965). *In Cold Blood*. New York: Random House, p. 216.
59. Capote, Truman. (1965). *In Cold Blood*. New York: Random House, p. 239.
60. Capote, Truman. (1965). *In Cold Blood*. New York: Random House, p. 241.
61. Capote, Truman. (1965). *In Cold Blood*. New York: Random House, p. 257.
62. Capote, Truman. (1965). *In Cold Blood*. New York: Random House, p. 266.
63. Capote, Truman. (1965). *In Cold Blood*. New York: Random House, p. 280.
64. Capote, Truman. (1965). *In Cold Blood*. New York: Random House, p. 307.
65. Capote, Truman. (1965). *In Cold Blood*. New York: Random House, p. 309.
66. Capote, Truman. (1965). *In Cold Blood*. New York: Random House, p. 317.
67. Capote, Truman. (1965). *In Cold Blood*. New York: Random House, p. 326.
68. Capote, Truman. (1965). *In Cold Blood*. New York: Random House, p. 327.
69. Capote, Truman. (1965). *In Cold Blood*. New York: Random House, p. 330.
70. Capote, Truman. (1965). *In Cold Blood*. New York: Random House, p. 336.
71. Capote, Truman. (1965). *In Cold Blood*. New York: Random House, p. 337.

72. Capote, Truman. (1965). *In Cold Blood*. New York: Random House, p. 339.

73. Capote, Truman. (1965). *In Cold Blood*. New York: Random House, p. 337.

74. Capote, Truman. (1965). *In Cold Blood*. New York: Random House, p. 340.

75. TruTV. (2011). The Clutter Family Killings – *In Cold Blood*. Retrieved online at http://www.trutv.com/library/crime/notorious_murders/family/clutter/8.html.

76. Capote, Truman. (1965). *In Cold Blood*. New York: Random House, p. 304; Internet Movie Database. (2011). *In Cold Blood* (1967). Retrieved online at http://www.imdb.com/title/tt0061809/.

77. TruTV. (2011). The Clutter Family Killings – *In Cold Blood*. Retrieved online at http://www.trutv.com/library/crime/notorious_murders/family/clutter/8.html.

78. Internet Movie Database. (2011). *In Cold Blood* (1967). Retrieved online at http://www.imdb.com/title/tt0061809/; TruTV. (2011). The Clutter Family Killings – *In Cold Blood*. Retrieved online at http://www.trutv.com/library/crime/notorious_murders/family/clutter/8.html.

CHAPTER 8

Escape from Alcatraz and the Alcatraz Prison (1962)

Alcatraz Island, home to many notorious criminals, but closed shortly after Frank Morris, John Anglin, and Clarence Anglin escaped from Cell Block B. Photo courtesy of the Library of Congress.

No one has ever escaped from Alcatraz and no one ever will.
— Warden to inmate (and escapee) Morris
upon his arrival at Alcatraz

Introduction

Alcatraz Island is a 12-acre land mass in the middle of San Francisco Bay. It has served as a military fort, a military prison, and a temporary jail after an earthquake struck California in 1906. The island seemed to be the perfect place to build an escape-proof prison. In the 1930s, when a public outcry erupted over rising violence associated with Prohibition, the Federal Bureau of Prisons turned the existing structures into a super-maximum security facility for America's worst criminals. On August 18, 1934, the first criminal inmates arrived on Alcatraz.

The first warden of the prison, James A. Johnston, was the former warden from Folsom and San Quentin.[1] To create his escape-proof prison, Johnson replaced iron bars in the cells with steel bars, installed automatic locking devices, tear-gas outlets were installed throughout the prison, gun galleries were set up at both ends of the cell-house, as well as an outside gun-walk for guards to watch inmates more closely. He asked for steel doors on the utility corridors that existed between the cell blocks, ordered gun towers connected with catwalks, and placed a barbed wire fence around the entire prison.[2] There were metal detectors placed at different locations in the prison, as well as the yard that inmates would have to pass through.

The prison was designed to hold the nation's most notorious prisoners— those men with the biggest behavioral problems and those who had killed others. Most men there had either escaped, or attempted to escape, from other prisons. It held men like "Machine Gun" Kelley, "Baby Face" Nelson, Al Capone, Alvin "Old Creepy" Karpis, George "Bugs" Moran, Mickey Cohen, and Robert Stroud, otherwise known as "The Bird Man of Alcatraz."

The prison had four blocks, A, B, C and D. A block was used only for storage. B and C blocks had a total of 336 cells in double banks of triple tiers. Between C and D blocks was a utility corridor, sometimes called "the tunnel," that included the sewer pipes, water mains, and electrical conduits for the cells. The tunnel was not accessible to the convicts. At the tier levels in the corridor were plank catwalks for plumbers and repairmen when they were needed. D was the isolation, or treatment, block.

Each inmate had his own cell. Each cell was five feet wide by eight feet long with a steel cot on the right side and a toilet without a lid or a seat in the back. On the side wall were two shelves, and the opposite wall was a washbowl with a faucet. Above the sink were two more shelves and two pegs for hanging clothes. The rear wall was concrete, and the side walls made of sheets of steel. The cell bars were cores of cable embedded with alloy steel.

The prison was run by a philosophy of punishment rather than treatment. As such, the prisoners were not permitted to speak to each other unless absolutely necessary for the first three years after it opened.[3] The inmates could talk only in the shops and during a three minute rest period in the morning and three minutes in the afternoon. They could also speak to each other in the yard on Sunday afternoons. The rule was rescinded in 1937.[4]

The inmates awakened at 6:30 AM and had ten minutes to wash and get dressed. After being counted, they marched to the dining hall and had 20 minutes to eat breakfast. They then went to the yard for work assignments until 11:40. Then, the inmates came in for lunch. At noon they were sent to their cells for another count, returning to the yard and to work detail. The work day ended at 4:15. The inmates were counted again before allowed 20 minutes to eat dinner. At 4:45, they would be locked in cells for the evening. The lights were turned out at 9:30 p.m.[5]

Alcatraz prison had the highest ratio of guards to inmates, with one guard for every three inmates. The inmates were counted every 15 minutes with many other unscheduled counts and cell inspections.[6] Many of the guards were transferred from other federal prisons and were expert marksmen with orders to "shoot to kill." They had special training in judo and how to cope with unruly inmates.[7] In the evenings after lock-up, the guards would have target practice and shoot at dummies dressed as inmates. They would then leave the torn-up dummies in the yard.[8]

By the 1960s, the rules at Alcatraz had softened a bit. There were fewer shakedowns. Some inmates had musical instruments they were allowed to play, and they were even allowed to knit, a hobby that required sharp needles. After the lights were turned off, the men could talk to their neighbors or the inmates across the corridor, or even to those in the tier above or below. With the more relaxed rules came a more relaxed atmosphere among guards.[9] The prison also had deteriorating conditions, a result of the salt water.

Over its history, there were many escape attempts from Alcatraz. While the prison was open, there were 14 escape attempts involving 36 men. Every one of them failed. Some of the inmates died violently; some were shot to death; some drowned. Those who did not die were recaptured.

But on June 11, 1962, three prisoners may have successfully escaped by use of an ingenious plan that took over a year to carry out. Three inmates, Frank Morris, along with brothers John and Clarence Anglin, devised a carefully planned and executed escape plot that may be the best prison escape in Alcatraz history, or even prison history. Whether the men survived has never been determined. While many say they drowned in the Bay, others are convinced the men survived and are living in Florida, Georgia, and even South America.

Escape from Alcatraz: The History

On January 14, 1960, a boat named the *Warden Johnston* left the dock to take some visitors to the prison at Alcatraz. Among its passengers was a new inmate named Frank Lee Morris, a bank burglar and escape artist from Georgia. The boat arrived at the island and the other passengers, including a doctor on his daily visit, disembarked. The new inmate left the boat, passed through a metal detector, and climbed into a bus. The bus travelled along a narrow road to the prison, where a guard opened the gate. The prisoner and guards stepped into a vestibule and turned into the visitors' room. The manacles, midriff chain and leg irons were removed from the inmate and he was ordered to strip. A doctor conducted a search of his ears, nose, mouth and rectum for contraband. The naked prisoner was led into the cell-house. The prisoner was surprised that the cell blocks were painted shocking pink and trimmed in red.

The naked inmate was escorted down the aisle between two cell blocks. The guard took him to the shower room, where the officer noted his tattoos. The inmate showered then received a set of fresh clothes and new shoes. He walked back to the cell house, climbed a circular stairway at the end of C Block and went to the middle tier to his cell. His name was already on the door. This cell was in a quarantine section (the inside half of C Block on Broadway), where he would stay locked up except to eat and shower until he was fully processed, which would take about a week or two. He would then be assigned a job in the prison. Later that day, the associate warden dropped by and explained the rules to the inmate. He told Morris the discipline is never inhumane. He said, "good behavior begets good time, and good time means a shortened term."10

Morris was a soft-spoken man, a loner, who appeared to be personable and courteous. He was identified as having superior intelligence (an IQ of 133),11 but at the same time a potential escape problem.12 Morris had a troubled background. His mother and father both abandoned him as a child and he was placed in a foster home.13 Later he told the FBI his parents died in 1937.14 As a youth, he turned to crime and spent time in various state prisons. He was eventually sent to the federal penitentiary in Atlanta for a bank robbery and, in January of 1960, he was transferred to Alcatraz to finish the remaining time on a ten-year sentence.

On his 12th day in Alcatraz, Morris was assigned the job of cleaning vegetables in the kitchen. He was moved into cell number 138 on the bottom row of B Block. In the cell next to him was Allen Clayton West. West was in Alcatraz for driving a stolen car across state lines, a federal crime. West played an accordion. A few weeks later, Morris was given another job as the library messenger in the mornings, delivering books and magazines to inmates. Later he was assigned to an industrial job.15

One night at dinner, Morris saw John Anglin, whom he had met in prison in Atlanta. John and his brother, Clarence, had been transferred from Leavenworth and were in cells 140 and 142, next to each other, four down from Morris. The Anglin brothers had all been in and out of jail since they were teenagers for petty offenses. They were sent to reform school but broke out. After they committed a bank robbery with a toy pistol, the brothers were given a sentence of over 30 years. Both Anglins were sent first to Leavenworth but tried to escape and were sent to Alcatraz.

At dinner one night in the spring of 1961, Morris told the Anglins about a plan for escape. They included a fourth inmate, Alan Clayton West. West had been in Alcatraz since June of 1958 and had spent a lot of time in solitary, giving him the opportunity to plot an escape. West was an inmate janitor who was responsible for painting the cell house. This meant that he had to stand on scaffolding in different places around the cell block. While he was on the scaffolding, he saw a vent in the ceiling of B Block that led to the roof of the prison. However, the vent was covered with bars that were out of his reach.[16] West claims to have told Morris about the vent, which gave him the idea for the escape.

To get to the vent, the inmates could use the utility corridor located behind the row of cells. It was filled with pipes for the plumbing for the cells. The inmates realized that if they could get into this corridor, they could easily climb to the top of cell block. Then they could enter the ventilator shaft and climb onto the roof of the prison. The prisoners could then climb down the building to the water's edge and leave the island.

The first obstacle was getting into the utility corridor from the cells. The only way to do this was to go through the air vent in the back of every cell. The vents were small and buried in eight-inch thick concrete. One fall evening in 1961, Morris was clipping his nails in his cell when he began to look more closely at the vent. It was covered by a small metal grille. Even if the grille could be removed, the hole would be too small to crawl through.[17] Nonetheless, Morris began to pick at the concrete surrounding the grille. When pieces of concrete fell off easily, he continued to dig.[18]

Morris told the three others what he discovered. The men started to dig around their vents with whatever tools they had. Morris found the nail clipper was hard to grip and wanted a better digging tool. One day he stole a spoon from the cafeteria, and Morris was able to use silver scrapings from a dime to weld the spoon and the nail clippers together to make a better digging tool.[19] At one point, Morris decided to make a wedge out of scrap metal at the prison shop where he worked to help him force the grille out. On the way out of the shop, Morris was searched by the guards. When the guard asked him about the wedge, Morris told him it was a clothes peg. Surprisingly, the guard let him go.[20]

The four inmates were able to conceal the noise made by their digging by working while other inmates practiced their instruments. In Alcatraz, the inmates were permitted to practice on musical instruments for one hour in the evening. Some inmates played saxophones, others guitars, accordions, or trumpets. This was quite loud, and allowed the inmates to dig undetected. There was also some construction in the cell house at that time which also helped to cover the noise from the digging.[21]

As the holes became bigger and more obvious, the inmates needed to find ways to disguise the openings. At first, Morris ordered an accordion that he placed strategically to hide the hole.[22] He then had the idea to make a fake grille out of cardboard which he could place in the opening. To do this, Morris told the others to order magazines and keep the pages with ads on both sides, which wouldn't be missed. He used the magazine pages to make a mash of pulp. With this, he formed a cardboard grille that he could place in the hole he was creating.

Soon Morris was able to squeeze his shoulders through the vent and stick his head into the utility corridor.[23] After several more months of digging, he could squeeze his entire body through the vent hole and enter the utility corridor. He could then leave his cell at night and explore the inside of the prison corridor. To do this, he needed to have a way to hide his absence from the guards. Using the same material he used to make the cardboard grille, Morris formed a dummy head.[24] Another inmate, "Whitey" Thompson, helped Morris order art supplies and showed him how to mix the color of flesh from the paint. The fake heads were covered with human hair that Clarence Anglin collected from his job in the prison barber shop. The men placed the dummy heads on their cots when they left their cells so it appeared to guards that they were sleeping.

One night Morris and Clarence Anglin met in the corridor to examine the air vent that led to the prison roof more closely. The vent was protected with bars. Discouraged, the inmates realized they would need a drill to remove the bars. At the end of a music session one evening in the prison, Morris was able to steal a fan. He took the blades off the fan and inserted a drill that he stole from the prison workshop. After trying the new drill on the bars, he realized it wasn't strong enough.[25]

The inmates then tried to remove the bars with "Carborundum" string, a cord impregnated with an abrasive such as raw grains of silicon carbine, aluminum oxide, or diamond powder. It was used in the shop for certain repairs. Most of the time, the guards measured the amount of string the inmates needed, and then measured it again when returned, but they had been forgetting to do so. Another inmate took a two-foot length of string but only returned one foot, giving the other foot to Morris.[26] The inmates were able to use this string to remove the bars from the vent.

Once the bars were off, the men faced another dilemma: How would they get off the island? They needed some type of boat to get across the Bay. While reading the November issue of *Popular Mechanics* and a May 21 article of *Sports Illustrated* magazine, the men found a solution. The articles explained how to create life jackets and an inflatable raft. Using this information, the men smuggled dozens of raincoats and stole liquid plastic from the workshops to make a raft and life preservers. Since the guards did not keep inventory of the raincoats, they did not notice when they disappeared. At one point, John Anglin wore two raincoats into the prison after work. When asked why he had two, he told the guard he was cold.

The raft took many months to complete. The final product was 14 feet by six feet and made out of 40–80 waterproof raincoats that were sewn together. The sleeves of the raincoats were stuffed with toilet paper and both ends tied to serve as "water wings," or flotation devices for the escapees.[27]

Throughout these preparations, the inmates needed to find a place to hide their tools and the raft materials. They found some space on top of the cell block during one of their nightly trips out of their cells. The area was a mesh-wire cage that was an unmanned east gun gallery. The men could stand up in it and could easily use the area as a workshop. West was able to convince the guards to hang up 40 to 60 blankets to prevent dust and paint from splatter-ing on the floors below while he cleaned and painted the top of the cell blocks. The real reason to hang blankets was to hide the materials they were collect-ing related to the escape. Not only did the guards allow West to hang the blan-kets, but they allowed them to hang for more than two months. At one point the inmates had around 50 raincoats, water wings, liquid plastic, a fan motor, an extra electric cord, part of a vacuum cleaner motor that had proved useless, two electric drills, six small saw blades, a file, two short pieces of steel and an eight-inch length of scrap metal, and two plywood oars that the inmates had shaped on the shop lathe, all in the top of the cell block, undetected by guards.[28]

The men were finally ready to attempt their escape. Morris read the tide charts and maps from the prison library. They decided to escape on a Mon-day night, June 11, 1962. Oddly, prison guards searched the cells of the An-glin brothers on the Saturday before the escape attempt. John's bathrobe was hanging over the fake vent grille, and during the search, the guards moved it to another peg. Clarence had a large towel with the original owner's name (UNITED STATES MARINE CORPS) hanging over his vent.[29]

Because the warden was on vacation, Arthur Dallus, the associate warden, was on duty the night of the escape. After lights out at 9:30 PM, each man placed his dummy head on his cot and pulled the blankets up around it to make it appear as if they were sleeping. Crawling through the vents, the men each left their cells, placing the fake grilles in the vents behind them. They en-tered the utility corridor and met there, but only three men appeared. West was not able to remove his grille because a few days before, West had put some glue on his grille because it kept falling out.[30] Morris and the Anglins could-n't wait for him and had to go without him.[31]

The three men climbed to the top of the cell block. During the climb, one inmate dropped a bar, making a loud clanging noise as it fell, but the guards did not react. The men made it to the top of the cell block. Once there, they had to complete the raft. When that was done, the men climbed onto the roof through the air vent. On the roof they scared some seagulls that flew away, but the guards ignored the commotion. When one inmate came out of the shaft, he leaned over to lay the top aside, but a gust of wind snatched it, and it clattered to the roof.[32] Again, no guard reacted to the noise.

The men climbed down the outside of the five-story prison building on a pipe. They scaled the barbed wire fence, carefully picked their way over the barbed wire and climbed down the other side.[33] They ran past the water tower and down a grassy hill,[34] where they entered the Bay. The guards did not see any of this activity. An imprint of the raft was found near the water. After that, the three men disappeared forever.

West was eventually able to get out of his cell and onto the roof of the prison around midnight, but the others were already gone. On the roof of the prison he found an unfinished pontoon, a paddle, three life preservers, and his own fake head.[35] He waited there awhile, but soon realized he was too late, he went back inside the prison and returned to his bed.

The next morning, when the wake-up bell rang, over nine hours had passed since the inmates left. The guards blew a whistle to indicate the first inmate count of the day, but the three escapees did not get out of bed or stand up. When the guards reached into the cell to wake them up, their heads fell onto the floor.[36] The acting warden Dollison got the call that inmates were possibly missing, and the search for the escapees began immediately. The siren went off. Because of the hole in the back of his cell, West had to acknowledge he was part of the escape plan. He was questioned and cooperated, providing some details about the escape, but not all.

Dozens of guards searched the island and the prison grounds, and the Coast Guard was called in to search for bodies in the water. They checked the many caves where the men could be hiding. The search was one of the largest manhunts in history, covering air, land, and sea. Even soldiers from the Presidio of San Francisco were called in to search Angel Island, but they discovered no clues to the whereabouts of the men. Other inmates were questioned, but none of them provided much information.

Prison officials doubted the men could make it to San Francisco on a raft made from old raincoats and announced they had drowned. FBI agents, who had been called in to help with the search, assumed that the men succeeded. Hundreds of leads poured in from public but there was little evidence as to what happened to the prisoners. A few months after the escape, US Attorney General Robert Kennedy announced that the prison would be phased out by 1963. He said, "it would be a savings to the taxpayers because it's so much more expensive to feed prisoners there than at any other federal prison."[37]

Escape from Alcatraz: The Film

The possible escape from Alcatraz has fascinated the public for many years. There have been many motion pictures about the escape attempt, including *Alcatraz Island, The Birdman of Alcatraz, King of Alcatraz, Alcatraz Express,* and *Escape from Alcatraz.* The movie *Escape from Alcatraz* is based on the book by J. Campbell Bruce.[38] The movie stars Clint Eastwood as Frank Morris, one of the escapees. The film's co-stars include Fred Ward as John Anglin, Jack Thibeau as Clarence Anglin, and Patrick McGoohan as the prison warden. The movie, released in 1979, is rated PG.[39]

The first scene takes place on a cold, rainy night as an inmate is being taken to Alcatraz Island on a small boat. He is heavily guarded and shackled for the entire trip. Upon arriving at the island, the inmate is taken off the boat, put in a van, and driven to the door of the prison. A spotlight follows it for the short drive. During the prisoner intake process, the viewer learns the prisoner's last name is Morris. He is checked by a doctor for lice, and the inside of his ears, mouth, nose, are examined, as are his eyes. He is forced to walk naked down the cell block to his cell. While locking him in the cell, a guard says, "Welcome to Alcatraz."

In the morning, the inmates are awakened and counted. The inmates leave their cells and walk to breakfast in a single file line. They are all wearing blue button-down shirts and gray pants. A fellow inmate tells Morris to button his collar. At breakfast, the inmates are not provided with forks with which to eat their pasta. Another inmate says, "I see pasta in my sleep." Morris gives his plate of food to the other inmate.

Morris watches as another inmate, whose name turns out to be Litmus, has brought his pet mouse to breakfast and was feeding it pasta. He explains that he is nicknamed Litmus because his face turns color based on the temperature. It turns blue when it is cold and red when it is hot. Morris sees another inmate from across the room and they make eye contact. It is not a friendly look.

The inmates have a short time to eat and then return to their cells. Morris is called out of his cell to see the prison warden. There, viewers discover the inmate's full name is Frank Lee Morris. The warden tells him that Alcatraz is not like any other prison in the US. Each inmate is confined alone to his individual cell. There are no programs for good conduct, and there are no counselors. Inmates have no say in what they do and must do as they are told. There are no newspapers or knowledge of the outside world other than what officials report. The inmates shave once a day, shower twice a week, and have their hair cut once a month. Work and talking are privileges that must be earned. He can receive two visitors a month but they cannot be former inmates. Morris responds that he has no family and will have no visitors.

The warden continues. He tells Morris that Alcatraz is a maximum security prison with few privileges. He notes that Morris has escaped from quite a few prisons. He tells the new inmate that the super-maximum facility was built to keep all the rotten eggs in one basket. Only a few people have tried to escape, and most have been recaptured. Those that have not been recaptured have been killed or drowned in the Bay. Upon leaving the office, the warden notes that Morris's file indicates that he has a high I.Q. and is of superior intelligence. Viewers also see Morris steal nail clippers from the warden, hiding them in a Bible in his cell.

Next is a shower scene in which Litmus brings his pet mouse to get washed. The inmate from the dining hall then comes over to Morris. Morris tells the inmate, named Wolf, that he came from Atlanta. Wolf tells Morris he is looking for a new punk. Morris responds by punching Wolf and stuffing a bar of soap in his mouth.

Morris is assigned to work in the prison library. Another inmate working there, English, tells Morris that he was in a bar in Alabama when two white men started hassling him. He pulled two 99-year sentences. Since being in Alcatraz, he slashed his Achilles tendon to get out. Morris leaves to deliver books on a cart to inmates.

The scene switches to the yard where inmates are outside. One inmate named Doc is painting a picture of himself with a chrysanthemum in his pocket. He tells Morris, "You hurt Wolf, now Wolf's gonna hurt you." Morris leaves Doc and goes to sit on the steps. He goes to see English, who tells him, the higher you sit on the steps the more status you have. Since English was at the top, he's the king. English tells Morris that no one's ever made it out of Alcatraz, because "there ain't any way out." There is one guard for every three cons. Each bar has six smaller bars set in a steel tube with extra steel cording. If a person does get out, it is over a mile swim to the land with currents make it seem like ten. English tells Morris the water so is cold it will numb arms in a matter of minutes. Plus, the inmates are counted 12 times every day.

Morris soon gets a permanent job in the carpentry building making 15 cents an hour. On the way to work, Litmus tells Morris he sniffs glue to help him sleep. He also tells him the ventilator shaft on top of the cells is the way out of the prison.

Out on the yard, Wolf approaches Morris, carrying a shank. He tries to stab Morris, but Morris fights him off. In the fight, Wolf slashes a guard. Wolf and Morris are both sent to solitary in D Block. While in the cell, Morris is sprayed with a hose as a *shower* by a guard. When the door to Morris's cell is finally opened, it is clear he has not seen any light in a few days and is blinded.

A new inmate is brought in to the prison and placed in the cell beside Morris. His last name is Butts. During the recreation period, Morris introduces Butts to Litmus and Doc. While the men are on the yard, the warden visits the cell block. He drops nail clippers in Doc's cell and goes in to retrieve them. He sees the paintings Doc has made. One of the pictures is of the Warden. This spooks the warden, who decides to take painting privileges away from Doc. Doc is clearly upset when he is told of the warden's decision, saying, "painting's all I have."

On their way to work the next day, guards are having shooting practice in front of the inmates. Morris asks Doc if he is OK. Without speaking, Doc puts on his overalls for work and puts something in Morris' overalls pocket. Doc then asks the guard for a hatchet to work on a new table. He raises the hatchet with one hand and chops off the fingers of his other hand. The guard takes Doc out and tells the other inmates to get back to work. Later, Morris discovers what Doc put in his pocket: a chrysanthemum. Morris collects Doc's fingers to gives them to the guard.

Later, in the dining hall, Morris notices the Anglin brothers, whom he knew from his time in prison in Atlanta. The brothers are serving 15 to 20 years in Alcatraz for previous escape attempts from other prisons. At first the brothers were sent to Atlanta, then to Leavenworth, but when caught trying to escape, they were sent to Alcatraz.

That night in his cell, Morris turns off his light and tries to remove the air vent grate in the back of the cell. He finds that he can easily chip away chunks of the wall with nail clippers.

The next day, Butts tells Morris that he stole cars and sold the parts. He was originally sent to a state penitentiary, but upon his release, he stole another car and drove it across state lines. That made it a federal offense, so he was sent to Alcatraz.

Morris tells the Anglins and Butts that he may have found a way out of the prison. He has discovered that the cell block is getting old and the moist air is corroding the concrete and the salt is rusting the metal. He tells them he was digging around the grill in the back of the cell with a nail clipper, and he can get the grill out of the wall, enlarge the hole and get into the utility corridor. The corridor will then lead to the top of the cell block and maybe out on the roof. The Anglins agree to be part of the escape, as does Butts.

Once out of the prison, they will need a way to get across the bay. John Anglin steals raincoats and contact cement from the clothing shop where he works. With that material, the inmates make a life raft and some life preservers, as described in *Popular Mechanics*. They tell each other that they would go to Angel Island, because officials will think they are going to San Francisco.

Morris starts to dig around the vent in his cell while Butts watches for the guards. Morris tells Butts to start whistling if he sees a guard coming. First Morris digs with nail clippers, but he realizes he needs a better tool. The next day, Morris slips an extra spoon into his pocket and leaves the dining room with it. English shows him how to weld two pieces of metal together using silver shavings from a dime and multiple matches. This creates a tool with which he could dig easier and more quickly.

To help him get the grill out of the wall, Morris makes a wedge in the wood shop. The wedge has metal on it and sets off the alarm in the metal detector as Morris walks through it. He tells the guard he made it as a clothes pin. The guard keeps the wedge, but Morris had another one in his shoe. Using the new tools, Morris is able to remove the grate. The other inmates begin digging to remove their grates and enlarge the holes so they can slip their bodies through.

To conceal the hole in the wall, Morris pretends to want to learn how to play the accordion and places the case in front of the hole. He also has the idea to make a fake grill with a mixture of paper, soap, and concrete from their digging. They can paint grills on the cardboard and put them back in the hole to disguise their work.

Morris is finally able to remove the grate from the wall and slips through the hole and enters the corridor to explore. At a meal the next day, he tells the other men he went on top of the cell. He saw the ventilator shaft to the roof but was unable to reach it.

In order to leave his cell undetected at night to explore the insides of the prison, Morris needs a way to trick the guards into thinking he is in his cell. He decides to make a dummy head out of cardboard. Since Clarence Anglin worked in the barber shop, he collected real human hair to use on the dummy heads. Butts orders paint for both the fake grills and dummy heads. The inmates put the dummy heads in their bunks on the pillow, with the blankets pulled up, to make it appear as if the men are sleeping.

In order to get through the ventilator shaft and onto the roof of the prison, the inmates need to remove the bars. Morris knows if he can get a motor and a drill bit he can drill through it. One day while leaving a music session, Morris sees a fan. He quickly puts it in his instrument case. On the way out of the session, the guards stop Morris to search his case, but they do not find the fan. Morris then asks Litmus for an extension cord and drill bit. Litmus agrees to supply the goods. Morris uses the motor from the fan and drill bit from Litmus to get the ventilator cover off. While cutting it off, the men drop something. The guard hears it but does nothing.

Meanwhile, John Anglin is working on putting the raft together. The men steal raincoats by wearing one back to the cell each day after work. They know that the guards won't know the raincoats are missing. He then reports to Morris that the rafts will be done Tuesday. Morris decides the inmates would leave on the next Tuesday night.

Butts reports to Morris that he is having a hard time with his grille because it keeps falling out. Morris tells him to put some contact cement around it to keep it in place.

The guards and warden inspect Morris' cell. The warden looks at the fake grate but doesn't notice anything wrong. The warden also talks about splitting up Butts and Morris, and decide to move Butts to another cell by Tuesday morning.

The men decide to all meet on top of the cell when the lights go out. Before they go, Wolf approaches Morris in the yard. He is holding a knife. English stops Wolf, reminding Wolf that he just spent six months in the hole and doesn't want to go back.

On the night of the escape, the men all leave their cells and enter the utility corridor. From there, they can climb onto the roof. Butts is unable to get out of his cell. The others decide they cannot wait for Butts and leave without him. They get onto the roof, taking the rafts with them. At one point, the top of a unit falls off. A bird on the roof is also scared and flies off, cawing. Again, the guard on duty does not notice. They slide down a pipe and climb over a fence. When they get to the water they are seen swimming away. Meanwhile, Butts continues to dig his grate out, and finally gets it off. When he gets out, the men are gone. He returns to his cell.

The guards are unaware of the escape until morning. They wake up the men for breakfast, and when the men do not get out of bed, the guard reaches into the cell to wake them. Morris' fake head rolls onto the floor, scaring the guard, who screams.

As officials search the island, they find a package of photos that belonged to Charles Anglin. They also find a chrysanthemum on the cliff. Someone tells the warden that the tides were mild that night and fog was light. The men had a nine and a half hour head start if they left at lights out. The bodies have never been found.

Escape from Alcatraz: Hollywood's Rendering

In order to lend credibility to the movie, it was filmed largely in the buildings on Alcatraz Island, in the actual cells where the escapees lived and in the workhouses on prison grounds. Additionally, the actual dummy masks made by the inmates are used in the film. This helps to ensure the events portrayed in the movie are largely realistic. Nonetheless, there are many mistakes in the movie that take away from the historical accuracy of the escape attempt.

First, there were many fictitious characters included in the film that never existed. One of those was the character named Charlie Butts. More than likely, this character was based on inmate Allen West, who played a major role in the escape in a few ways. After the escape was completed, West took credit for masterminding the entire escape, telling many people that the idea for the plan was his. However, the movie showed that Morris took the lead and planned the escape.[40]

The night of the escape, West did not leave his cell and stayed behind. Some accounts claim that he failed to fully excavate the hole in the back of his cell hole. As he tried to leave, he discovered a steel bar he did not anticipate that prevented him from removing the grate completely. Clarence Anglin attempted to assist West by kicking at it from inside the corridor, but it didn't loosen.[41] The movie shows that the character Butts did not leave his cell, but is unclear as to why. In an earlier scene in the film, Butts is shown telling Morris that his cardboard grille kept falling out. Morris tells him to use a small amount of glue to tack it into place. It could be that Butts did not leave his cell on the night of the escape because he used too much glue and could not remove the grille. However, the film also makes it appears as if he was simply too scared to leave, a suggestion made in some reviews of the film.

In the real escape, West, as an inmate janitor, was painting B Block. As he was doing so, he continued to drip paint and kick dust all over the floor below him. He was able to convince the guards to let him hang up about 30 blankets for a long period of time. In doing so, he was able to create a space within the prison where no one could see what he was doing, giving him and Morris plenty of room to build a raft and store tools. This was not made clear in the movie. The film does not show blankets hanging to create a workspace for the inmates.

Another falsehood concerning the Butts/West character has to do with the arrival of the inmates to Alcatraz. West was in the prison before Morris arrived. John Anglin arrived in Alcatraz in October 1960, while his brother Clarence did not arrive until three months later, in January of 1961. The film made it appear as if Morris arrived before the others involved in the escape plan.

Many other main characters in the movie were fictitious. In the movie, there were characters named Litmus, English, Wolf, and Doc. None of these were real inmates at Alcatraz as one might think from watching the film. There is some possibility that the character called English (King of the Hill in the yard) may have been "Bumpy" Johnson, a high ranking member of organized crime who, as some theorize, may have arranged for an escape boat to meet the three escapees once they were out of the prison. He is seen in the film sitting at the top of the stairs in the exercise yard, telling Morris that the higher the inmates sit, the more status they have. Throughout the movie he seemed to have a great deal of respect from other inmates, who listened to him when he gave advice or told them something. This was made clear when English stopped Wolf from attacking Morris just before the escape.

The fictitious characters may have been written into the movie to enhance viewers' feelings towards the inmates and show the human side of the prisoners, and what they endured as inmates in a high-security prison at the time. Their interactions could help explain the dynamics of the prison as well as the daily routine of the facility. Their conversations, both with each other and with the guards and warden, inform the viewers about the prison policies. This can be seen when, early in the film, the character of English tells Morris to button his shirt collar on the way to breakfast. Or when English tells Morris about how difficult it is to escape during their conversation in the yard.

Some of the fictitious inmates took on traits or portrayed things that really happened to other inmates in Alcatraz. For example, many inmates had pets and would take them to the dining hall or even the shower, as shown by the fictional character Litmus. Some inmates in the prison used razor blades to cut their Achilles' tendons as a way to express their unhappiness with prison policies, or even as a way out. The character English describes doing this to himself in a conversation with Morris. Yet another example is the character Doc, who chopped his fingers off with a hatchet in the early part of the movie. In 1937, convict Rufe Persful, a robber from Arkansas, was working with the dock gang when he laid his left hand on a block and chopped off his fingers with a hatchet, one by one.[42] Thus, although many of the main characters in the movie are fictional, they help to portray the historical accuracy of the events within the prison.

Moreover, the character of Doc was associated with a chrysanthemum throughout the film, which is also not realistic as there were no chrysanthemums on the island, nor were there flowers readily available to the inmates. In an early scene, Doc is shown painting a picture of himself with a yellow chrysanthemum. Later, before he chops his fingers off with a hatchet, he places a yellow chrysanthemum in Morris' overalls. At the end of the movie, the warden stumbles across the flower. The flower is used as a symbol of freedom, or the struggle for hope, for the inmates.

The film shows that several tools were used by the inmates in their escape attempt. Although the movie makes it appear that Morris was the only one who knew how to make the necessary tools needed, in reality, West was the one who made the majority of the tools. For example, the movie shows Morris taking an electric fan to help him cut through the steel bars on the ventilator shaft. He actually used an extra motor from a prison vacuum. The inmates tried to use the fan motor, but found it was too small to cut through the metal bars. That is when West learned that the prison's vacuum was broken and he convinced the guards to attempt a repair on the machine. In doing so, he discovered the vacuum had two motors and removed one. He got one motor to work, which fixed the vacuum so the guards were not suspicious of his behavior. He kept the second motor and the escapees tried to use it to remove the bars on the shaft. However, in the end, the motor was too noisy and did not work well.[43]

The role that Morris played in the escape was exaggerated in other ways as well. The movie indicated that only the four men and maybe a few others knew about the plan to escape. The movie made Morris look as if he collected all the materials and made all the plans. In reality, somewhere around 80 (or more) inmates reportedly knew the men were trying to escape. Many other inmates helped them get the right tools and materials they needed. For example, inmate Darwin Coon helped them steal tools. Coon worked in the kitchen and would *accidentally* break things so that a friend of his on the maintenance crew would have to come and fix them. The friend would leave tools behind, which Coon would take to Anglin.[44]

Another tool used by the inmates that was not shown in the movie was a concertina, a musical instrument similar to an accordion that was used by the escapees to inflate their raft. The movie shows the inmates manually blowing up the raft they made.

There are other historical inaccuracies about the equipment the men used to escape. As they leave the island, they are shown holding on to a small raft. However, the raft they made was about 14 feet by six feet and made out of 60 to 80 raincoats. This would make the raft quite large, probably bigger than the tube-shaped object shown in the movie.

The film shows some inaccurate facts about events that occur after the men are found to be missing, The warden in the film is shown as being one of the first people who was notified of the escape. In reality, the warden was not even present at the time of the escape. He had gone on vacation and the deputy warden, Arthur Dollison, was in charge of the prison at the time. Further, the warden is shown picking up a packet containing photos during the initial search of the island. However, not only was the warden not present, this packet was discovered several days after the escape, floating in the water. These changes were probably made to shorten the length of the movie and to keep it less complicated for viewers.

Another technique used to compress the events was simply to speed up the entire escape plan. Planning for the escape took the prisoners about two years to accomplish, which was not noted in the movie. The events of the movie imply that it was fairly easy to dig out the vent grills in the cells, and to open the vent to the top of the prison. In reality it took months for the inmates to dig out the holes in their cells, loosen the ventilator grill, build a raft, and complete all the other preparations for the escape. The film's producers had to omit some of this timing in order to keep the film at a reasonable time length.

Another fact omitted from the film, possibly to save time, was that the escapees had made plans for their lives after they left the prison and reached San Francisco. They told other inmates about their intentions to steal a car and carry out a burglary to get some cash. Additionally, the movie did not show that the inmates were learning Spanish, and one had a map of Mexico in his cell. This indicates that the men had a plan to disappear once they crossed the Bay.

There were some other minor errors in the film that take away from the historical impact of the movie. First, the movie shows Morris being taken to Alcatraz on the boat by himself. But when Morris was taken to the prison in reality, he was on the boat with other people. Second, the film shows Morris had a meeting with the warden in his office upon arriving at Alcatraz, whereas in reality the warden came to his cell.[45] The last minor difference is when Morris snuck the wedge into the prison from the workshop. The movie indicated that he had made two wedges, one of which was confiscated by the guards, allowing him to sneak in the other. But in reality, the guard simply questioned Morris about the wedge but allowed him to take it in when he said it was for hanging up his clothing.

Conclusion

By the time of the possible escape from Alcatraz, the prison building had been deteriorating as a result of the cold, damp salt water from the Bay. In addition, some claim that the security procedures within the prison were becoming lax and the guards were not as careful as they once had been.[46] This allowed four inmates to spend months, undetected and under the noses of the guards, preparing for, and possibly carrying out, the first and only successful escape from the *unescapable* federal prison. To this day, it is unknown if the men successfully made it to shore or if they drowned in the San Francisco Bay. Nonetheless, the story has fascinated people for many years. The movie *Escape from Alcatraz* serve to inform viewers of this historical event in criminal justice, despite several inaccuracies, and entertain them at the same time.

Further Reading

Babyak, Jolene. (1988). *Eyewitness on Alcatraz*. Berkeley, CA: Ariel Vamp Press.

Beyeler, Ed. (1988). *Alcatraz: The Rock*. Flagstaff, AZ: Northland Press.

Bruce, J. Campbell. (1963). *Escape From Alcatraz*. Berkeley, CA: Ten Speed Press.

Cecil, Richard. (1992). *Alcatraz*. West Lafayette, IN: Purdue University Press.

Fuller, James. (1982). *Alcatraz Federal Penitentiary, 1934–1963.* San Francisco: Asteron Production.

Gaddis, Thomas E. (1976*). Birdman of Alcatraz.* Mattituck, NY: Aeonian Press.

George, Gregory H. (2002). *Alcatraz Screw: My Years as a Guard in America's Most Notorious* Prison. Columbia, MO: University of Missouri Press.

Johnson, Troy R. (1996). *The Occupation of Alcatraz Island.* Urbana, IL: University of Illinois Press.

Johnston, James A. (1937). *Prison Life is Different.* Boston: Houghton Mifflin Company.

Lageson, Ernest B. (2002). *Alcatraz Justice: The Rock's Most Famous Murder Trial.* Berkeley, CA: Creative Arts Book Co..

Lageson, Ernest B. (1999). *Battle at Alcatraz: A Desperate Attempt to Escape the Rock.* Omaha, NE: Addicus Books.

Presnall, Judith Janda. (2001). *Life on Alcatraz.* San Diego, CA: Lucent Books.

Quillen, Jim. (1991). *Alcatraz from Inside: The Hard Years, 1942–1952.* San Francisco, CA: Golden Gate National Park Association.

Ward, David A. (2009). *Alcatraz: The Gangster Years.* Berkeley, CA: University of California Press.

Endnotes

1. Johnston, James A. (1937) *Prison Life is Different* Boston: Houghton Mifflin Company.

2. Babyak, Jolene. (1988). *Eyewitness on Alcatraz.* Berkeley, CA: Ariel Vamp Press.

3. Bruce, J. Campbell. (1963). *Escape From Alcatraz.* Berkeley, CA: Ten Speed Press, p. 17.

4. Bruce, J. Campbell. (1963). *Escape From Alcatraz.* Berkeley, CA: Ten Speed Press, p. 44; Quillen, Jim. (1991). *Alcatraz from Inside: The Hard Years, 1942–1952.* San Francisco, CA: Golden Gate National Park Association.

5. Babyak, Jolene. (1988). *Eyewitness on Alcatraz.* Berkeley, CA: Ariel Vamp Press, p. 27.

6. Quillen, Jim. (1991). *Alcatraz from Inside: The Hard Years, 1942–1952.* San Francisco, CA: Golden Gate National Park Association.

7. Bruce, J. Campbell. (1963). *Escape From Alcatraz.* Berkeley, CA: Ten Speed Press, p. 17.

8. Bruce, J. Campbell. (1963). *Escape From Alcatraz.* Berkeley, CA: Ten Speed Press, p. 70.

9. Quillen, Jim. (1991). *Alcatraz from Inside: The Hard Years, 1942–1952.* San Francisco, CA: Golden Gate National Park Association.

10. Bruce, J. Campbell. (1963). *Escape From Alcatraz.* Berkeley, CA: Ten Speed Press, p. 162.

11. Bruce, J. Campbell. (1963). *Escape From Alcatraz*. Berkeley, CA: Ten Speed Press, p. 163.

12. Bruce, J. Campbell. (1963). *Escape From Alcatraz*. Berkeley, CA: Ten Speed Press, p. 148.

13. Bruce, J. Campbell. (1963). *Escape From Alcatraz*. Berkeley, CA: Ten Speed Press, p. 150.

14. Bruce, J. Campbell. (1963). *Escape From Alcatraz*. Berkeley, CA: Ten Speed Press, p. 154.

15. Bruce, J. Campbell. (1963). *Escape From Alcatraz*. Berkeley, CA: Ten Speed Press, p. 166.

16. Bruce, J. Campbell. (1963). *Escape From Alcatraz*. Berkeley, CA: Ten Speed Press, p. 172.

17. Bruce, J. Campbell. (1963). *Escape From Alcatraz*. Berkeley, CA: Ten Speed Press, p. 7.

18. Bruce, J. Campbell. (1963). *Escape From Alcatraz*. Berkeley, CA: Ten Speed Press, p. 173.

19. Bruce, J. Campbell. (1963). *Escape From Alcatraz*. Berkeley, CA: Ten Speed Press, pp. 179–80.

20. Bruce, J. Campbell. (1963). *Escape From Alcatraz*. Berkeley, CA: Ten Speed Press, pp. 182–183.

21. Bruce, J. Campbell. (1963). *Escape From Alcatraz*. Berkeley, CA: Ten Speed Press, p. 177.

22. Bruce, J. Campbell. (1963). *Escape From Alcatraz*. Berkeley, CA: Ten Speed Press, p. 174.

23. Bruce, J. Campbell. (1963). *Escape From Alcatraz*. Berkeley, CA: Ten Speed Press, p. 184.

24. Bruce, J. Campbell. (1963). *Escape From Alcatraz*. Berkeley, CA: Ten Speed Press, p. 175.

25. Bruce, J. Campbell. (1963). *Escape From Alcatraz*. Berkeley, CA: Ten Speed Press, pp. 189–91.

26. Bruce, J. Campbell. (1963). *Escape From Alcatraz*. Berkeley, CA: Ten Speed Press, p. 192.

27. Bruce, J. Campbell. (1963). *Escape From Alcatraz*. Berkeley, CA: Ten Speed Press, p. 187.

28. Bruce, J. Campbell. (1963). *Escape From Alcatraz*. Berkeley, CA: Ten Speed Press, p. 193.

29. Bruce, J. Campbell. (1963). *Escape From Alcatraz*. Berkeley, CA: Ten Speed Press, pp. 194–95.

30. Bruce, J. Campbell. (1963). *Escape From Alcatraz*. Berkeley, CA: Ten Speed Press, p. 196.

31. Some accounts report that West was not able to get through his opening because there was a steel bar in the grate that he did not anticipate.

32. Bruce, J. Campbell. (1963). *Escape From Alcatraz*. Berkeley, CA: Ten Speed Press, p. 197.

33. Other accounts claimed that they escapees cut their way through two eight-foot fences that were covered with barbed wire.

34. Bruce, J. Campbell. (1963). *Escape From Alcatraz*. Berkeley, CA: Ten Speed Press, p. 199.

35. Bruce, J. Campbell. (1963). *Escape From Alcatraz.* Berkeley, CA: Ten Speed Press, p. 200.

36. Sullivan, L. (2011). Escape from Alcatraz and a 47-year manhunt. Retrieved online at http://www.npr.org/templates/story/story.php?storyid=112746496&ps=cprs.

37. Bruce, J. Campbell. (1963). *Escape From Alcatraz.* Berkeley, CA: Ten Speed Press, p. 200.

38. Bruce, J. Campbell. (1963). *Escape From Alcatraz.* Berkeley, CA: Ten Speed Press.

39. Internet Movie Database. (2011). Escape from Alcatraz (1979). Retrieved online at http://www.imdb.com/title/tt0079116/.

40. Hamlin, J. (1996). Breakout! Escape from Alcatraz. Retrieved online at PERLINK"http://www.alcatrazhistory.com/alcesc1.htm"http://www.alcatrazhistory.com/alcesc1.htm.

41. Hamlin, J. (1996). The Great Escape from Alcatraz. Retrieved online at http://www.alcatrazhistory.com/alcesc2.htm.

42. Bruce, J. Campbell. (1963). *Escape From Alcatraz.* Berkeley, CA: Ten Speed Press, p. 44.

43. Hamlin, J. (1996). The Great Escape from Alcatraz. Retrieved online at http://www.alcatrazhistory.com/alcesc2.htm.

44. Sullivan, L. (2011). Escape from Alcatraz and a 47-year Manhunt. Retrieved online at http://www.npr.org/templates/story/story.php?storyid=112746496&ps=cprs

45. Other reports indicate that inmates, upon arrival in Alcatraz, would meet with the warden in his office (see Quillen).

46. Quillen, Jim. (1991). *Alcatraz from Inside: The Hard Years, 1942–1952.* San Francisco, CA: Golden Gate National Park Association.

CHAPTER 9

MISSISSIPPI BURNING AND THE MURDER OF THREE CIVIL RIGHTS WORKERS (1964)

The FBI wanted poster for the three missing civil rights workers in Philadelphia, Mississippi: Andrew Goodman, James Earl Chaney, and Michael Henry Schwerner. Photo courtesy of the Associated Press.

Mr. President ... I wanted to let you know we have found the car.
—FBI Director J. Edgar Hoover to President Lyndon B. Johnson
on June 23, 1964, 4:05 p.m. two days after the disappearance
of three civil rights workers

Introduction

On June 21, 1964, three civil rights workers, Michael Schwerner, Andrew Goodman, and James Chaney, were arrested on suspicion of having some involvement in a church arson. They had just been visiting that church and members of the congregation when Schwerner was warned that the Ku Klux Klan had burned the church because they were looking for him. It was their intent to kill him. The three young men were heading back to the Congress of Racial Equality (CORE) office, in Meridian, Mississippi, when Deputy Sheriff Cecil

Price of the Neshoba County Sheriff's Office arrested them. Held for seven hours, they were released at approximately 10 that night. It was a set up. The deputy, along with three other cars filled with members of the Ku Klux Klan, captured the three men. They were shot at pointblank range, and then buried in an earthen dam. The car was set on fire.

The next morning, the Federal Bureau of Investigation (FBI) descended on the little town of Philadelphia and launched an investigation referred to as MIBURN—Mississippi Burning. Later that day they would find the smoldering car; 44 days later, the three bodies; and three years later, they obtained the conviction of seven conspirators. The case received not only special attention from FBI Director J. Edgar Hoover and President Lyndon B. Johnson, it received the attention of the entire world. Mississippi and similar small southern towns could no longer discriminate against blacks; the southern world was changing.

In 1988, a film by director Alan Parker used the title of the FBI case as the title for the motion picture—*Mississippi Burning.*[1] While the film brings to life Mississippi in the summer of 1964 and the plight of the three missing civil rights workers, the film was greatly lacking in historical accuracy, and chose rather to tell the story of the civil rights workers and Mississippi blacks through the eyes of two FBI agents, played by Gene Hackman and Willem Dafoe. Although generally considered an excellent movie, its grade for historical accuracy falls far short.

Mississippi Burning: The History

The summer of 1964, an election year for the Presidency of the United States, was to become known as "Freedom Summer."[2] It was so named because of the civil rights activities of numerous groups that mobilized that summer for the Mississippi Summer Project—a project to register all Mississippi black people in the state to vote and to encourage them to participate in the political process that November. Among the groups participating and sending volunteers were the Congress on Racial Equality (CORE), the National Association for the Advancement of Colored People (NAACP), the Southern Christian Leadership Conference (SCLS), and the Student Nonviolent Coordinating Committee (SNCC). All of these operated under a coalition organization known as the Council of Federated Organizations (COFO).[3]

While these groups and their black members had previously been working toward the same goal for years, that summer the director of the Mississippi Summer Project, Robert Moses, began recruiting white students to participate. His goal was to "produce a confrontation between federal and state authorities that could not be ignored, precipitating a crisis that finally would force the federal government to protect civil rights and Mississippi's black citizens who were trying to register to vote."[4] Moses and members of the project began recruiting on college campuses across the nation in the academic year prior to the summer of 1964. They recruited a number of white students from many of the northern colleges and universities who were willing to travel to Mississippi to participate that summer.

The Mississippi Summer Project was no ordinary summer position, nor was it by any stretch of the word a vacation, and Moses ensured that students understood that. He advised that there would be risks and that in order to prepare for these risks they had certain requirements for the students. First, they had to raise $500 bail money to be fully prepared in the event they were arrested by the local police authorities. Second, they had to provide a list of next of kin who could be contacted in the event of their death. Third, they had to be photographed with a sandwich board that detailed their personal information, again, so they could later be identified in case of their demise.[5] Made aware of the potential threats they would face, many backed out of the summer volunteer work in Mississippi. Others, such as Andrew Goodman, remained convinced it was the right thing to do and it was worth the risk. As he told his mother before he left for Mississippi, he wanted to go because "it's the most important thing going on in the country."[6]

The Mississippi Summer Project actually had multiple goals, one of which was to establish "Freedom Schools," where volunteers would spend their summer educating young black students. Another was to increase the number of blacks registered to vote. The black population of Mississippi at the time was approximately 45%, but only 6% of those were actually registered to vote, and most of those did not vote on election day out of fear.[7] The other function of the project, more out of necessity than anything, was to track the members of the Ku Klux Klan and the positions of authority they happened to fill in order to better protect the Summer Project workers.

The Ku Klux Klan (KKK) had an enormous amount of control over the state of Mississippi, largely because of their close ties to those in government positions, especially in law enforcement. The KKK was estimated to have over 10,000 members in Mississippi. To show their power, on April 24, 1964, there were 61 simultaneous cross burnings across the state.[8] One prime example of the KKK's close ties with law enforcement was found in Sheriff Lawrence Rainey, of Neshoba County. Rainey was elected sheriff in November of 1963, and he campaigned as "the man who can cope with situations that might arise."[9] The "situations" referred to outsiders who were planning to come into Neshoba

County and to tell them how to treat their black citizens, which they saw as an affront.

Threats like this had already been aimed at one of the CORE workers—Michael Schwerner. Schwerner had earned a reputation for being an advocate for civil rights, one of the bravest whites working for C.O.R.E., and one of the most hated individuals by the KKK. Schwerner had become the first white civil rights worker to work in the field, as the other whites spent their time primarily in Jackson, Mississippi, the capital, working on policy. Because he was a white working with blacks, he gained special attention by the Klan and they referred to him derogatorily as "Goatee" and "Jew Boy." The KKK hated Schwerner so much they launched a plan to assassinate him.

Schwerner visited the Mount Zion Church in Longdale on Memorial Day. His reason for being there was to try and establish a "Freedom School." The Klan learned of his meeting, and because there was a business meeting of the church scheduled for the evening of June 16, 1964, the KKK decided to try and kill him during the meeting. At approximately 10 that evening, the meeting broke up and seven black men and three black women left the building. The KKK was waiting for them, armed with rifles and shotguns. The Klan members searched for Schwerner, but they did not find him. So they took out their frustrations by beating the blacks and burning the church.[10]

The following day, news of the church burning reached the office of C.O.R.E. and ultimately Schwerner, who was in Ohio at the time helping to train new college student volunteers, including Andrew Goodman. Schwerner talked Goodman into coming back to Meridian, Mississippi, with him, along with James Chaney, a native black of Meridian who was helping to train the new recruits. The three piled into a blue Ford station wagon owned by C.O.R.E. and drove straight to Meridian. They arrived late at night, caught a little sleep and breakfast, before heading out to the burned church in Longdale.

Prior to leaving, as was their practice, Schwerner coordinated with the C.O.R.E. office, notifying them that they would return by 4 p.m. If they were not back by then, the office should begin calling law enforcement offices and hospitals starting at 4:30 p.m. If for any reason they were delayed, they would attempt to contact the C.O.R.E. office.

On the afternoon of June 21, 1964, the three civil rights workers arrived at the charred remains of the Mount Zion Church.[11] They then went to the home of a family who were members of the church congregation in order to learn more about the church burning. There they were warned that the KKK was looking for Schwerner and that he was in grave danger. At 3 p.m., the three men decided it would be best to head back to Meridian. It was decided that Chaney would drive the vehicle and most likely Schwerner and Goodman ducked in the back seat so as not to be seen. They decided of the two routes they could take, the best would be Highway 16, which would take them through Philadelphia, the Neshoba County seat. It turned out to be a poor choice.

As they were driving along the highway, Deputy Sheriff Cecil Price was driving on patrol and passed the blue Ford station wagon.[12] He recognized it as a C.O.R.E. vehicle and proceeded to pull a u-turn. Price pulled the vehicle over inside Philadelphia's jurisdiction, and arrested the three young men on suspicion of having committed the burning of the church. Arrested for arson, they were then booked into the Neshoba County Jail.

Schwerner asked to make a phone call in the hopes of contacting the C.O.R.E. office, but he was denied his request. Schwerner, upset, probably at least took comfort in the fact that the sheriff's office would soon receive a phone call anyway from the C.O.R.E. office. At 5:20 p.m., that phone call was made to the Neshoba County Jail. The caller from C.O.R.E. was told the three civil rights workers were not there. At 10 p.m., Deputy Cecil Price arrived back at the jail, released the three men, and followed them out of town on Highway 19, accompanied by a Philadelphia police officer.

At that point, Schwerner, Goodman, and Chaney had to know they were being led into a trap, a trap that the KKK had been working on all afternoon. When the Ford station wagon left Philadelphia, Price turned around and headed back into town to drop off the Philadelphia police officer and then raced back out onto Highway 19. Chaney was again driving and saw the flashing lights in his rearview mirror. They decided it was best to try and escape. What then occurred was a high speed chase, but the slow Ford station wagon was no match for the fast Chevy police cruiser. Chaney tried turning onto Highway 492 to avoid capture, but Price followed. Chaney then slammed on his breaks and the three surrendered.

Court testimony reconstructs what happened next.[13] The three were removed from their car and placed in the back of the police car. Three other cars arrived and they proceeded down an unmarked dirt road known as Rock Cut Road. The car stopped and they were removed from the vehicle. There is some evidence to suggest that Chaney was first beaten, but in the end, dishonorably discharged Marine and member of the KKK Wayne Roberts killed Schwerner, then Goodman, and finally Chaney, with a gunshot at point-blank range.[14] The bodies were then taken to a dam on the Old Jolly Farm owned by Olen Burrage, a Philadelphia businessman and member of the KKK. Their bodies were placed together in a hole and, literally, a ton of dirt was dumped on their bodies by an earth-moving Caterpillar machine.

The C.O.R.E. office became very concerned by midnight that the three civil rights workers had not checked in, so they contacted John Doar, their contact person for the U.S. Department of Justice in Mississippi.[15] Doar contacted the Meridian office of the Federal Bureau of Investigation (FBI) and Agent John Proctor was dispatched immediately.[16]

The next day, New Orleans-based supervising agent Joseph Sullivan arrived, along with 10 other special agents and the MIBURN (Mississippi Burning) case was opened. That day a tip was received. Someone had found the blue Ford station wagon smoldering. Harry Maynor contacted J. Edgar Hoover, the director of the FBI, who contacted President Johnson. The FBI was giving this top priority and by June 25, more agents had arrived along with a busload of nearby sailors who began searching the woods and swamps for the bodies.[17] After failing to find the bodies, Maynor focused more heavily on the investigation. A $30,000 reward was offered for information leading to the bodies. This motivated highway patrolman Maynard King, who had been tipped off by Klan member Pete Jordan, to provide the location of the bodies, and on August 4, 1964, the bodies were recovered.[18]

As the investigation continued, Agent Proctor began to put pressure on James Jordan, a Meridian businessman who ran a bar in a dry county. Proctor offered Jordan a reduced sentence and some money to help relocate, and after five long interviews, Jordan turned state's evidence. On December 4, 1964, armed with enough evidence, 19 men were arrested for conspiracy to violate the civil rights of Schwerner, Goodman, and Chaney. Six days later, the charges were dismissed. A month later, the Justice Department secured indictments from a federal grand jury in Jackson, Mississippi. These charges were also challenged until eventually a new grand jury was formed and 18 Klansmen were finally indicted on February 28, 1967.[19]

The trial took place that October and eventually seven of the men were found guilty—Deputy Sheriff Cecil Price, Imperial Wizard Sam Bowers, trigger man Wayne Roberts, Jimmy Snowden, Billey Posey, and Horace Bennett.[20] Seven others were acquitted, including Sheriff Lawrence Rainey. In three other cases, including that of Edgar Ray Killen, the jury could not reach a decision. In 2004, the case of Killen was reopened and the following year, on the 41st anniversary of the killings, he was convicted in three counts of manslaughter.[21]

Mississippi Burning: The Film

The film *Mississippi Burning*, by Orion Pictures, premiered December 11, 1988.[22] It was directed by Alan Parker and starred Gene Hackman and Willem Dafoe as the two FBI agents investigating the three missing civil rights workers. The motion picture was filmed primarily in Mississippi, with the exception of the town square scenes, which were filmed in Lafayette, Alabama. The film was rated R and was 128 minutes in length. Sales for the opening weekend were poor, but in the end the film grossed $34 million, while the budget was estimated to have been $15 million to produce, making it a successful film.[25]

The film opens with gospel music being sung, while it pans across a small white clapboard church burning to the ground. The scene then transitions to a nighttime, where a blue Ford station wagon, driven by a white male with his two companions, a white male in the front passenger seat and a black male in the back seat, are driving along a country road. They are ominously being followed by several vehicles without their headlights on. Eventually they are rammed from behind, and it would appear only the black male in the back seat understands the severity of the situation.

The car eventually leaves the road and drives across the meadows, but then the lights come on from the trailing cars, as does a red flashing light from the police cruiser. The driver with a goatee says, "Let me talk." A sheriff's deputy is seen at the window as the driver rolls down his window, words are exchanged, and the driver is shot by the deputy. The scene fades to black and two more shots are heard before the onscreen caption reads, "Mississippi, 1964."

The film transitions to daylight and another station wagon, driving along the highway, is occupied by two men. Through their discussions, they are introduced as Mr. Anderson and Mr. Ward, two FBI agents sent to investigate the three missing civil rights leaders. The primary in the case, Mr. Ward, is introduced as an agent who has previously investigated missing civil rights workers, while Mr. Anderson is introduced as a person who was born and raised nearby in Mississippi. Mr. Ward is a young agent, strait-laced and by-the-book. Mr. Anderson is a seasoned veteran, a good-ole-boy, and one who often takes liberties with the rules and regulations.

They arrive in a small town sheriff's office where the deputy sheriff treats them poorly, before the sheriff himself intervenes. The FBI agents press the deputies to know why the three men were arrested at 3 p.m., only to be released at 10 p.m. Agent Ward wants to know, "Why didn't they make a phone call?" They receive no help from the sheriff and very quickly it becomes clear that they are to be the antagonists in the story.

The two FBI agents arrive at a diner for lunch, but the place is full. Agent Ward sees two counter seats in the back, but they are reserved for black patrons due to segregation laws. Agent Ward says he wants those seats, but Agent Anderson advises against it. As they make their way to the two counter seats, the whole diner goes silent. Agent Ward sits next to a young black male at the lunch counter and asks him if he has any information; the black male responds, "I ain't got nothing to say to you, Sir."

The two agents are then seen visiting the church that burned to the ground at the opening of the film. They review the facts of the case. The three civil rights workers had been at the church for voter registration. The church had been burned before and was rebuilt. After the three Freedom Summer workers left, they were arrested, and later the church was burned. Mr. Ward wants to talk to the local black community. Mr. Anderson advises they will not talk. Mr. Ward states it is "Bureau procedure."

The scene transitions briefly to a number of the local members of the Ku Klux Klan going after the black male who refused to speak to the FBI agents at the lunch counter. It then transitions back to the agents in a local motel, discussing the case and southern hatred for blacks. Gunshots are fired through their motel window and a cross is found burning in the motel courtyard. Mr. Ward states he is going to call Washington for more agents. The scene then cuts to agents arriving and setting up a headquarters in an old movie theater that was closed, before transitioning back to the black male from the lunch counter who has been beaten and left in a cotton cage in a cotton field.

The film then returns to the town square, where a car sporting several Confederate flags pulls up to the Town Hall. The occupants are identified as being members of the Ku Klux Klan. The key occupant is later identified as Townley, a local leader and Grand Wizard of the KKK.

Mr. Anderson is then shown heading into the local barbershop, where he meets the sheriff and the mayor. The mayor argues that since the missing boys have not shown up, they are probably in Chicago drinking beer and that the agents should stay out of local business. Mr. Anderson is then shown entering a beauty shop, where the locals identify the occupant of the car as Clayton Townley. The lady he is talking to is Deputy Pell's wife. He was the deputy that gave Ward and Anderson a hard time when they first arrived at the sheriff's office.

All of a sudden, a car screams into the town square, the door opens, and the black male from the lunch counter is dumped into the street. Anderson and Ward arrive at the same time to assist the man, and Ward informs Anderson that they found the car. The scene then shifts to a backwoods Cajun family, who shows the agents to the location of the car. Heavy equipment is seen removing the car, but there are no bodies. They find a watch stopped at 12:45 p.m. Ward calls for 100 more men, the "entire Army," if need be.

A series of short film shots are then shown. First the freedom house blows up, as buses full of Navy soldiers are shown arriving at the swamp to search for the bodies. Then two more nighttime fire bombings are shown, while this is interspersed with footage of the Navy searching for the bodies through the swamp. Then a black male is thrown out of a house and another church is burned. Then more agents are shown arriving, but the motel wants all of the agents to leave. Mr. Ward tells his agent to buy the motel. The locals and the sheriff are shown being interviewed by the local media, and they deny the boys were murdered or even still in Mississippi.

The next scene has agents once again at a burned church to investigate. The local church members are having a service and a young child is preaching to the adults. As the FBI agents show up, the people all leave. Mr. Anderson asks the name of a flower and the father tells him it is a trumpet pitcher. The only member of the black community who appears willing to talk to the agents is the young child who tells them that their investigation should "start with the sheriff's office."

So, in the next scene, Anderson and Ward visit the home of Deputy Pell. Ward begins questioning the deputy as to his location on June 21, the night the civil rights workers went missing. Anderson slips into the kitchen to talk to Pell's wife. They then leave. Anderson, now nervous, leaves for Hogie's Place, a KKK hang out. Anderson returns with a trumpet pitcher for Pell's wife. They talk, he gives her the flower, and then leaves.

The scene then turns to another church where a service is being held. As the members of the church community begin to leave, the KKK arrives, and the people begin to run. The members of the KKK begin to beat those they catch. This is then followed by another series of fast-changing scenes with local interviews, the search for the bodies continuing, the deputy and his wife having a brief confrontation, the mayor and Townley being interviewed, and a KKK speech.

Anderson is then shown arriving at Hogie's Place where the sheriff and the deputy are hanging out, drinking beer in a dry town. Anderson is told he has to be a member, but they allow him in and give him a beer. Eventually one of the locals gets in Anderson's face, and Anderson grabs the individual by the crotch, squeezes hard, and tells him never to threaten him again.

The agents are next shown reviewing KKK propaganda film and then a civil rights march proceeds through town. Anderson arrives back at the beauty parlor, and watches the parade go by, but Pell sees Anderson next to his wife.

That night, Ward and Anderson are waiting for a black male to be released from the sheriff's office. As he walks away, a car follows him. The sheriff and his deputy watch. Anderson tells Ward to move, but Ward wants to wait until the sheriff and deputy go back inside so they are not seen. A chase ensues, and the black male is picked up, the sheriff and deputy go back inside, and the agents give chase. They are then delayed by a train and when they finally find the black male, he has been beaten and is bleeding.

Once again, a series of fast-changing scenes show the FBI talking to a family, asking for the son to testify against the sheriff and deputies. The FBI then questions Pell about his involvement in the KKK whereupon he walks out on them. The mayor confronts Anderson and Ward and rages against them. Then Anderson is shown later that evening following the deputy sheriff's wife home. An incendiary device is thrown at another house. Anderson then returns to talk to the young boy, who drives with them through town disguised by a box over his head, in order to point out the perpetrators.

A courtroom scene is then shown regarding the burning house case. The defendants all plead guilty and the judge sentences them to five years each — with five years suspended. They are free to go. Then another series of fire bombings occurs at churches, until finally a firebomb is thrown into a shack and the father tells the family to run as he goes outside with a shotgun. He is knocked out and lynched. The son returns to take the body of his father down from the tree. Ward and Anderson show up the next day and Ward tells Anderson the key is the 50 minutes that Pell was with his wife for which he otherwise has no alibi.

While a KKK rally is going on and agents are noting the license plates of cars parked nearby, Anderson goes to the deputy wife's house, presumably to get the key information. He stays and it is insinuated that he has a one-night stand with the deputy's wife.

Then the break in the case occurs: they find the bodies of the three men. The bodies are loaded into an ambulance and taken to the hospital. There, the sheriff pulls Deputy Pell aside and tells him he has problems at home. He later arrives with three other KKK members and they beat his wife and put her in the hospital. Ward tells Anderson about the beating and he becomes outraged. They then get into an argument about the proper investigative methods for solving the case. Eventually, Ward agrees to try it Anderson's way.

The mayor of the town is kidnapped and taken to a house, where a black male threatens him by way of a story of a black male having his scrotum cut off with a razor. The black male pulls out a razor, and it is insinuated that the mayor talks. The black male is identified as a bureau agent who is a specialist as he gets on a plane and flies away. Ward and Anderson decide to go after federal charges of civil rights violations, knowing they will never get a state charge against any of the perpetrators.

The agents then set up a series of encounters with the KKK members, first by calling an erroneous emergency meeting of the KKK to see who shows, then pressuring other members through false lynchings and physical threats. Eventually the KKK members are arrested and indicted, and the number of years they were sentenced appears on the screen in subtitles. The FBI then finds the mayor hanging in his basement, having committed suicide. Anderson visits Deputy Pell's wife. And, once again, the agents, Ward and Anderson, appear at a burned church, where whites and blacks are mingled together, listening to a Martin Luther King-like sermon. The scene transitions to a cemetery where the same white and blacks begin singing "Walk On" together and the camera focuses on a headstone that says "1964, Not Forgotten."

Mississippi Burning: Hollywood's Rendering

From the beginning, there is a clear distinction to be made in regard to the Hollywood rendering of *Mississippi Burning* and the true historical events, and that lies with names.[24] The names in real life, names that became such a fixture in the tragedy, have been changed in the film. The three civil rights workers, Schwerner, Goodman, and Chaney, become "the boys," Neshoba County becomes Jessup County, and people like Jimmy Lee Townsend becomes Clayton Townley. Even the two FBI agents that the film follows have their names changed, John Proctor becomes Agent Anderson and Joseph Sullivan becomes Agent Ward. There is no overt explanation as to why the names were changed in the film, no subtitle about protecting the names and reputations of the individuals involved. One is left to believe that because many of the people involved in the case, such as Edgar Ray Killen (who had not been convicted at the time of the film), were either still alive or their family members were, the film producers created fictional names in order to prevent lawsuits arising from the use of their names and how those individuals were presented. While this does diminish the historical accuracy of the film, it can be seen as justifiable, and once it is understood that the names are different, it is relatively easy to move on from this inaccuracy. It should be noted, however, that this particular historical inaccuracy does not excuse any of the other errors which appear in the film.

Once again, like the first film in this book, *Amistad*, this film is about an event that centered on mostly the lives of black Americans. While it is true many of the key players were white (the FBI agents, some members of C.O.R.E.), the majority of the principles involved in this case and overcoming the injustice of the day were black. In the film, nearly all of the blacks are played as background people all waiting for someone to help them or to be told what to do. The only one black character who steps up and seems to want to right these injustices is an 11-year-old boy. Black citizens are relegated to background material and their role in *Mississippi Burning* is all but eliminated. Thus, it is two diametrically opposed white men, in the guise of the two FBI agents, Ward and Anderson, that come to town to save the day. They are the heroes that finally crack the case and bring justice to Jessup (Neshoba) County. Like *Amistad* this film is entirely a white wash, aimed at a largely white American audience, with two white men as heroes, who can save the blacks in the film, thus saving American guilt for past injustices against black citizens.[25] Director Alan Parker conceded that it was his belief, if the two protagonists had not been white, "the film would probably have never been made."[26]

In addition to the only black willing to take a stance, there are other examples of the white wash. At the very end there is a black preacher voice-over during the funeral of the "three boys," yet the words do not resound like the Reverend Dr. Martin Luther King, Jr.'s words, nor is it like his voice. Dr. King had won the Nobel Peace Prize that same year as the disappearance of the three civil rights workers and, in fact, made an appeal for any information leading to their whereabouts. Yet, none of this was shown in the film. Further, in a number of cases, the director chose to show blacks singing spiritual gospels, standing on the side-lines singing and praying, but never doing anything. This is disingenuous at best. And, as if to make a point, the final spiritual is sung by a mixture of blacks and whites, males and females, which in the context of the funeral was historically inaccurate.[27] The only other scene where the blacks (and whites) appear to take a stand is the civil rights march through town, where they are once again seen singing. The historical discrepancy here, however, is during the FBI's investigation, there were no civil rights marches in Philadelphia or the surrounding towns.

Turning to the specifics of the film, in the opening scene there is a blue Ford station wagon being driven by a white male with a goatee (allegedly Schwerner). Next to him, in the passenger seat is another white male (Goodman) and a black male sitting in the back seat (Chaney). There are cars pursuing the Ford station wagon with their lights off. When the lights go on, the two white boys act as if they are not sure what is going on, while only the black male in the back seat seems to understand the gravity of their situation. In order to escape the cars, they veer off the road into a field, and then the flashing lights of a police car appear behind them. The exchange in the car goes something like this, "What do they want? I don't know. What are these—playing at? I don't know."

In real life, Chaney was the driver and it is believed that both Schwerner and Goodman were in the back seat trying not to be seen.[28] All three had just been arrested, held in jail for seven hours, were not allowed to use the phone, and had been released. The three real civil rights workers would have known exactly what was going on and would not have been so clueless. Especially Schwerner (Goatee), for he had been working for C.O.R.E. in Mississippi the longest. Not to mention, Schwerner had learned earlier, before being arrested, that the reason the church was burned to the ground was because the KKK was looking to assassinate him. These three guys were more knowledgeable than they appear in the film. The director makes it appear as if these three clueless guys are out for a ride, late at night, and all of a sudden some KKK guys (including one cop) decide to pull them over and kill them.

The film presents the three men leaving the road and driving hopelessly into a field. In reality, Chaney tried turning off the main road onto a dirt road in the hopes of losing the deputy sheriff. It did not work. When the deputy pulls over the car in the film, he immediately takes a threatening tone, and then a gunshot rings out, followed by a pause, then two more. The film suggests that the three civil rights workers were murdered in their vehicle, but this was not the case. The three were placed in the back of the patrol car, driven to the dam, and then shot outside of the vehicle. While evidence of any beatings prior to the three being shot is tenuous, it is generally concluded that only Chaney was beaten and shot. The other two, Schwerner and Goodman, were not beaten and were shot before Chaney. Regardless, there was no evidence from the blue Ford station wagon, despite the burned nature of the recovered vehicle, that anyone had been shot inside the vehicle.[29]

After the FBI agents arrive, the pressure on black citizens begins to rise on film. The real FBI agents, from the time they arrived to the time they found the bodies was 44 days, yet the film shows numerous incidents and attacks aimed at black citizens. At best this could be referred to as time compression, but the reality of even compressing an entire decade of events in Neshoba County (Jessup in the movie) would not amount to all of the events that transpire in the film. For instance, during the film, there are four churches being burned in the vicinity. There were 31 churches burned in Mississippi from June of 1964 to January of 1965, but that was across the entire state.[30] In fact, the only church burned during the investigation was the one that prompted all of the events in the first place.

In addition, there is a repeated attack on Willie the black at the lunch counter. At one point, his house is attacked and the young boy gets away, while the father, tired of the attacks, takes his shotgun and goes outside to confront the attackers. He is then lynched from a tree. The boy returns to let him down. This is entirely Hollywood fiction. There were no lynchings of any blacks during the Neshoba County investigation.

When the agent in charge runs into difficulties, part of the recurring theme in the film is that he calls for more agents to put more pressure on the locals. While it is true the agent in charge, Maynor, did ask for more FBI agents, he never received the 100 or more requested in the film. J. Edgar Hoover, the director of the FBI, did send more agents, but he rotated them through, so while approximately 150 agents worked MIBURN, at most there were 50 agents on hand at any given time.

One scene where Agent Ward calls for more men is when he wants to search the swamp for the bodies. In the film, sailors are brought in to search. While it would seem incongruous, this was historically accurate, for hundreds of sailors from the Long Naval Air Station were brought in to search the swamps. In the film, they have no real success. In real life, they found seven missing bodies, unrelated to MIBURN, that had been dumped in the swamp. This was not depicted in the film.

When the agents do find the bodies, buried in the earthen dam, they are in a wide open area, between what appear to be two dams or a channel, with a river in the background. In reality, the area was so heavily forested, the dam could not be seen from the air and it was difficult to access. Had it not been for the information provided to the FBI, it is doubtful they would have ever found the location of the bodies.

In the film, the case is ultimately broken by the tenacity of the FBI agents, and the less than by-the-book ways of the one agent, Anderson. Throughout the film there is an antagonism that builds between the agent in charge, Ward, and his sidekick, Anderson. Ward is by-the-book, Anderson is by-whatever-means-necessary. Throughout much of the film, it is done Ward's way. By the end of the movie, it is done Anderson's way and the case is resolved. The film makes it appear that this is what solved MIBURN, but that could not be farther from the truth.

First, there is the issue of missing time on the part of Deputy Sheriff Pell (Price). The only one who provides him cover is his wife. So, Anderson, ever the renegade, seduces Pell's wife and has a one-night stand with her. When Pell finds out, he invites three of his KKK buddies to come to the house and beat her, putting her in the hospital. Anderson gets angry and he and Ward have a fight where Ward finally gives in to Anderson and says they will do it his way. The reality is, Anderson (Proctor) never had an affair with the deputy sheriff's wife, his wife was never beaten, she did not end up in the hospital, and Proctor (Anderson) and Sullivan (Ward) never had a fight. This was not how they solved the case.

Second, there is the issue of pursuing some of the shaky participants and scarring them. In one example, they go after Lester (Killen) and a number of agents pretend to be KKK members who are targeting Lester because he was seen talking with the FBI. They go to lynch him, but Ward and Anderson show up to save him. They fire shots at the KKK members, who run into the field, unharmed, before taking off their white sheets which reveals themselves as FBI agents. It is a great scene, played with great effect. But it never happened.[31]

Third, and probably the most difficult of the methods employed, was the use of the "special agent." In the film, a black male FBI agent is called in to assist. He kidnaps the mayor and threatens to "cut off his balls." The mayor gives in and tells all. The agent leaves the area. This is, in part, historically inaccurate; at best, built on half-truths. There were no black FBI agents in 1964, so the film is entirely incorrect in making that assertion.[32] There is, however, some conjecture, based on reports that are flimsy at best, that the FBI called in Gregory Scarpa, Sr., a member of the Mafia (Colombo family), and FBI informant, to kidnap an appliance salesman and member of the KKK. So, if this story is true, it was not a black FBI agent versus the mayor, but rather a Mafioso versus an appliance salesman. The problem with believing this story is the FBI has never confirmed this story (and likely never would), so the primary source is Gregory Scarpa, Jr., not exactly an unbiased source. While some former FBI agents have also made this claim, it is sketchy at best.[33] The director, Alan Parker, made the comment in an interview that he changed the Mafioso to a black FBI agent as "almost a metaphor for what was happening in real life, the assertion of black anger, and black rights reasserting themselves."[34] Bad metaphors clearly make for bad history.

The way in which the real information was obtained regarding the location of the missing bodies, which broke the case, was to simply play on good old-fashioned greed. The FBI offered $30,000 to anyone providing them information on the location of the three civil rights workers.[35] The person who provided this information became known as Mr. X in order for his identity to be protected. In subsequent years it has been learned that Mr. X was in fact, highway patrolman Maynard King.[36] He had heard information from KKK member Pete Jordan; specifically, that the three bodies were buried on the Old Jolly Farm, and King passed that information along to the FBI. What has not been answered to date is who received the award money—King, Jordan, or both. King died in 1966 from a massive heart attack and Jordan never spoke about it.

There are a number of other historical inaccuracies that are minor, but do not necessarily detract from the film. In one scene, the mayor of the town makes the comment that the three civil rights workers are probably in Chicago, drinking a beer, and laughing at all the fuss they caused. This line was not spoken by the mayor of Philadelphia, Mississippi, but rather in real life it was said by U.S. Senator James Eastland. This same fictional mayor, at the very end of the film, is found hanging in his basement from a suicide. The real mayor of Philadelphia did not commit suicide.

There are some oddities in the film as well. At one point, Agent Anderson is asked if he would like sugar in his tea. Mississippi is assuredly in the South, and Southerners always have pre-sweetened iced tea. Only in the North would one be asked if they would like sugar in their iced tea in 1964. Another odd historical mistake is when Ward and Anderson go to Deputy Sheriff Pell's house one evening and he is watching baseball on television. In 1964, baseball games were still played in the afternoons.[37]

Conclusion

When the film was released in December of 1988, it brought with its release a new level of criticism over historically based films that had elements of fiction in them. The majority of the reviews and comments were negative toward what appeared to be the passing off of fiction on a historically based movie. As one critic summed up the criticism in his review of *Mississippi Burning* for the American Historical Association, "A number of commentators have criticized director Alan Parker for taking liberties with the facts and producing a film that contains as much fiction as the truth."[38] In fact, the film was so filled with fiction that half the film used entirely fictional elements (e.g., the affair with the deputy sheriff's wife, the near-lynching of Lester, etc.) while the other half, containing historically based information, was greatly lacking in accuracy.

Parker, however, defended his film by making the argument that the film "is a fiction."[39] He explained, "It's a movie. There have been a lot of documentaries on the subject. They run on PBS and nobody watches them. I have to reach a big audience, so hopefully the film is accessible to reach millions of people in 50 different countries."[40] Parker further asserted, "It's fiction in the same way that 'Platoon' and 'Apocalypse Now' are fictions of the Vietnam War. But the important thing is the heart of the truth, the spirit. I keep coming back to truth, but I defend the right to change it in order to reach an audience who knows nothing about the realities and certainly don't watch PBS documentaries."[41]

Interestingly, Parker went beyond the argument for artistic license and did not defend his film as being historical and accurately based as many directors have done with other films, many of those featured in this book. What Parker raises, however, is an important question. If the director makes a film about a historical subject that most people do not know about, but the film is one that they will watch, has the director done a service to the nation's historical memory? The average American did not know much about the plight of the Amistads, but after Spielberg's film, it nearly became a household name. Many Americans do not remember or know about the Mississippi Burning investigation by the FBI, but with the success of the film, now they do. So, the crux of the question comes down to this: would it be better for an entertaining historical film to be made, one that makes a wide audience aware of the historical events/situation, even if it is historically inaccurate, or would it be better to not have the film made, and allow people to remain mostly ignorant? In simpler terms, is it better to be inaccurately knowledgeable or wholly ignorant?

Perhaps there is an answer to this question. Toplin concludes that "In basing his film on an actual and significant historical event, Parker invites scrutiny over details and concern for authenticity."[42] This would mean that it would be better to have the inaccurate film made, but then invite the criticism to correct the historical inaccuracies, the specific goal of this book. However, Toplin also notes that perhaps there is an alternative answer, and that is—"the truth behind the Mississippi story is so dramatic that there was no need to apply liberal doses of fiction."[43] In other words, Parker was wrong. A historically accurate motion picture could have been made, that would have reached a wider audience. It is only, perhaps, implied that it would just have been a little more difficult to direct.

Further Reading

Alston, Alex A., Jr. and James L. Dickerson. (2009). *Devil's Sanctuary: An Eyewitness History of Mississippi Hate Crimes.* Chicago: Lawrence Hill Books.

Ball, Howard. (2006). *Justice in Mississippi: The Murder Trial of Edgar Ray Killen.* Lawrence, KS: University Press of Kansas.

Ball, Howard. (2004). *Murder in Mississippi: United States v. Price and the Struggle for Civil Rights.* Lawrence, KS: University Press of Kansas.

Cagin, Seth and Philip Dray. (2006). *We Are Not Afraid: The Story of Goodman, Schwerner, and Chaney, and the Civil Rights Campaign for Mississippi.* New York: Nation Books.

Huie, William Bradford. (2000). *Three Lives for Mississippi.* Jackson, Mississippi: University Press of Mississippi.

Linder, Doug. (2011). *U.S. v. Cecil Price et al.* ("Mississippi Burning" Trial). *Famous Trials Website.* Retrieved online at http://law2.umkc.edu/faculty/projects/ftrials/price&bowers/price&bowers.htm.

McCord, William. (1965). *Mississippi: The Long Hot Summer.* New York: W.W. Norton & Company.

Watson, Bruce. (2010). *Freedom Summer: The Savage Season that Made Mississippi Burn and Made America a Democracy.* New York: Viking Press.

Whitehead, Don. (1970). *Attack on Terror: The FBI Against the Ku Klux Klan in Mississippi.* New York: Funk & Wagnalls Company.

Williams, Juan. (1988). *Eyes on the Prize: America's Civil Rights Years, 1954–1965.* New York: Penguin Books.

Endnotes

1. *Mississippi Burning.* (Orion, 1988) (Alan Parker, Director).
2. Watson, Bruce. (2010). *Freedom Summer: The Savage Season that Made Mississippi Burn and Made America a Democracy.* New York: Viking Press.
3. Cagin, Seth and Philip Dray. (2006). *We Are Not Afraid: The Story of Goodman, Schwerner, and Chaney, and the Civil Rights Campaign for Mississippi.* New York: Nation Books; Watson, Bruce. (2010). *Freedom Summer: The Savage Season that Made Mississippi Burn and Made America a Democracy.* New York: Viking Press.
4. Kotz, Nick. (2005) . *Judgment Days: Lyndon Baines Johnson, Martin Luther King, Jr., and the Laws that Changed America.* 3rd Edition. New York: Houghton Mifflin, p. 159.
5. Cagin, Seth and Philip Dray. (2006). *We Are Not Afraid: The Story of Goodman, Schwerner, and Chaney, and the Civil Rights Campaign for Mississippi.* New York: Nation Books.
6. Kotz, Nick. (2005) . *Judgment Days: Lyndon Baines Johnson, Martin Luther King, Jr., and the Laws that Changed America.* 3rd Edition. New York: Houghton Mifflin, p. 158.
7. Watson, Bruce. (2010). *Freedom Summer: The Savage Season that Made Mississippi Burn and Made America a Democracy.* New York: Viking Press.
8. Alston, Alex A., Jr. and James L. Dickerson. (2009). *Devil's Sanctuary: An Eyewitness History of Mississippi Hate Crimes.* Chicago: Lawrence Hill Books; McCord, William. (1965). *Mississippi: The Long Hot Summer.* New York: W.W. Norton & Company.
9. Linder, Doug. (2011). *U.S. vs Cecil Price et al.* ("Mississippi Burning" Trial). *Famous Trials Website.* Retrieved online at http://law2.umkc.edu/faculty/projects/ftrials/price&bowers/price& bowers.htm.
10. Huie, William Bradford. (2000). *Three Lives for Mississippi.* Jackson, Mississippi: University Press of Mississippi.
11. Cagin, Seth and Philip Dray. (2006). *We Are Not Afraid: The Story of Goodman, Schwerner, and Chaney, and the Civil Rights Campaign for Mississippi.* New York: Nation Books.
12. Cagin, Seth and Philip Dray. (2006). *We Are Not Afraid: The Story of Goodman, Schwerner, and Chaney, and the Civil Rights Campaign for Mississippi.* New York: Nation Books.
13. Linder, Doug. (2011). *U.S. vs Cecil Price et al.* ("Mississippi Burning" Trial). *Famous Trials Website.* Retrieved online at http://law2.umkc.edu/faculty/projects/ftrials/price& bowers/price&bowers.htm.
14. Cagin, Seth and Philip Dray. (2006). *We Are Not Afraid: The Story of Goodman, Schwerner, and Chaney, and the Civil Rights Campaign for Mississippi.* New York: Nation Books.
15. Linder, Douglas. (2002). Bending Toward Justice: John Doar and the Mississippi Burning Trial. *Mississippi Law Journal, 72.* Retrieved online at http://law2.umkc.edu/faculty/projects/ftrials/price&bowers/doaressay.html
16. Whitehead, Don. (1970). *Attack on Terror: The FBI Against the Ku Klux Klan in Mississippi.* New York: Funk & Wagnalls Company.

17. Linder, Doug. (2011). *U.S. vs Cecil Price et al.* ("Mississippi Burning" Trial). *Famous Trials Website.* Retrieved online at http://law2.umkc.edu/faculty/projects/ftrials/price&bowers/price&bowers.htm.

18. Ball, Howard. (2006). *Justice in Mississippi: The Murder Trial of Edgar Ray Killen.* Lawrence, KS: University Press of Kansas; Ball, Howard. (2004). *Murder in Mississippi: United States v. Price and the Struggle for Civil Rights.* Lawrence, KS: University Press of Kansas; Cagin, Seth and Philip Dray. (2006). *We Are Not Afraid: The Story of Goodman, Schwerner, and Chaney, and the Civil Rights Campaign for Mississippi.* New York: Nation Books.

19. Ball, Howard. (2004). *Murder in Mississippi: United States v. Price and the Struggle for Civil Rights.* Lawrence, KS: University Press of Kansas.

20. For more information on the trial itself, see Linder, Doug. (2011). *U.S. vs Cecil Price et al.* ("Mississippi Burning" Trial). *Famous Trials Website.* Retrieved online at http://law2.umkc.edu/faculty/projects/ftrials/price&bowers/price&bowers.htm.

21. Ball, Howard. (2006). *Justice in Mississippi: The Murder Trial of Edgar Ray Killen.* Lawrence, KS: University Press of Kansas.

22. *Mississippi Burning.* (Orion, 1988). (Alan Parker, Director).

23. Internet Movie Database. (2011). *Mississippi Burning* (1988). Retrieved online at http://www.imdb.com/title/tt0095647/.

24. *Mississippi Burning* .(Orion, 1988). (Alan Parker, Director).

25. Gabriel, John. (1998). *Racialized Politics and the Media.* New York: Routledge; White, Jack E. (1989). "Show Business: Just Another Mississippi White Wash." *Time,* 34.

26. Ringel, E. (1989). Truth Isn't as Simple as Black and White in Mississippi Burning. *Atlanta Journal and Constitution,* K01.

27. One excellent reference for understanding the activities of black civil rights workers during that summer in Mississippi is the book by Ann Moody. See Moody, Ann. (1968). *Coming of Age in Mississippi.* New York: Doubleday.

28. Cagin, Seth and Philip Dray. (2006). *We Are Not Afraid: The Story of Goodman, Schwerner, and Chaney, and the Civil Rights Campaign for Mississippi.* New York: Nation Books; Toplin, Robert Brent. (1989). "*Mississippi Burning* Scorches Historians." *Perspectives: American Historical Association.* Retrieved online at http://www.historians.org/perspectives/issues/1989/8904/8904FIL.cfm.

29. Cagin, Seth and Philip Dray. (2006). *We Are Not Afraid: The Story of Goodman, Schwerner, and Chaney, and the Civil Rights Campaign for Mississippi.* New York: Nation Books; King, Wayne. (1988). "Film, Fact vs. Fiction in Mississippi." *The New York Times.* Retrieved online at http://www.nytimes.com/1988/12/04/movies/film-fact-vs-fiction-in-mississippi.html?pagewanted=all; Toplin, Robert Brent. (1989). "*Mississippi Burning* Scorches Historians." *Perspectives: American Historical Association.* Retrieved online at http://www.historians.org/perspectives/issues/1989/8904/8904FIL.cfm.

30. King, Wayne. (1988). "Film, Fact vs. Fiction in Mississippi." *The New York Times.* Retrieved online at http://www.nytimes.com/1988/12/04/movies/film-fact-vs-fiction-in-mississippi.html?pagewanted=all.

31. Cagin, Seth and Philip Dray. (2006). *We Are Not Afraid: The Story of Goodman, Schwerner, and Chaney, and the Civil Rights Campaign for Mississippi.* New York: Nation Books; DuPont, Katie, Jim Bube, Devin Johnson, Dan Stets, and Emily Papendieck. (2011). Approaches to Film: Context of *Mississippi Burning.* Retrieved online at http://course1.winona.edu/pjohnson/h140/mississippi.htm.

32. King, Wayne. (1988). "Film, Fact vs. Fiction in Mississippi." *The New York Times*. Retrieved online at http://www.nytimes.com/1988/12/04/movies/film-fact-vs-fiction-in-mississippi.html?pagewanted=all.

33. Linder, Doug. (2011). *U.S. vs Cecil Price et al.* ("Mississippi Burning" Trial). *Famous Trials Website*. Retrieved online at http://law2.umkc.edu/faculty/projects/ftrials/price&bowers/price&bowers.htm.

34. King, Wayne. (1988). "Film, Fact vs. Fiction in Mississippi." *The New York Times*. Retrieved online at http://www.nytimes.com/1988/12/04/movies/film-fact-vs-fiction-in-mississippi.html?pagewanted=all.

35. Cagin, Seth and Philip Dray. (2006). *We Are Not Afraid: The Story of Goodman, Schwerner, and Chaney, and the Civil Rights Campaign for Mississippi*. New York: Nation Books; King, Wayne. (1988). "Film, Fact vs. Fiction in Mississippi." *The New York Times*. Retrieved online at http://www.nytimes.com/1988/12/04/movies/film-fact-vs-fiction-in-mississippi.html?pagewanted=all; Toplin, Robert Brent. (1989). "*Mississippi Burning* Scorches Historians." *Perspectives: American Historical Association*. Retrieved online at http://www.historians.org/perspectives/issues/1989/8904/8904FIL.cfm.

36. Mitchell, Jerry. (2007). "Documents Identify Whistle Blower." *ClarionLedger.com*. Retrieved online at http://www.clarionledger.com/article/20071203/NEWS/712030343/Documents-identify-whistle-blower.

37. Internet Movie Database. (2011). *Mississippi Burning* (1988). Retrieved online at http://www.imdb.com/title/tt0095647/.

38. Toplin, Robert Brent. (1989). "*Mississippi Burning* Scorches Historians." *Perspectives: American Historical Association*. Retrieved online at http://www.historians.org/perspectives/issues/1989/8904/8904FIL.cfm.

39. King, Wayne. (1988). "Film, Fact vs. Fiction in Mississippi." *The New York Times*. Retrieved online at http://www.nytimes.com/1988/12/04/movies/film-fact-vs-fiction-in-mississippi.html?pagewanted=all.

40. King, Wayne. (1988). "Film, Fact vs. Fiction in Mississippi." *The New York Times*. Retrieved online at http://www.nytimes.com/1988/12/04/movies/film-fact-vs-fiction-in-mississippi.html?pagewanted=all.

41. King, Wayne. (1988). "Film, Fact vs. Fiction in Mississippi." *The New York Times*. Retrieved online at http://www.nytimes.com/1988/12/04/movies/film-fact-vs-fiction-in-mississippi.html?pagewanted=all.

42. Toplin, Robert Brent. (1989). "*Mississippi Burning* Scorches Historians." *Perspectives: American Historical Association*. Retrieved online at http://www.historians.org/perspectives/issues/1989/8904/8904FIL.cfm.

43. Toplin, Robert Brent. (1989). "*Mississippi Burning* Scorches Historians." *Perspectives: American Historical Association*. Retrieved online at http://www.historians.org/perspectives/issues/1989/8904/8904FIL.cfm.

CHAPTER 10

All the President's Men and the Watergate Scandal (1972)

President Richard Nixon gives his victory sign to those gathered on the White House lawn to send him off in the wake of the Watergate Investigation, on August 9, 1974, the day he became the only President of the United States to resign from office. Photo courtesy of the Richard Nixon Library.

Nothing's riding on this except the first amendment of the Constitution, freedom of the press and maybe the future of this country.
— Washington Post Editor Ben Bradlee to reporters Woodward and Bernstein after they discovered the extent of the cover-up

Introduction

In 1972, President Richard M. Nixon was seeking reelection. Many top Republicans, and possibly Nixon himself, were convinced that the Democrats were planning to use "dirty tricks" to get their candidate elected into office.[1] In order to get information on the Democrats' plans, members of the Committee to Reelect the President (CRP) broke into the office of Larry O'Brien, the head of the Democratic National Committee (DNC), in the Watergate office building in Washington, D.C. Their plan was to put bugging equipment on his phone to listen to his conversations. On Sunday, May 28, the burglars broke into the Democratic Headquarters and placed wiretaps on three phones. It was later discovered that the wiretap on O'Brien's phone did not work, so the burglars decided to go back in and replace the wiretap. They did so on the night of June 17, 1972.

That night, a security guard making rounds through the building discovered tape on the lock of a door to the parking garage, preventing the door from locking shut. Not thinking much of it, he removed the tape and went on his way. Fifteen minutes later he returned to find the tape had been replaced. This time, the guard called the police. The police responded and discovered the offices of the DNC had been opened. They arrested five burglars, and later discovered two other men who were helping the burglars from a hotel room across the street. The burglars were quickly linked to the White House.

After a long investigation, two reporters from the *Washington Post* uncovered evidence that the White House and the President were aware of, and possibly ordered, the break-in, and then devised complex cover stories to hide the role of the administration in the burglary. They also found evidence that hush money was paid to the burglars from a secret slush fund to keep them from talking, *dirty tricks* were used by CRP to influence the outcome of the election, and federal campaign finance laws had been violated. When it became clear that impeachment was probable, Nixon announced his resignation and Vice President Gerald Ford was sworn in as President of the United States.

Many of the events surrounding the Watergate scandal may not have been known had it not been for the reporters who pursued the story. For months, the reporters chased leads and asked questions to uncover the facts. Throughout, they discovered that following the story was not always easy, and they were sometimes afraid for their lives. But in the end, they revealed a true story of dishonesty and unethical actions at the top level of government. The reporters' experience in tracking down wrongdoing was the basis of the movie *All the President's Men*.[2]

All the President's Men: The History

On Saturday, June 17, 1972, at 9:00 AM, *Washington Post* reporter Bob Woodward received a phone call from the city editor, who told him about the arrest of five men earlier that morning at the national offices of the Democratic Party in the Watergate building complex. The burglars were arrested at 2:30 AM, and had in their possession photographic material and electronic gear including a walkie-talkie, rolls of film, cameras, lock picks, tear-gas guns, and bugging devices. They were wearing business suits and carrying large amounts of money, some of which included consecutive $100 bills, ranging in amounts from $215 to $814.[3]

The burglars had a preliminary hearing scheduled for later that afternoon, so Woodward went to the courthouse to watch the hearing. Woodward discovered that three of the burglars were Cuban-American. When the defendants appeared in court, the judge asked the defendants if they had jobs. One burglar, James McCord, replied that he was a security consultant for the Central Intelligence Agency (C.I.A.).[4]

Woodward found this to be quite unusual and wrote the story for the paper, but he continued to look into the burglars' background. To assist him, another more experienced reporter, Carl Bernstein, was also assigned to the story alongside Woodward. Together, they discovered that McCord was the security coordinator for the Committee to Reelect the President (CRP). When they contacted the head of CRP, John Mitchell (the former U.S. Attorney General) for comments, he denied any relationship with McCord.

That evening, Woodward received information that two address books belonging to the burglars contained the name and phone number of Howard Hunt, next to notations that said "W. House" and "W.H." When contacted, Hunt seemed nervous and did not want to answer any questions. Not long after, Ken Clawson, a former reporter at the *Post* who had become the deputy director of White House communications, denied Hunt had anything to do with the break-ins. The White House press secretary Ronald Ziegler also denied any relationship and called it a "third-rate burglary attempt."[5] Later, the President himself denied any involvement by the White House.[6] Despite the denials, the possible connection between the burglars, the White House, and CRP was curious to Woodward and Bernstein, and they stayed on the story.

Meanwhile, the Federal Bureau of Investigation (FBI) was investigating the possible link between the burglars and the White House. They assigned about 150 agents to the story. It is now known that the information the agents had was largely the same as that found by Woodward and Bernstein. Often, the FBI thought the reporters were getting their information directly from FBI reports.[7] However, the focus of the FBI investigation was very narrow and was limited only to the burglary itself and bugging at the DNC rather than the possible conspiracy behind it, which was the focal point for Woodward and Bernstein.

At one point, Bernstein discovered that a check for $89,000 had been deposited in the bank account of one of the burglars, Bernard Barker. He found it curious that the check originated in Mexico City, and soon realized that money was being laundered through Mexico in an effort to hide its origins. The reason for this was new campaign finance laws. Before April 7, the date the new law went into effect, anonymous contributions could be accepted by the CRP[8] At this time, Democrats, business executives, or labor leaders could contribute to the campaign of a Republican candidate with their anonymity ensured. To take advantage of the last-minute opportunity for secret contributions, Maurice Stans (the finance chair for the CRP) went on a fund-raising swing across the southwest United States, bringing in thousands of dollars. The Midwestern campaign manager for the CRP, Kenneth Dahlberg, also collected last-minute contributions.

As the two *Post* reporters continued to investigate their leads, the General Accounting Office (GAO) also decided to investigate the events of Watergate, focusing on the possible connection between the break-in and the new campaign finance law. Bernstein's contact at the GAO told him that there were hundreds of dollars in unaccounted cash—a slush fund of cash that totaled at least $100,000.[9] When Bernstein asked a former official in the Nixon administration about the slush fund, he was told that G. Gordon Liddy had supervision over the fund. He was to spend the money as needed "if the crazies made an attack on the President."[10] The GAO report also indicated 11 possible violations of the campaign finance law and that the CRP maintained a secret slush fund of at least $350,000.[11] Based on that information, the *Post* reported that the GAO had determined that the CRP had mishandled more than $500,000 in campaign funds.[12]

By this time there were many calls for a special prosecutor to investigate some of these charges, but Nixon refused to appoint one. Instead, he told the public that his legal counsel, John Dean, had conducted an internal investigation and found that no one on the White House staff was involved with the break-in.[13]

The findings from these outside investigations did not satisfy Bernstein and Woodward, and they continued to probe the story. They were able to find a confidential list of CRP employees and called many of them, but quickly discovered that none of the employees were willing to talk to the reporters on the phone. In another tactic to get interviews, the reporters began to show up at employees' homes during evenings. Many employees asked the reporters to leave "before they see you."[14] Despite this, Woodward and Bernstein began to get some inkling that documents and records had been destroyed immediately after the break-in, but no one would provide details as to what documents were destroyed and by whom.

On one visit to a CRP employee's home, Bernstein was allowed into the house by the employee's sister. The sister asked Bernstein if he wanted coffee and he accepted it, a move that got him into their home. The employee, a bookkeeper, reluctantly spoke to the reporter. The woman said that she knew who received payments from the CRP and who approved the payments. Six people were paid separately from the slush fund, all in small amounts, but all of the evidence had been destroyed.[15] One of those who received payments was G. Gordon Liddy, a CRP employee. Another person to receive money was Jeb Stuart Magruder, a special assistant to the President. At first, the bookkeeper refused to give Bernstein any names. Instead, she used their initials. It was becoming very clear to Bernstein that the slush fund held by CRP was related to the break-in and bugging operation of the Democratic Headquarters and he wanted to know more.

On September 15, the five men arrested in the Watergate complex were indicted by a grand jury, as were Hunt and Liddy, the lookout men across the street. They were each charged with eight separate counts, all related to conspiracy, burglary, and the federal wiretapping statute.

The indictment did not stop the reporters from continuing to explore the twists in the complex story. Woodward developed a source who helped the reporters when they ran out of leads. This man worked in the executive branch and had access to inside information from the White House. Since he was on *deep background*, editors at the *Post* dubbed him "Deep Throat," after the popular pornographic movie at the time.[16] At first, the two spoke on the phone, but Deep Throat became nervous about that. So they devised a system whereby Woodward would leave a red flag on his apartment balcony in an old flower pot if he needed to meet Deep Throat. They would then meet at 2 a.m. in a parking garage. To get there, Woodward took two or more taxis in order to prevent being followed. Once in the garage, the two men would often talk for an hour or more. If Deep Throat wanted a meeting, he would indicate that on page 20 of the *New York Times* that was delivered to Woodward's apartment each day. The page number would be circled and the hands of a clock indicating the time of the meeting. The source never gave Woodward exact information, but led him in the right direction.

From what the bookkeeper had told him earlier, Bernstein knew that Hugh Sloan, the treasurer of the CRP, was aware of the payments from the secret slush fund. One night, Bernstein decided to visit Sloan at his house and ask him some questions. Sloan told Bernstein that he paid Herbert Porter, a CRP employee, close to $300,000—more money than the reporter had originally thought. When asked, Sloan would not say who ordered him to make the payments. But he did say the fund had been in existence for more than 18 months. Knowing that information, Bernstein wrote a story indicating what happened in the CRP after the break-in. He wrote that Mitchell's assistants at the CRP, Robert C. Mardian and Fred LaRue, directed others to destroy documents. Mitchell forbade employees from talking to the press, and gave specific responses that might be asked by investigators.

Woodward returned to see Sloan on another occasion. This time, Sloan said there were five people who could authorize payments from the slush fund, including Mitchell and Stans.[17] When Sloan was approached for money, he would usually call Mitchell, who would approve the payment. This meant that while he was attorney general of the U.S., Mitchell authorized the expenditure of campaign funds for illegal activities against political opposition.[18] Later Magruder was also able to approve payments. This meant that Mitchell, Stans, and Magruder were three of the five people who could approve payment from the slush fund. Both reporters wanted to know who else was responsible for handing out the secret money and for what reason.

Later that night, Woodward called Mitchell for a response to the charge that he authorized payment of hush money from an illegal fund. At first, Mitchell panicked, then denied the charges. After some later meetings with Sloan, Woodward and Bernstein agreed that Kalmbach knew all about the finances of the Nixon campaign, and he was one of the five people with the authority to approve payments from the slush fund.[19] The fifth person, they were told, was an official in the White House, but Sloan would not divulge that name. The reporters believed it to be Bob Haldeman, the White House Chief of Staff.

Sloan told the reporters that the slush fund was used for espionage and political sabotage,[20] and that he had paid Donald Segretti to carry that out. Woodward and Bernstein discovered that Segretti crossed the country more than 10 times during the latter part of 1971, visiting cities in key political states for the 1972 campaign. They also discovered that as an undergraduate student at the University of Southern California (USC), Segretti had been friends with several people who later worked at the White House. At USC, they carried out what they called "ratfucking," which referred to their attempts to influence a campaign by stuffing ballot boxes, planting spies in opposition camps, and sending out bogus campaign literature.[21] Bernstein immediately wondered if the secret fund held in the CRP financed "ratfucking" against the Democrats in the 1972 campaign.[22]

One particularly effective sabotage technique was the Canuck letter. This was a forged, poorly written letter to the editor that appeared in the *Manchester Union Leader*. In the letter, the author claimed that a member of Muskie's staff made a derogatory remark about Americans with a French-Canadian background, calling them *Canucks*. Muskie, the Democratic candidate for president, responded to the allegations on the steps of the *Union Leader's* offices. In an emotional speech, Muskie reportedly broke down and cried numerous times. Many voters considered his response to be unstable, and threw their support to George McGovern instead. Muskie ended up losing the Democratic nomination, largely due to the letter.

Deep Throat told Woodward that the Canuck Letter was really written by someone inside the White House.[23] A fellow reporter at the *Post* provided more evidence of that when she told Bernstein and Woodward that the letter was actually written by Ken Clawson. Clawson admitted to writing the story while they were having a drink together one night at her apartment. Bernstein thought that it may have been an initiation rite for the White House in which new members of the President's staff had to prove themselves by "screwing" an enemy of the White House.[24] When asked about it by Woodward and Bernstein, Clawson seemed concerned that it would be reported that the conversation took place in her apartment because he was married, with a wife and family and a dog and a cat.[25] The reporters wrote the story, headlined, "FBI Finds Nixon Aides Sabotaged Democrats."[26]

Meanwhile, the White House began a counterattack on the *Post* and the two reporters. There were challenges made against the *Post's* ownership of two television stations in Florida. Some of the people challenging the licenses were people who had long associations with Nixon.[27] The CRP then subpoenaed Bernstein's and Woodward's files.[28]

The criminal trial of the burglars began with Judge John Sirica presiding. After the opening statement, Hunt changed his plea to guilty, as did the Cubans.[29] Allegations arose that Hunt urged the other defendants to change their pleas to guilty with the promise that their families would be cared for financially and they could count on executive clemency after a few months in jail.[30] It took the jury less than 90 minutes to find Liddy and McCord guilty of all counts against them.

At the same time, the Senate began their investigation of the events surrounding Watergate. The Senate Committee was headed by Democratic Senator Sam Ervin from North Carolina. Before the hearings began, Ervin called Woodward as a means to learn more about what the reporters knew. Woodward told Ervin the key to the events was the secret campaign cash, and told Ervin the committee should trace the secret slush fund. He also told Ervin that the evidence pointed toward a massive Haldeman undercover operation.[31]

It was becoming very clear to the reporters that the break-in at the Watergate was a small part of a massive campaign of espionage and sabotage against anyone who opposed the administration.[32] More evidence of this was provided as people from within the administration chose to testify about what they knew about the break-in and subsequent cover-up. Dean agreed to testify that there were many meetings about Watergate and the cover-up, and that Nixon attended them.[33] Continuing testimony indicated that secret investigations into the Democrats by the Nixon administration started as early as 1969. In 1971, Haldeman ordered an FBI investigation of Daniel Schorr, a C.B.S. news reporter.

In one of their last meetings, Deep Throat told Woodward that electronic surveillance was being used against them, and that they were being watched.[34]

In the Senate Watergate Committee meeting, McCord testified behind closed doors to seven Senators. McCord reportedly testified that Liddy stated that the plans and budget for the Watergate operation were approved by Mitchell when he was still the attorney general. He also testified that the White House Special Counsel Charles Colson knew about Watergate in advance.[35] After hearing so many allegations about the President's involvement in the cover-up, the House Judiciary Committee started an investigation into the possibility of impeaching Nixon.

McCord then faced sentencing in his criminal trial. At the hearing, McCord gave a letter to the judge in which he indicated that people had committed perjury during the trial and that they were under pressure to keep quiet.[36] He wrote that others were involved in Watergate who were not identified in testimony.[37]

By this time, things were falling apart in the administration. Both Haldeman and Dean resigned. Throughout early 1974, many of those associated with the administration pled guilty to various offenses. Mitchell and Stans were on trial for obstructing justice and perjury. Additionally, eight officers from different corporations also pled guilty to making illegal contributions to the CRP. On March 1, the Washington grand jury charged seven former White House employees and campaign aides with conspiracy to obstruct justice. This included Haldeman, Ehrlichman, and Mitchell, among others.

In the end, Woodward and Bernstein followed a story of lies and corruption, and an extensive cover-up, carried out by the President and his administration. Without their continued investigative reporting, it is not known if the public would have ever known the full story behind the Watergate break-in. The reporters and others at the *Post* had little doubt that the events were orchestrated and, if not ordered by the President, made with his knowledge and approval.[38] The scandal ruined political and personal careers of many involved. Some top officials from the Nixon administration went to prison. Nixon, almost certain to be impeached, resigned before hearings could begin. He was later pardoned by Ford and did not face criminal charges for his actions concerning the break-in and subsequent cover-up.

All the President's Men: The Film

The book describing the reporters' role in exposing the scandal sold nearly 300,000 copies when it was published. Robert Redford bought the rights to the movie and later played a starring role in it.[39] The movie version also included Dustin Hoffman as Carl Bernstein, Jason Robards as Ben Bradlee (executive editor of the *Washington Post*), and Hal Holbrook as Deep Throat. The movie was nominated for the Academy Award for Best Picture and for seven other Oscars. To ensure accuracy of the events, the actors visited the newsroom prior to filming, although the film itself was shot on a sound stage.

The movie begins with a typewriter's keys informing viewers it is June 1, 1972. President Nixon is shown arriving at the Capitol. His destination is the House of Representatives, where he is to give a speech.

The scene switches to the Watergate building. A guard on rounds sees a door taped open. He removes the tape and calls the police. Two plain clothes officers are called to investigate the possible burglary. The officers enter the building and go into the offices of the Democratic headquarters. Across the street, lookouts for the burglars are in contact with them via walkie-talkies and tell the men that there are people entering the building. The police enter the offices and catch the burglars, who are dressed in suits and holding walkie-talkies. They also have two 35 mm cameras and different amounts of money in sequential $100 bills. Later, a *Washington Post* editor calls reporter Bob Woodward and tells him to go to the courthouse to watch the burglars' arraignment. Another reporter, Carl Bernstein, overhears the call and asks if he can check out some sources at the Watergate.

At the arraignment Woodward discovers that the five burglars are all charged with burglary of the second degree. When the judge asks the men about their jobs, one defendant tells the judge that he is a security consultant, recently retired from the Central Intelligence Agency (CIA).

Back at the *Washington Post* offices, Woodward tells other reporters that it was obvious that the burglars were trying to bug Larry O'Brien, the head of the DNC. In the meantime, Bernstein has checked the background of some of the men. Woodward notes that the CIA would not confirm that McCord worked for them.

Later, Woodward gets a call from another reporter who tells him that two of the burglars had address books containing strange entries. The notations were "H.H. at W.H." and "Howard Hunt at W. House." Woodward calls the White House directly to speak to Hunt. When he finally gets ahold of Hunt and asks him why his name and phone number were in the address book of the men arrested at Watergate, he has no comment. In another call, a public relations person from the White House denies Hunt was part of the burglary.

Woodward is then shown calling a source from a pay phone. He identifies himself and says that he wants to talk about Watergate. The source would not talk about it, and tells Woodward not to call him again. The next morning, Woodward finds an envelope tucked into his newspaper, on which is a message from the source. The note indicates if Woodward wants to see him, he should put a red flag in the pot on the balcony. They will then meet at 2 a.m. in a specified parking garage.

To get to the parking garage, Woodward takes multiple taxis. Once there, he tells the source that he will never be quoted but will be on deep background. Woodward informs the source that he knows some basic information about those involved in the break-in but that the reporters can't figure out the pieces to the story. The source tells Woodward that things got out of hand in the White House, and tells Woodward to follow the money. He promises to keep the reporters in the right direction, but warns that he will not provide specific information.

The reporters are frustrated when they see a story in the *New York Times* describing 15 phone calls that were made from the burglars while in Miami to the CRP prior to the break-in. There was also $89,000 issued in checks by a prominent Mexican lawyer. Bernstein calls an investigator in Miami and arranges to meet with him. Bernstein waits all day to see him. Posing as an employee of the clerk's office, Bernstein fakes a phone call to get the secretary away from her desk. He is then able to enter the official's office. He asks to see phone records and money records. He is able to see the cashier's checks from Mexico, including a $25,000 check to a Watergate burglar from Kenneth H. Dahlberg.

Back in Washington, Woodward calls Dahlberg and asks him about the check deposited into the bank account of Bernard Barker, a burglar of the Watergate complex. Dahlberg explains that as Midwest Finance Chair, he raised money for the CRP. When asked again how the check got into the bank account of the burglar, he hangs up.

Woodward calls Clark McGregor, head of the CRP, and asks why the check for $25,000 ended up in the bank account of one of the burglars. McGregor says he does not know. Dahlberg calls Woodward back and explains that he gave the money he raised to Stans, the head of finance for Nixon. Right away, Woodward wrote a story with the headline, "Bug Suspect got Campaign Funds."

Not all of the editors at the *Washington Post* are enthusiastic about the Watergate story. Some question why other reporters are not following the story, and the *Post* had two relatively unknown reporters on it. Further, they question why the Republicans would commit such acts, especially when the Democratic candidate, McGovern, was self-destructing. They note being afraid that the story, if wrong, will ruin the paper.

The General Accounting Office starts an investigation into possible campaign finance violations by CRP. The reporters note that since the GAO is responsible to Congress, the White House cannot control the investigation. A source at the GAO tells the reporters that there were illegal activities at the CRP, including a slush fund with hundreds of thousands of dollars.

Woodward and Bernstein retrieve a list of CRP employees and immediately begin to call those listed. When no one will talk to them on the phone, the reporters begin visiting people at their homes in the evening hours. Still, no one will talk. They find one former employee, Betty Milan, who admits that shredding took place at the CRP and that Mitchell helped shred documents. Because the reporters have more questions, they returned to question her again. She says, "Please leave before they see you." The reporters think it is odd, even unnatural, that none of the employees are willing to talk to them.

Bernstein visits Sloan's bookkeeper. Her sister opens the door. Bernstein asks for a cigarette and works his way into the apartment. The bookkeeper slowly begins giving Bernstein information. She tells him there was a list of 15 names and the amount of money given to each person, but it was destroyed. She said she could not be positive the money was used for the break-in, but some people were worried about it. She tells Bernstein that during a two-day period, $6 million cash came into the Committee and the employees did not know where to put it all. He asks her how many people received money, and she answers about five. When Bernstein asks the woman to identify who got the money, the bookkeeper will only give him their initials. Later, Woodward wants specific names rather than initials of who got money, so they return to see the bookkeeper. She tells them that Mitchell was in control of the slush fund and that it held thousands of dollars. Porter got more than $50,000 and Magruder also got money.

Woodward and Bernstein go to the home of Hugh Sloan. He tells them that the White House controlled everything in the CRP and that the amount of money in the fund was close to $1 million. As treasurer, he could release the funds when ordered to do so. The reporters guess that the person from the White House who oversaw the fund was Haldeman. When asked how the money was handed out, Sloan says he called Mitchell, who would tell him to hand it out. It was all done verbally.

Woodward and Bernstein tell Bradlee that Mitchell, while he was attorney general, approved payment of secret funds. Bradlee is concerned that the sources have refused to go on the record, so Bernstein calls Mitchell to tell him that the *Post* is going to print a story that would report that Mitchell, while attorney general, controlled a secret cash fund. Mitchell calls the story "crap" and denies it. Nonetheless, Bradlee agrees to print the story, entitled, "Mitchell Controlled Secret Slush Fund."

Woodward and Bernstein discovered that in 1971, Donald Segretti recruited others to sabotage Democratic candidates. They found that Segretti crossed the country multiple times, staying in cities where there were Democratic primaries. But the reporters realize since Segretti was doing this a year before the break-in, the break-in was just one incident in the sabotage campaign that began a whole year before.

To get more information, Bernstein went to see Segretti in California. Segretti admitted that he was the head coordinator of the Nixon sabotage campaign against the Democrats, and that they did things like accuse Senator Humphrey of going out with call girls, or that another candidate, Scoop Jackson, was having an illegitimate child. Segretti said that in college, he and some others stuffed ballot boxes to get their guy elected, called "rat-fucking." They did the same things to help Nixon.

In Washington, Woodward met with Deep Throat and they talked about "rat-fucking." Deep Throat explained that it meant the infiltration of the Democrats. When Woodward tells Deep Throat that they knew the slush fund funded the "rat-fucking," Deep Throat explains that the fund was used to destroy the Muskie campaign because Nixon was afraid that Muskie would win. The Republicans placed bugs on people, followed people, leaked false press statements, wrote fake letters, cancelled Democratic campaign rallies, investigated the private lives of Democrats, planted spies inside Democratic campaigns, and stole documents.

Later, a fellow reporter at the *Post* tells Bernstein that as she and Ken Clawson were having drinks one night in her apartment, he admitted to writing the letter in which Muskie was slurring French-Canadians, known as the Canuck letter. This meant that the deputy director of White House communications wrote the letter that destroyed Muskie. When asked, Clawson denied the charges, claiming he does not remember the entire incident. He also said the reporters could not write about it because he was married with a wife and a family and a dog and a cat. Clawson calls Bradlee to deny writing the letter.

The reporters return to speak to Sloan, and ask him if the fifth man to control the slush fund was Haldeman. Although Sloan refuses to acknowledge it forthright, he indicates that to be the case. Bernstein also gets a confirmation of that information from an FBI source. But Bradlee tells the reporters to get another confirmation, just to be sure. Bernstein calls a source at the Justice Department. The source confirms by not hanging up as Bernstein counts to ten. The paper printed the story under the headline, "Testimony Ties Top Nixon Aide to Secret Fund."

After the story ran, Sloan denies naming Haldeman as the fifth man in his grand jury testimony. White House Press Secretary Ziegler attacked the reporters, saying the story was inaccurate, and it was clear that the *Washington Post* did not support Nixon. Further, he said he did not support the type of journalism being practiced by the *Washington Post*. Clark McGregor also denied the story. Throughout it all, Bradlee supported the reporters.

Woodward meets again with Deep Throat and demands real answers instead of hints, so Deep Throat admitted that the whole thing was run by Haldeman. Deep Throat tells Woodward that the covert operations involved the entire U.S. intelligence community: the FBI, CIA, and Justice Department. Before leaving, he told Woodward the reporters' lives were in danger.

The reporters tell Bradlee that Haldeman was the fifth person to control the fund and he tells them to print the story.

The movie shows that Nixon won his reelection bid for the presidency. A teletype informs viewers that Hunt pled guilty to three counts of conspiracy and burglary related to the break-in. Magruder pled guilty to helping plan Watergate. Segretti was sentenced to six months in prison for his role in carrying out dirty tricks against the Democrats. Kalmbach pled guilty to taking illegal White House funds. Chapin pled guilty to lying to the grand jury. Porter received 30 days in jail for lying to the FBI. Former Attorney General Kleindeinst entered a guilty plea. Colson pled guilty to a felony, admitting lying to the Justice Department. Stans admitted his guilt in charges involving illegal fundraising. Mitchell, Haldeman, and Ehrlichman were found all guilty on all counts. Nixon resigned from the presidency, and Gerald Ford was sworn in as President.

All the President's Men: Hollywood's Rendering

In an interview in 2006, Robert Redford said that accuracy was a major objective as they made the movie. He sought to tell the story from the perspective of the reporters, showing what they did to uncover the facts of the scandal. To make the movie more realistic, the actors spent time with the reporters at their jobs in order to get a feel for the tasks and the people involved. They even took trash from the actual newsroom to use as props on the movie set. Because of that desire for correctness, the film is notably accurate.[40]

In 2007, Woodward was asked what, in his opinion, was the biggest error of the film. He stated that the biggest inaccuracy was that several secondary characters in the investigation had to be dropped or combined together in order to save time and money. Most notable was Barry Sussman, the head city news editor at the *Washington Post*. His character was completely missing from the movie. In reality, Sussman helped Woodward and Bernstein organize their thoughts and coverage of Watergate into meaningful patterns, even helping the two recognize connections they had not noticed before. He played a vital role in helping the reporters put the story together.

Another editor, Howard Simons, was portrayed in the film but not accurately. Simons was the managing editor of the *Post*, played by actor Martin Balsam. Simon's character often came across as less serious, and at times even goofy. In reality, Simons was considered to be the one senior editor most involved in

Watergate story. He came up with the moniker "Deep Throat" for Woodward's source.[41]

A group of people left out of the movie was called *The Plumbers*. The Plumbers were a secret team created by Nixon to investigate and fix the leaks of classified information coming from the White House to the news media. Among their members were Hunt, Liddy, and McCord, all of whom were involved in the Watergate scandal.[42] In April 1973, it was revealed that Watergate burglars/Plumbers Hunt and Liddy broke into the office of the psychiatrist Daniel Ellsberg to uncover evidence that could be used to discredit Ellsberg after he leaked the Pentagon Papers to the *New York Times*.[43] The Pentagon Papers showed that Nixon had lied about the US government's role in the Vietnam War. Nixon's possible role in ordering the burglary was later questioned. There was also evidence that the administration (and possibly Nixon himself) proposed a burglary of the Brookings Institution, or even the use of a fire bomb to hide a break-in.[44] In the end, the idea to attack Brookings was aborted and there was no fire bomb. But it was clear that some of the same people in Nixon's administration were involved in both the Watergate break-in and cover-up as well as the Plumbers, and there was more evidence of wrongdoing by the administration. Nonetheless, the Plumbers were never mentioned in the movie.

One tactic used by the Plumbers and the Nixon administration to track down the leaks was to use wiretaps against those suspected of being the source of the secret information. *Time* magazine reported that the FBI wiretapped the telephones of news reporters and other government officials and aides under the guise of *domestic security*. The taps started in 1969 when J. Edgar Hoover was head of the FBI. He ordered the taps only after the attorney general, John Mitchell, authorized them. The taps were then continued under acting FBI Director Gray, who succeeded Hoover. Deep Throat told Woodward that in 1969, the first targets of Nixon's aggressive wiretapping policies were the reporters and others in the administration who were suspected of being disloyal to the President, or people who supported McGovern.[45] After that, the emphasis was shifted to those who were involved in the anti-war protests.[46] Eventually, the wiretaps were used against anyone considered to be an enemy of the President.

The movie does not show the extent of the wiretapping that was conducted by the Nixon administration. Throughout the Watergate investigation, the President's wiretapping activities came under attack. The policy toward, and use of, extensive warrantless wiretaps,[47] called the Mitchell Doctrine, or their *national security* wiretap policy, allowed the President and his men to have the authority to conduct electronic surveillance when they felt it was necessary. The Justice Department could use electronic bugging against anyone they suspected of conducting domestic *subversive activity* without prior authorization from the Court. This lasted until the Supreme Court declared the policy illegal on June 19, 1972, two days after the Watergate burglary. The extensive use of illegal wiretaps by the President was the basis of the second article of impeachment passed by the House of Representatives in 1974.[48] Despite their importance for Nixon and the role they played in the possible impeachment of the President, they were omitted from the film.

While these events were omitted from the film, other scenes were included in the film that never happened. One was a scene in which Bernstein waits all day to see the Miami prosecutor, but is not allowed to enter his office. Bernstein is shown making a phone call to the secretary from the hallway, posing as an employee of the clerk's office, in a successful effort to get her away from her desk and allowing him to enter the prosecutor's office. This scene is not described in the book and can be assumed to have never happened. Another scene in the movie that does not appear in the book was between Woodward and Deep Throat during one of their clandestine meetings. Woodward is shown being frustrated at Deep Throat because he will only provide hints rather than real facts. Woodward raises his voice at Deep Throat and demands he provide real information rather than just suggestions. This event was also not described in the book.

There are some minor discrepancies found throughout the film that, more than likely, are there to keep the film at a reasonable length. Many of them have to do with the events surrounding the break-in and occur at the beginning of the movie. For example, the film begins with a few men breaking into the headquarters of the Democratic Party. The film made it seem as if this was the first and only break in attempt. In actually, the burglars attempted to break into the office on May 26, but were unsuccessful, and tried again on May 27, but failed a second time. On Sunday, May 28, the men successfully entered the office and placed wiretaps on three phones in the office. It was later discovered that the wiretap on Larry O'Brien's phone did not work. So the burglars decided to go back in on the night of June 17, 1972, the night they were caught.[49]

In that same part of the movie, the film shows the security guard discovering tape on the door to prevent the door from becoming locked. He immediately suspects a burglary and calls the police. In reality, the guard found tape on the door and removed it, but did nothing further. Later, when he checked the door a second time, he found the tape had been placed back onto the lock. At this point he removed the tape for a second time and called police.[50]

As the burglars entered the Democratic headquarters, there were two men serving as lookouts across the street in a hotel room. In the film, only one of the lookouts was shown, but in reality, there were two people in the room. In the end, both were charged with crimes. These men were G. Gordon Liddy and E. Howard Hunt.[51]

Inaccuracies in the film exist regarding the reporters and their role in the story. The movie implied that Woodward and Bernstein had an amicable working relationship from the start. But in reality, the pair did not like each other. They came from different backgrounds and had a different levels of experience in the news field. Woodward was new to the *Post* and had little experience. In fact, he was writing stories about health violations in local restaurants at the time of the Watergate break-in. Bernstein, on the other hand, had been working at the *Washington Post* for some time and was known to be *street smart* when it came to investigating stories. The reporters would often butt heads and publicly argue over their stories. The movie did not explain or focus on this relationship.

Further, the film often presents Bernstein and Woodward working alone in an empty newsroom late at night, and hints that these two reporters were the only ones who pursued the story. But the story was an important one, and almost everyone who worked in the newsroom was involved in the investigation of the Watergate story in some way. Other reporters did what they could to help Woodward and Bernstein. At times, there were over a dozen reporters on the story.[52] The other reporters often stayed late, fielded questions, passed along tips, and generally offered their assistance when needed. The editors helped track the events of the story and kept a broad perspective. But Woodward and Bernstein were not on their own.

Further, in their book, Woodward and Bernstein did not mention the roles that federal prosecutors, investigators for the FBI, grand juries, different congressional committees in both the House and Senate, and Judge Sirica played in the discovery of the Watergate story. Although this added to their heroic stature and made it appear as if they were the primary ones to discover the wrongdoing,[53] there were certainly others who assisted them.

The movie implies that the *Washington Post* reporters were the only news reporters following the story. It is true that many other newspapers did not follow the Watergate story initially, and when the stories were printed, they were often on back pages.[54] This made some believe that nobody was paying any attention to the story.[55] But Woodward and Bernstein kept the story alive,[56] and toward the end of the investigation, as more information became public, many other newspaper companies were running the story in their papers.[57] They also had journalists checking their sources and running around for their own stories. When other papers published stories that reinforced those published by the *Post*, the reporters were pleased. It was a change to have support of other sources as opposed to the constant attacks they received from the White House.

The reporters were not the only ones portrayed inaccurately in the movie. Deep Throat was portrayed as sinister, lurking in a parking garage. However, he was described by Woodward as being an incurable gossip who was not good at concealing his feelings. He ended up being a major source of information and help to the reporters. The movie has Deep Throat telling the reporters to "follow the money," but this was never actually spoken by Deep Throat, nor was it written by Woodward and Bernstein in their book. The quote was made up for the movie.[58]

At the end of the movie, keystrokes from a typewriter inform the viewers of the outcome of the individual cases. There was no mention of Liddy, when he was one of the two people who oversaw the operations of Watergate and arrested in the break-in. He served four-and-a-half years in prison for his role in Watergate.

The movie does not show much information about the taping system in the Oval Office, or the fight between Nixon and the prosecution about them. When the taping system was discovered, it was clear that Nixon could be on tape discussing the break-in and other events with his assistants. After many legal battles, the courts ordered Nixon to provide the tapes to both the court and to the Senate committee investigating the scandal. When he did, it was discovered that one of the tapes had an 18.5 minute gap. This gap included a key conversation between Nixon and Haldeman that took place three days after the original break-in.

Conclusion

All the President's Men was produced to show the public the role the media played in investigating the wrongdoing by the President and his administration. It was an attempt to present the reporters' perspective of the events. The reporters faced many challenges as they delved into the story, facing constant roadblocks in their attempts to discover the truth. But they never stopped their investigation, even when other media outlets seemed to have given up on the story. Because of their perseverance, the *Washington Post* won a Pulitzer Prize for its coverage of the story. The movie that was made based on the story was intended to be factual and an accurate portrayal of events and despite some minor inaccuracies, turned out to be a realistic film.

Further Reading

Bernstein, Carl and Bob Woodward. (1974). *All the President's Men*. New York: Warner Books.

Dean, John. (1976). *Blind Ambition*. New York: Avon Books.

Ehrlichman, John. (1982). *Witness to Power*. New York: Simon & Schuster.

Emery, Fred. (1994). *Watergate: The Corruption of American Politics and the Fall of Richard* Nixon. New York: Touchstone Books.

Haldeman, H.R. (1978). *The Ends of Power.* New York: Times Book.

Haldeman, H. R. (1994). *The Haldeman Diaries: Inside the Nixon White House.* New York: G.P. Putnam's Sons.

Jaworski, Leon. (1976). *The Right and the Power.* New York: Pocket Books.

Jeffrey, Harry P. and Thomas Maxwell-Long, Eds. (2004). *Watergate and the Resignation of* Richard Nixon. Washington, D.C.: CQ Press.

Kutler, Stanley I. (1998). *Abuse of Power: The New Nixon Tapes.* New York: Touchstone.

Kutler, Stanley I. (1992). *The Wars of Watergate: The Last Crisis of Richard Nixon.* New York: W.W. Norton & Company.

Liddy, G. Gordon. (1980). *Will: The Autobiography of G. Gordon Liddy.* New York: St. Martin's Press.

Reeves, Richard. (2002). *President Nixon.* New York: Simon & Schuster.

Schudson, Michael. (1992). *Watergate in American Memory.* New York: Basic Books.

Sussman, Barry. (2010). *The Great Coverup: Nixon and the Scandal of Watergate.* New York: Catapulter Books.

Woodward, Bob and Carl Bernstein. (1976). *The Final Days.* New York: Avon Books.

Endnotes

1. Liddy G. Gordon. (1980). *Will: The Autobiography of G. Gordon Liddy.* New York: St. Martin's Press.

2. *All the President's Men* (Warner Brothers, 1976). (Alan J. Pakula, Director).

3. Schultz, Jeffrey. (2000). *Presidential Scandals.* Washington, D.C.: CQ Press.

4. Emery, Fred. (1994). *Watergate: The Corruption of American Politics and the Fall of Richard Nixon.* New York: Touchstone Books.

5. Klein, Woody. (2008). *All the President's Spokesmen.* Westport, CT: Praeger Publishers, p. 122.

6. In light of the fact the film was largely based on the book, the Bernstein and Woodward book is critical to the review of facts of the case. When their book is cited in this chapter, reference page numbers will be included even where there is no direct quote. Bernstein, Carl and Bob Woodward. (1974). *All the President's Men.* New York: Warner Books, p. 30.

7. Bernstein, Carl and Bob Woodward. (1974). *All the President's Men.* New York: Warner Books, p. 90.

8. Emery, Fred. (1994). *Watergate: The Corruption of American Politics and the Fall of Richard Nixon.* New York: Touchstone Books.

9. Bernstein, Carl and Bob Woodward. (1974). *All the President's Men.* New York: Warner Books, p. 48.

10. Bernstein, Carl and Bob Woodward. (1974). *All the President's Men.* New York: Warner Books, p. 48.

11. Bernstein, Carl and Bob Woodward. (1974). *All the President's Men.* New York: Warner Books, p. 58.

12. Bernstein, Carl and Bob Woodward. (1974). *All the President's Men.* New York: Warner Books, p. 49.

13. Emery, Fred. (1994). *Watergate: The Corruption of American Politics and the Fall of Richard Nixon.* New York: Touchstone Books.

14. Bernstein, Carl and Bob Woodward. (1974). *All the President's Men.* New York: Warner Books, p. 61

15. Bernstein, Carl and Bob Woodward. (1974). *All the President's Men.* New York: Warner Books, p. 69.

16. Palermo, Joseph A. (2004) "Politics, Public Opinion, and Popular Culture." In Harry P. Jeffrey and Thomas Maxwell-Long (Eds.), *Watergate and the Resignation of Richard Nixon.* Washington, D.C.: CQ Press, pp. 17–29.

17. Bernstein, Carl and Bob Woodward. (1974). *All the President's Men.* New York: Warner Books, p. 101.

18. Bernstein, Carl and Bob Woodward. (1974). *All the President's Men.* New York: Warner Books, p. 102.

19. Bernstein, Carl and Bob Woodward. (1974). *All the President's Men.* New York: Warner Books, p. 167.

20. Bernstein, Carl and Bob Woodward. (1974). *All the President's Men.* New York: Warner Books, p. 167.

21. Bernstein, Carl and Bob Woodward. (1974). *All the President's Men.* New York: Warner Books, p. 131.

22. Emery, Fred. (1994). *Watergate: The Corruption of American Politics and the Fall of Richard Nixon.* New York: Touchstone Books.

23. Bernstein, Carl and Bob Woodward. (1974). *All the President's Men.* New York: Warner Books, p. 142.

24. Bernstein, Carl and Bob Woodward. (1974). *All the President's Men.* New York: Warner Books, p. 143.

25. Bernstein, Carl and Bob Woodward. (1974). *All the President's Men.* New York: Warner Books, p. 147.

26. Bernstein, Carl and Bob Woodward. (1974). *All the President's Men.* New York: Warner Books, p. 151.

27. Bernstein, Carl and Bob Woodward. (1974). *All the President's Men.* New York: Warner Books, p. 247.

28. Bernstein, Carl and Bob Woodward. (1974). *All the President's Men.* New York: Warner Books, p. 288.

29. Van Tassel, Emily Field and Paul Finkelman. (1999). *Impeachable Offenses.* Washington, D.C.: Congressional Quarterly, Inc..

30. Emery, Fred. (1994). *Watergate: The Corruption of American Politics and the Fall of Richard Nixon.* New York: Touchstone Books.

31. Bernstein, Carl and Bob Woodward. (1974). *All the President's Men.* New York: Warner Books, p. 276.

32. Bernstein, Carl and Bob Woodward. (1974). *All the President's Men.* New York: Warner Books, p. 399.

33. Bernstein, Carl and Bob Woodward. (1974). *All the President's Men.* New York: Warner Books, p. 339.

34. Bernstein, Carl and Bob Woodward. (1974). *All the President's Men*. New York: Warner Books, p. 348.

35. Bernstein, Carl and Bob Woodward. (1974). *All the President's Men*. New York: Warner Books, p. 309.

36. Bernstein, Carl and Bob Woodward. (1974). *All the President's Men*. New York: Warner Books, p. 304.

37. Van Tassel, Emily Field and Paul Finkelman. (1999). *Impeachable Offenses*. Washington, D.C.: Congressional Quarterly, Inc..

38. Bernstein, Carl and Bob Woodward. (1974). *All the President's Men*. New York: Warner Books, pp. 172–3.

39. Palermo, Joseph A. (2004). "Politics, Public Opinion, and Popular Culture." In Harry P. Jeffrey and Thomas Maxwell-Long (Eds.), *Watergate and the Resignation of Richard Nixon*. Washington, D.C.: CQ Press, pp. 17–29.

40. Associated Press. (2006). "Redford Remembers 'All the President's Men.'" Retrieved online at http://today.msnbc.msn.com/id/11373722/ns/today.

41. Internet Movie Database. (2011). "Goofs for All the President's Men." Retrieved online at http://www.imdb.com/title/tt0074119/goofs.

42. Dean, Howard. (1977). *Blind Ambition*. New York: Pocket Books; Rather, Dan. (1975). *The Palace Guard*. New York: Warner Paperback Library Edition; Jaworski, Leon. (1977). *The Right and the Power*. New York: Pocket Books.

43. Emery, Fred. (1994). *Watergate: The Corruption of American Politics and the Fall of Richard Nixon*. New York: Touchstone Books; Jeffrey, Harry P. and Thomas Maxwell-Long (Eds.). (2004). *Watergate and the Resignation of Richard Nixon*. Washington, D.C.: CQ Press.

44. Bernstein, Carl and Bob Woodward. (1974). *All the President's Men*. New York: Warner Books, pp. 355–356.

45. Emery, Fred. (1994). *Watergate: The Corruption of American Politics and the Fall of Richard Nixon*. New York: Touchstone Books.

46. Bernstein, Carl and Bob Woodward. (1974). *All the President's Men*. New York: Warner Books, p. 299.

47. Friedman, Leon. (2004). "Separation of Powers." In Harry P. Jeffrey and Thomas Maxwell-Long (Eds.), *Watergate and the Resignation of Richard Nixon*. Washington, D.C.: CQ Press, pp. 31–46.

48. Friedman, Leon. (2004). "Separation of Powers." In Harry P. Jeffrey and Thomas Maxwell-Long (Eds.), *Watergate and the Resignation of Richard Nixon*. Washington, D.C.: CQ Press, pp. 31–46.

49. Marion, Nancy E. (2010). *The Politics of Disgrace*. Durham, North Carolina: Carolina Academic Press.

50. Emery, Fred. (1994). *Watergate: The Corruption of American Politics and the Fall of Richard Nixon*. New York: Touchstone Books; Schultz, Jeffrey. (2000). *Presidential Scandals*. Washington, D.C.: CQ Press.

51. Ringle, K. (1992). "Journalism's Finest 2 Hours and 16 Minutes. *The Washington Post*: National, World & D.C. Area News and Headlines" *The Washington Post*. Retrieved online at http://www.washingtonpost.com/wp-srv/national/longterm/watergate/; Washington Post. (2011). "Watergate." Retrieved online at http://www.washingtonpost.com/wp-srv/politics/special/watergate/hunt.html;

Washington Post. (2011). "The Watergate Story: The Post Investigates." Retrieved online at http://www.washingtonpost.com/wp-srv/politics/special/watergate/part1.html.

52. Bernstein, Carl and Bob Woodward. (1974). *All the President's Men*. New York: Warner Books, p. 223.

53. Palermo, Joseph A. (2004). "Politics, Public Opinion, and Popular Culture." In Harry P. Jeffrey and Thomas Maxwell-Long (Eds.), *Watergate and the Resignation of Richard Nixon*. Washington, D.C.: CQ Press, pp. 17–29.

54. Palermo, Joseph A. (2004). "Politics, Public Opinion, and Popular Culture." In Harry P. Jeffrey and Thomas Maxwell-Long (Eds.), *Watergate and the Resignation of Richard Nixon*. Washington, D.C.: CQ Press, pp. 17–29.

55. Bernstein, Carl and Bob Woodward. (1974). *All the President's Men*. New York: Warner Books, p. 82.

56. Witcher, Russ. (2004). "The Media." In Harry P. Jeffrey and Thomas Maxwell-Long (Eds.), *Watergate and the Resignation of Richard Nixon*. Washington, D.C.: CQ Press, pp. 113–124.

57. Marion, Nancy E. (2010). *The Politics of Disgrace*. Durham, North Carolina: Carolina Academic Press.

58. Safire, William. (1997). "Follow the Proffering Duck." *New York Times Magazine*. Retrieved online at http://www.nytimes.com/1997/08/03/magazine/follow-the-proffering-duck.html.

INDEX